HOUSE of WHITE BIRCHES

Crochet Gifts to Go!™

Edited by Laura Scott

HOUSE of WHITE BIRCHES
PUBLISHERS
SINCE 1947

Crochet Gifts to Go!

Editor: Laura Scott
Pattern Editor: Agnes Russell
Associate Editor: Cathy Reef
Editorial Coordinator: Laura Polley
Copy Editors: Mary Nowak, Nicki Lehman
Technical Artist: Allison Rothe
Publication Coordinator: Kelly Keim
Design Coordinator: Tanya Turner

Photography: Tammy Christian, Jeff Chilcote, Justin P. Wiard
Photography Stylist: Arlou Wittwer
Photography Assistant: Linda Quinlan

Production Coordinator: Brenda Gallmeyer
Book Design: Erin Augsburger
Graphic Artist: Pam Gregory
Cover Design: Jessi Butler
Production Assistants: Janet Bowers, Marj Morgan
Traffic Coordinator: Sandra Beres

Publishers: Carl H. Muselman, Arthur K. Muselman
Chief Executive Officer: John Robinson
Marketing Director: Scott Moss
Book Marketing Manager: Craig Scott
Product Development Director: Vivian Rothe
Publishing Services Manager: Brenda Wendling

Printed in the United States of America
First Printing: 2001
Library of Congress Number: 00-109646
ISBN: 1-882138-68-6

Every effort has been made to ensure the accuracy and completeness of the instructions in this book. However, we cannot be responsible for human error or for the results when using materials other than those specified in the instructions, or for variations in individual work.

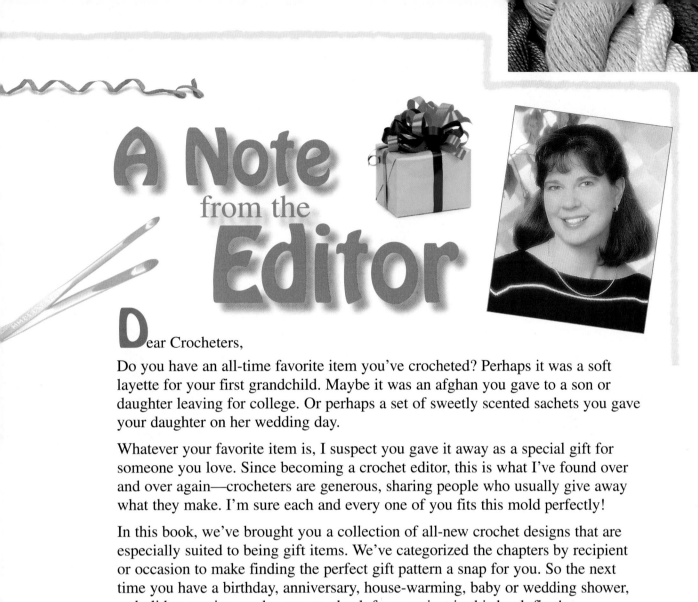

A Note from the Editor

Dear Crocheters,

Do you have an all-time favorite item you've crocheted? Perhaps it was a soft layette for your first grandchild. Maybe it was an afghan you gave to a son or daughter leaving for college. Or perhaps a set of sweetly scented sachets you gave your daughter on her wedding day.

Whatever your favorite item is, I suspect you gave it away as a special gift for someone you love. Since becoming a crochet editor, this is what I've found over and over again—crocheters are generous, sharing people who usually give away what they make. I'm sure each and every one of you fits this mold perfectly!

In this book, we've brought you a collection of all-new crochet designs that are especially suited to being gift items. We've categorized the chapters by recipient or occasion to make finding the perfect gift pattern a snap for you. So the next time you have a birthday, anniversary, house-warming, baby or wedding shower, or holiday coming up, be sure to check for a project in this book first!

Most of the items are portable, too, so you can work on them while you're on the go. Just tuck your project and yarn into a bag and take it in the car or to your child's next basketball game!

We hope you enjoy this collection. Who knows—maybe one of these patterns will become your new all-time favorite!

With warm regards,

Laura Scott

Conte

1 Creative Gifts for Her

2 Kid-Pleasing Presents

3 Pampered-Pet Pleasers

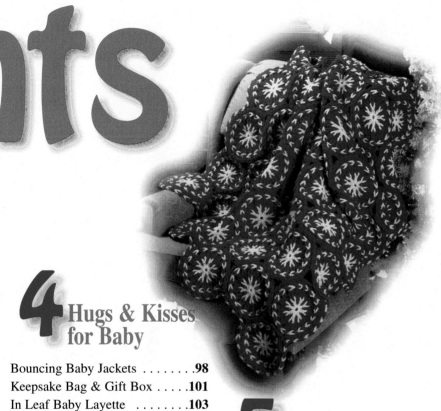

ts

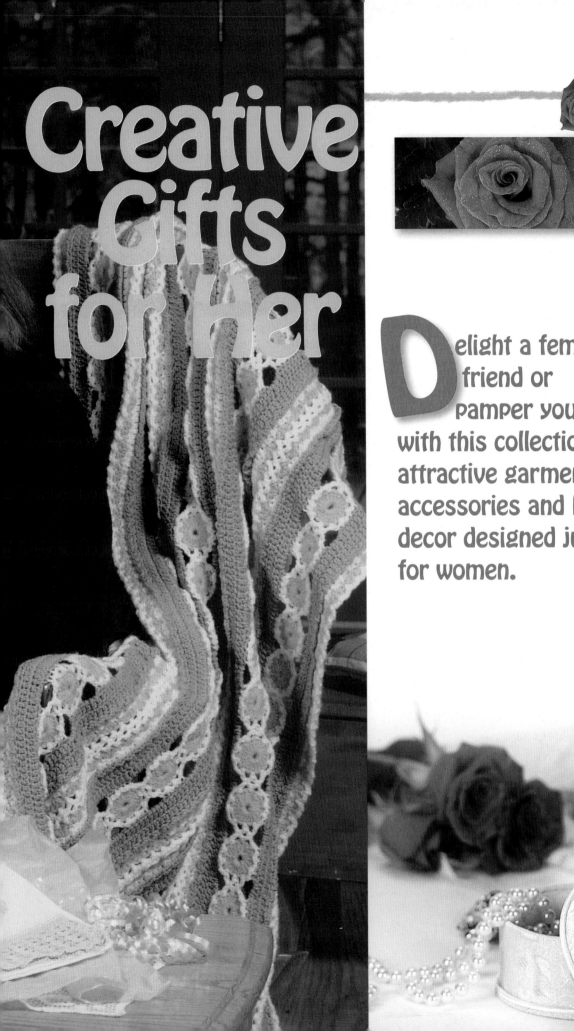

Creative Gifts for Her

Delight a female friend or pamper yourself with this collection of attractive garments, accessories and home decor designed just for women.

Drawstring Purses

By Sue Childress

Pearly Drawstring Purse

Skill Level: Beginner

Size: 2½ x 3 inches

Materials

- ✓ Crochet cotton size 10: 150 yds ecru
- ✓ Size 7 steel crochet hook or size needed to obtain gauge
- ✓ 525 (3mm) pearls
- ✓ 1 yd ¼-inch-wide cream satin ribbon
- ✓ Bead needle

Delicate and dainty, these tiny purses are wonderful gifts for the bride and her wedding party, or for anyone who loves those big gifts that come in small packages!

Gauge

3 shell rnds = 1 inch

Check gauge to save time.

Pattern Notes

Weave in loose ends as work progresses.

Join rnds with a sl st unless otherwise stated.

String pearls onto cotton, push along as work progresses until needed.

Pattern Stitch

Bead st: Push up 3 pearl beads, holding pearls on RS, sl st in top of last hdc.

Purse

Rnd 1: Ch 3, 7 hdc in 3rd ch from hook, join in top of beg ch-3. (8 hdc)

Rnd 2: Ch 2 (counts as first hdc throughout), hdc in same st as beg ch-2, 2 hdc in each st around, join in top of beg ch-2. (16 hdc)

Rnd 3: Ch 2, hdc in next hdc, [bead st, hdc in each of next 2 hdc] rep around, join in top of beg ch-2. (8 groups of pearls)

Rnd 4: Ch 2, 2 hdc in same st as beg ch, 2 hdc in each rem hdc around, join in top of beg ch-2. (33 hdc)

Rnd 5: Ch 2, hdc in each of next 2 hdc, bead st, [hdc in each of next 3 hdc, bead st] rep around, join in top of beg ch-2.

Rnd 6: Ch 2, hdc around, inc 15 hdc evenly sp around, join in top of beg ch-2. (48 hdc)

Rnd 7: Rep Rnd 5.

Rnd 8: Rep Rnd 6. (63 hdc)

Rnd 9: Rep Rnd 5.

Rnd 10: Ch 2, hdc in each st around, join in top of beg ch-2.

Rnds 11 & 12: Rep Rnds 5 and 10.

Rnd 13: Rep Rnd 5.

Rnd 14: Ch 2, hdc around, inc 12 hdc evenly sp around, join in top of beg ch-2. (75 hdc)

Rnd 15: Rep Rnd 5.

Rnd 16: Ch 2, hdc around, inc 29 hdc evenly sp around, join in top of beg ch-2. (104 hdc)

Rnd 17: Rep Rnd 5.

Rnd 18: Ch 4 (counts as first dc, ch 1), sk next hdc, [dc in next hdc, ch 1, sk next hdc] rep around, join in 3rd ch of beg ch-4. (52 ch-1 sps)

Rnd 19: Sl st into ch-1 sp, ch 3 (counts as first dc), 6 dc in same ch-1 sp, sc in next ch-1 sp, [7 dc in next ch-1 sp, sc in next ch-1 sp] rep around, join in top of beg ch-3.

Rnd 20: Ch 1, sc in same st as beg ch-1, sc in each of next 2 dc, *draw up a lp in next dc, push up 1 bead, complete sc, sc in each of next 3 dc, draw up a lp in next sc, push up 1 bead, complete sc **, sc in each of next 3 dc, rep from * around, ending last rep at **, join in beg sc, fasten off.

Finishing

Cut ribbon in half. Weave first length through ch-1 sps of Rnd 18 entirely around opening, knot ends tog approximately 1 inch from end. Starting at center on opposite side of first ribbon, weave around opposite previous weave, knot ends tog. Holding each knot at side, pull outward to close bag opening.

Pineapple Drawstring Purse

Skill Level: Beginner

Size: 4 x 4 inches

Materials

- ✓ Crochet cotton size 10: 150 yds pink
- ✓ Size 7 steel crochet hook or size needed to obtain gauge
- ✓ 9-inch circle lining material
- ✓ 12 inches ½-inch-wide decorative lace
- ✓ Sewing needle and thread

Gauge

3 shell rnds = 1 inch
Check gauge to save time.

Pattern Notes

Weave in loose ends as work progresses.

Join rnds with a sl st unless otherwise stated.

Pattern Stitches

Shell: [2 dc, ch 2, 2 dc] in indicated st.

Beg shell: Sl st into indicated sp, [ch 3, dc, ch 2, 2 dc] in same sp.

Double shell (dshell): [2 dc, ch 2] twice and 2 dc in same ch-2 sp of shell.

V-st: [Dc, ch 1, dc] in indicated sp.

Purse

Rnd 1: Ch 8, sl st to join to form a ring, ch 3 (counts as first dc throughout), 11 dc in ring, join in top of beg ch-3. (12 dc)

Rnd 2: Ch 1, sc in same dc as beg ch, ch 3, [sc in next dc, ch 3] rep around, join in beg sc. (12 ch-3 sps)

Rnd 3: Beg shell in ch-3 sp, shell in each rem ch-3 sp around, join in top of beg ch-3. (12 shells)

Rnd 4: Beg shell in ch-2 sp of shell, 7 dc in next ch-2 sp of shell, [shell in next ch-2 sp of shell, 7 dc in next ch-2 sp of shell] rep around, join in top of beg ch-3. (6 shell; 6 pineapple bases)

Rnd 5: Beg shell in ch-2 sp of shell, *dc in first dc of 7-dc group, [ch 1, dc in next dc] 6 times **, shell in ch-2 sp of shell, rep from * around, ending last rep at **, join in top of beg ch-3.

Rnd 6: Beg shell in ch-2 sp of shell, *sc in next ch-1 sp, [ch 2, sc in next ch-1 sp] 5 times **, shell in ch-2 sp of shell, rep from * around, ending last rep at **, join in top of beg ch-3.

Rnd 7: Sl st into ch-2 sp of shell, ch 3, dc, [ch 2, 2 dc] twice in same ch-2 sp, *sc in next ch-2 sp, [ch 2, sc in next ch-2 sp] 4 times **, dshell in next ch-2 sp of shell, rep from *

around, ending last rep at **, join in top of beg ch-3.

Rnd 8: Beg shell in ch-2 sp of shell, shell in ch-2 sp of next shell, *sc in next ch-2 sp, [ch 2, sc in next ch-2 sp] 3 times **, [shell in next ch-2 sp of shell] twice, rep from * around, ending last rep at **, join in top of beg ch-3.

Rnd 9: Beg shell in ch-2 sp of shell, ch 2, shell in ch-2 sp of next shell, *sc in next ch-2 sp, [ch 2, sc in next ch-2 sp] twice **, shell in next ch-2 sp of shell, ch 2, shell in next ch-2 sp of shell, rep from * around, ending last rep at **, join in top of beg ch-3.

Rnd 10: Beg shell in ch-2 sp of shell, *shell in ch-2 sp between shells, shell in next ch-2 sp of shell, [ch 2, sc in next ch-2 sp] twice, ch 2 **, shell in next ch-2 sp of shell, rep from * around, ending last rep at **, join in top of beg ch-3.

Rnd 11: Beg shell in ch-2 sp of shell, [shell in next

ch-2 sp of shell] twice, *sk next ch-2 sp, shell in next ch-2 sp, sk next ch-2 sp **, [shell in next ch-2 sp of shell] 3 times, rep from * around, ending last rep at **, join in top of beg ch-3. (24 shells)

Rnds 12–16: Beg shell in ch-2 sp of shell, [shell in ch-2 sp of next shell] 23 times, join in top of beg ch-3.

Rnd 17: Sl st into ch-2 sp of shell, ch 4 (counts as first dc, ch 1), dc in same ch-2 sp, V-st in sp between shells, [V-st in ch-2 sp of shell, V-st in sp between shells] rep around, join in 3rd ch of beg ch-4. (48 V-sts)

Rnd 18: Sl st into ch-1 sp, ch 3, 4 dc in same ch-1 sp, 5 dc in each rem ch-1 sp around, join in top of beg ch-3.

Rnd 19: Ch 1, sc in same dc as beg ch, ch 3, [sc in next dc, ch 3] rep around, join in beg sc, fasten off.

Drawstring cord

(Make 2)

Ch 150, sl st in 2nd ch from hook, sl st in each rem ch across, fasten off.

Finishing

Place fabric inside of purse, sew to Rnd 15. Sew lace over top edge of lining.

Weave first drawstring cord through dc sts of Rnd 17, sew or tie ends tog. Weave 2nd drawstring cord opposite of first through same rnd, sew or tie ends tog.

Holding each cord at opposite side of bag, pull drawstrings outward to close opening of purse. ❀

Spring Floral Pillow

By Michele Wilcox

Skill Level: Beginner

Size: 16¼ x 16¼ inches

Materials

✓ Bernat Berella "4" worsted weight yarn: 2 skeins light ocean #8761, 1 skein white #8942, small amount each pale antique rose #8814, rose #8921, light tapestry gold #8886

✓ Size G/6 crochet hook or size needed to obtain gauge

✓ 16-inch pillow form

✓ Tapestry needle

Gauge

4 sc rows and 4 sc sts = 1 inch

Check gauge to save time.

Pattern Notes

Weave in loose ends as work progresses.

Join rnds with a sl st unless otherwise stated.

Pillow Front

(Make 4)

Row 1: With white, ch 25, dc in 3rd ch from hook, [sk 1 ch, {sc, dc} in next ch] rep across to last 2 chs, sk 1 ch, sc in next ch, turn.

Rows 2–17: Ch 1 loosely, dc in first sc, [sk 1 dc, {sc, dc} in next sc] rep across to last 2 sts, sk 1 st, sc in top of turning ch, turn.

At the end of Row 17, fasten off.

Sew the 4 squares tog to form a block.

Stem

(Make 4)

Row 1: With light ocean, ch 19, sl st in 2nd ch from hook, sl st in each rem ch across, leaving a length of yarn, fasten off.

Beg ½ inch from center joining of squares, sew stem diagonally from center outward. Rep with rem 3 stems on each rem square.

Leaf

(Make 8)

Rnd 1: With light ocean, ch 6, sc in 2nd ch from hook, sc in each of next 3 chs, 3 sc in last ch, working on opposite side of foundation ch, sc in each of next 3 chs, 2 sc in same ch as beg sc, join in beg sc. (12 sc)

Rnd 2: Ch 1, 2 sc in same sc as beg ch, sc in each of next 2 sc, hdc in next sc, 2 hdc in next sc, [hdc, ch 2, sl st in 2nd ch from hook, hdc] in next sc, 2 hdc in next sc, hdc in next sc, sc in each of next 2 sc, 2 sc in each of next 2 sc, join in beg sc, leaving a length of yarn, fasten off.

Sew 1 leaf to each side of each stem half way up each stem.

Flower

(Make 4)

Rnd 1: With light tapestry gold, ch 6, sl st to join to form a ring, ch 1, 12 sc in ring, join in beg sc, fasten off. (12 sc)

Rnd 2: Attach pale antique rose in any sc, ch 1, sc in same sc as beg ch, sc in next sc, [2 sc in next sc, sc in each of next 2 sc] 3 times, sc in next sc, join in beg sc, fasten off. (15 sc)

Rnd 3: Attach rose in any sc with sl st, [hdc, dc] in next sc, [dc, hdc] in next sc, [sl st in next sc, {hdc, dc} in next sc, {dc, hdc} in next sc] rep around, join in same st as beg sl st, fasten off.

Sew 1 flower to the end of each stem.

Center Ring

Rnd 1: With light ocean, ch 8, sl st to join to form a ring, ch 1, 16 sc in ring, join in beg sc. (16 sc)

Rnd 2: [Sl st in each of next 2 sc, ch 3] rep around, join in same sl st as beg st, leaving a length of yarn, fasten off.

Sew center ring over stems at center of pillow front.

Front Edging

Note: *Front edging is worked on each straight edge of pillow front across the joined blocks.*

Row 1: Attach light ocean at right edge, ch 1, work 46 sc evenly sp across edge, turn.

Rows 2–8: Ch 1, sc in each of next 46 sc, turn.

At the end of Row 8, fasten off. Rep front edging on each rem 3 sides.

Corner Square

(Make 4)

Rnd 1: With rose, ch 4, sl st to join to form a ring, ch 5 (counts as first dc, ch 2), [3 dc in ring, ch 2] 3 times, 2 dc in ring, join in 3rd ch of beg ch-5.

Rnd 2: Sl st into ch-2 sp, ch 3 (counts as first dc), 2 dc, ch 2, 3 dc in same ch-2 sp as beg ch-3, dc in each of next 3 dc, [{3 dc, ch 2, 3 dc} in next corner ch-2 sp, dc in each of next 3 dc] 3 times, join in top of beg ch-3, fasten off.

Place pillow front on a flat surface, sew 1 corner square at each corner of pillow front.

Pillow Back

Row 1: With light ocean, ch 61, dc in 3rd ch from hook, [sk 1 ch, {sc, dc} in next ch] rep across to last 2 chs, sk 1 ch, sc in last ch, turn.

Rows 2–58: Rep Row 2 of pillow front.

At the end of Row 58 do not fasten off.

Joining

With WS of front and back tog and working through both thicknesses, ch 1, [sc evenly sp across edge, work 3 sc in corner st] 3 times, insert pillow form, sc evenly sp across last edge, 3 sc in corner st, join in beg sc, fasten off. ✿

Delight your female friends with this beautiful folk-art pillow. Harmoniously arranged flowers decorate the front, while the pillow back echoes the shell pattern of the front squares. Tiny granny squares add just the right detail to the borders.

Linen Heart Doilies

By Sue Childress

Skill Level: Beginner

Size:

White edging: 1⅛ inch wide

Red edging: 1 inch wide

Materials

- ✓ Crochet cotton size 10: 100 yds each red and white
- ✓ Size 7 steel crochet hook or size needed to obtain gauge
- ✓ 1 each red and white 7¾ x 8-inch hemstitched edge linen heart doilies
- ✓ Assorted appliqués
- ✓ Sewing needle and thread

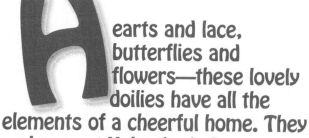

earts and lace, butterflies and flowers—these lovely doilies have all the elements of a cheerful home. They make great Valentine's Day or Mother's Day gifts!

Gauge

11 stitches = 1½ inches

Check gauge to save time.

Pattern Notes

Weave in loose ends as work progresses.

Join rnds with a sl st unless otherwise stated.

Red Edging

Rnd 1 (RS): With white heart upside down, attach red in first sp to the left of point, ch 1, sc in same sp, sc evenly sp around entire outer edge, working 3 sc tog at center top of heart between lobes and 3 sc in center bottom point of heart, join in beg sc. (87 sc each side; 3 sc in center bottom; 1 sc between lobes)

Rnd 2: Ch 1, sc in each sc around, join in beg sc. (178 sc)

Rnd 3: Ch 1, sc in same sc as beg ch, [ch 3, sk 2 sc, sc in next sc] rep around to 3-sc group at bottom point, ch 3, sk first sc, sc in center sc, ch 3, sk next sc, join in beg sc. (60 ch-3 sps)

Rnd 4: Sl st into ch-3 sp, ch 1, 5 sc in each ch-3 sp up side edge to the 2 ch-3 sps between lobes, 1 sc in each of next 2 ch-3 sp, 5 sc in each rem ch-3 sp across opposite side, join in beg sc.

Rnd 5: Sl st into 3rd sc, ch 1, sc in same sc, [ch 5, sc in 3rd sc of next 5-sc group] rep around, except dec 1 sc over next 2 sc between lobes, ending with ch 5, join in beg sc.

Rnd 6: Sl st into ch-5 sp, ch 1, work 7 sc in each ch-5 sp around, working 1 sc in the sc between lobes, join in beg sc, fasten off.

White Edging

Rnd 1: With white cotton, rep Rnd 1 of red edging using red linen doily.

Rnd 2: Ch 2 (counts as first hdc), hdc in each sc around, dec 1 hdc over next 2 sc between lobes and 3 hdc in center sc at bottom point of heart, join in top of beg ch.

Rnd 3: Ch 1, sc in same hdc as beg ch, [sk next 2 hdc, 5 dc in next hdc, sk 2 hdc, sc in next hdc] 9 times, [sk next hdc, 5 dc in next hdc, sk next hdc, sc in next hdc] 7 times, sk next hdc, dec 1 sc over next sts between lobes, sk next hdc, sc in next hdc, [sk next hdc, 5 dc in next hdc, sk next hdc, sc in next hdc] 7 times, [sk next 2 hdc, 5 dc in next hdc, sk next 2 hdc, sc in next hdc] 9 times, 9 dc in center hdc at bottom point of heart, join in beg sc.

Rnd 4: Sl st into 3rd dc of next 5-dc group, ch 3, 6 dc in same dc, [7 dc in 3rd dc of next 5-dc group] 15 times, sc in each of next 2 sc between lobes, [7 dc in 3rd dc of next 5-dc group] 16 times, 2 dc in first dc of 9-dc group, [2 dc in next dc] 3 times, 3 dc in next dc, [2 dc in next dc] 4 times, join in top of beg ch-3, fasten off.

Finishing

Decorate each doily with appliqués as desired. ❀

Bath Gift Basket

By Roberta Maier

Skill Level: Beginner

Size: 9 x 9 inches

Materials

✓ Acrylic sport weight cotton (1.75 oz per skein): 4 skeins melon, 5 skeins aquamarine

✓ Size F/5 crochet hook or size needed to obtain gauge

✓ 3 x 9-inch wall basket

✓ 2 decorative bars of soap

✓ Tapestry needle

Stitch the perfect gift! Worked in sport-weight cotton in the palest of hues, these attractive washcloths will look right at home in any bath.

Gauge

4 rows and 5 sts = 1 inch
Check gauge to save time.

Pattern Notes

Weave in loose ends as work progresses.

Each cloth requires 1½ oz; use leftovers to make striped washcloth.

Solid Washcloths

(Make 4 melon and 5 aquamarine)

Row 1: Ch 48, sc in 2nd ch from hook, sc in each rem ch across, turn. (47 sc)

Rows 2 & 3: Ch 1, sc in each sc across, turn.

Row 4: Ch 1, sc in each of next 3 sc, [ch 1, sk next sc, sc in next sc] 21 times, sc in next 2 sc, turn. (26 sc; 21 ch-1 sps)

Row 5: Ch 1, sc in each of next 3 sc, sc in next ch-1 sp, [ch 1, sk next sc, sc in next ch-1 sp] 20 times, sc in each of next 3 sc, turn.

Row 6: Ch 1, sc in each of

next 3 sc, [ch 1, sk next sc, sc in next ch-1 sp] 20 times, ch 1, sk next sc, sc in each of next 3 sc, turn.

Rows 7–32: Rep Rows 5 and 6.

Row 33: Rep Row 5.

Row 34: Ch 1, sc in each

sc and in each ch-1 sp across, turn. (47 sc)

Rows 35 & 36: Ch 1, sc in each sc across, turn. At the end of Row 36, fasten off.

Striped Washcloth

Rep Rows 1–36 of solid washcloth with leftover cotton working [3 rows aquamarine, 3 rows melon] rep until 36 rows are completed.

Assembly

Rolled humped cloths

Fold cloth in half, beg at opposite edge of fold

keeping edges even, roll cloth to fold, pick up and with folded edge at underside fold cloth in half.

Flower cloths

Fold cloth in half, grasp cloth at center of fold with fingers and allow open edges to flare out like a flower.

Place 2 rolled humped cloths end to end in the bottom of the basket.

Fold rem cloths as desired and fill basket placing soap inside flower cloths to accent. ❀

Flower Face Pins

By Sue Childress

Skill Level: Beginner

Size:

Pink pin: 2¼ inches in diameter

Yellow pin: 2½ inches in diameter

Materials

- ✓ Crochet cotton size 10: 40 yds each pink and yellow
- ✓ Size 7 steel crochet hook or size needed to obtain gauge
- ✓ 2 (1-inch) fabric face shank buttons
- ✓ Glue
- ✓ 2 (1-inch) pin backs
- ✓ Flower appliqués

Gauge

8 sts = 1 inch

Check gauge to save time.

Pattern Notes

Weave in loose ends as work progresses.

Join rnds with a sl st unless otherwise stated.

Ch 3 counts as first dc throughout.

For a truly unique and special pin, try these adorable smiling flowers. You'll love the way they complement a spring dress or straw hat.

Pink Flower

Rnd 1: With pink, ch 8, sl st to join to form a ring, ch 3, 29 dc in ring, join in top of beg ch-3. (30 dc)

Rnd 2: Ch 3, 2 dc in same st, 3 dc in each rem dc around, join in top of beg ch-3. (90 dc)

Rnd 3: Ch 1, sc in same dc, ch 3, [sc in next dc, ch 3] rep around, join in beg sc, fasten off.

Yellow Flower

Rnd 1: With yellow, ch 8, sl st to join to form a ring, ch 3, dc in ring, ch 2, [2 dc, ch 2] 13 times in ring, join in top of beg ch-3. (14 ch-2 sps)

Rnd 2: Sl st into ch-2 sp, ch 3, 9 dc in same ch-2 sp, 10 dc in each rem ch-2 sp around, join in top of beg ch-3. (140 dc)

Rnd 3: Ch 1, sc in same dc as beg ch, sc in next dc,

ch 5, [sc in each of next 2 dc, ch 5] rep around, join in beg sc, fasten off.

Finishing

Glue fabric face button to center of flower, glue appliqué centered below face on flower and glue pin back centered on back of flower. ❀

Elegant Christmas Cardigan

By Vicki Blizzard

Skill Level: Beginner

Size: 40 (42½, 45½, 48) inches

Materials

- ✓ Bernat Silky Soft worsted weight yarn (5 oz per skein): 4 skeins black #376, 1 oz scarlet #375
- ✓ Sizes G/6 and I/9 crochet hooks or size needed to obtain gauge
- ✓ Yarn needle
- ✓ #24 tapestry needle
- ✓ Beading needle
- ✓ Black and green sewing thread
- ✓ 8mm gold loose sequins
- ✓ Gold rocaille beads
- ✓ 3 yds green strung sequins

Gauge

With crochet hook size I, 4 rows and 7 sts = 1 inch

Check gauge to save time.

Pattern Notes

Weave in loose ends as work progresses.

Join rnds with a sl st unless otherwise stated.

Cardigan Body

Row 1 (RS): With crochet hook size I and black, ch 141, (149, 161, 169), sc in 2nd ch from hook, sc in each rem ch across, turn. (140, 148, 160, 168 sc)

Row 2: Ch 1, sc in each sc across, turn.

Rep Row 2 until body measures 15 inches or desired length to underarm, ending with a WS row, turn.

Right Front

Row 3: Ch 1, sc in each of next 35 (37, 40, 42) sc, turn.

Rep Row 3 until right front from underarm measures 5 inches, ending with a WS row, turn.

Neck shaping

Row 4: Sl st in each of next 10 (12, 14, 16) sc, ch 1, sc in each rem sc across, turn. (25, 25, 26, 26 sc)

Row 5: Ch 1, sc in each sc across to last 2 sc, dec 1 sc over next 2 sc, turn. (24, 24, 25, 25 sc)

Row 6: Ch 1, sc in each sc across, turn.

Rep Row 6 until right front from underarm measures 9½ (10, 10½, 10½) inches, ending with a RS row, fasten off.

Back

With RS facing, attach black with a sl st in next unworked sc on last row of body, ch 1, sc in same sc as beg ch-1, sc in each of next 69 (73, 79, 83) sc, turn. (70, 74, 80, 84 sc)

Work even in sc until back measures even with right front, fasten off.

Left Front

With RS facing, attach black with a sl st in next unworked sc on last row of body, ch 1, sc in same sc as beg ch-1, sc in each rem sc across, turn. (35, 37, 40, 42 sc)

Work as for right front, reversing shaping. Continue in pattern until left front measures the same as right front, fasten off.

Lifelike poinsettias and sparkling sequins fall like glittering snow down the front of this charming cardigan. Soft, warm and magically elegant, this is the ideal garment for holiday entertaining.

Sleeve

(Make 2)

Row 1 (RS): With crochet hook size I and black, ch 41, sc in 2nd ch from hook, sc in each rem ch across, turn. (40 sc)

Row 2: Ch 1, sc in each sc across, turn.

Row 3: Rep Row 2.

Row 4: Ch 1, 2 sc in first sc, sc in each sc across to last sc, 2 sc in last sc, turn. (42 sc)

Rows 5–7: Rep Row 2.

Row 8: Rep Row 4. (44 sc)

Rep Rows 5–8 until there are 56 (60, 64, 68) sts.

Work even until sleeve measures 15 (16, 16½, 17) inches from beg or desired length to underarm, ending with a RS row, fasten off.

Poinsettia

Large

(Make 6)

With crochet hook size G and scarlet, *ch 10, sl st in 2nd ch from hook, sc in next ch, hdc in next ch, dc in next ch, 3 tr in next ch, dc in next ch, hdc in next

Continued on page 38

Summer Afternoon Afghan

By Brenda Stratton for
Crochet Trends and Traditions

Skill Level: Intermediate

Size: 45½ x 63 inches

Materials

✓ Bernat Berella "4" worsted weight yarn: 6 skeins light vista green #8732, 5 skeins cameo white #8716, 4 skeins pale antique rose #8814

✓ Size H/8 crochet hook or size needed to obtain gauge

✓ Tapestry needle

Rows and rows of delicate flowers with leafy-green borders climb their way up the panels of this beautiful afghan. A versatile gift, this afghan looks equally elegant in the sunroom or on the porch.

Gauge

Three joined center motifs measure approximately 7 inches; each strip measures approximately 7½ x 62 inches

Check gauge to save time.

Pattern Notes

Weave in loose ends as work progresses.

Join rnds with a sl st unless otherwise stated.

Beg ch 3 counts as first dc throughout.

Pattern Stitch

Joining ch-3: Ch 1, sl st in matching ch-3 on opposite strip, ch 1.

First Strip

First motif

Rnd 1: With pale antique rose, ch 4, sl st to join to form a ring, ch 3, 19 dc in ring, join in 3rd ch of beg ch-3, fasten off. (20 dc)

Rnd 2: Attach cameo white with a sl st in any st, ch 1, sc in same st, ch 3, sk next st, [sc in next st, ch 3, sk next st] 9 times, join in beg sc, fasten off. (10 ch-3 sps)

Second motif

Rnd 1: Rep Rnd 1 of first motif.

Rnd 2: Attach cameo white with a sl st in any st, ch 1, sc in same st, ch 3, sk next dc, [sc in next dc, ch 3, sk next dc] 7 times, [sc in next st, ch 1, sl st into ch-3 sp on previous motif, ch 1, sk 1 st on working motif] twice, join in beg sc, fasten off.

Remaining motifs

Continue working and joining motifs according to instructions given for 2nd motif until 24 motifs have been worked for each strip, leaving 3 ch-3 sps free on each side of motif between joining.

Border

Rnd 1: Holding strip lengthwise with narrow end at top, attach light vista green with a sl st in back lp of center ch-3 of 3rd ch-3 group from last joining, working in back lps for this rnd only of each center ch of each ch-3 around, [sc, ch 3, 2 sc] in same ch, *[2 sc in center ch of next ch-3] twice, [2 sc, ch 3, 2 sc] in center ch of next ch-3, [2 sc in center ch of next ch-3] twice, ch 4, [{2 sc in center ch of next ch-3} 3 times, ch 4] rep across to last motif, [2 sc in center ch of next ch-3] twice **, [2 sc, ch 3, 2 sc] in center ch of next ch-3, rep from *, ending last rep at **, sc in same ch as beg sc, join in beg sc.

Rnd 2: Sl st into ch-3 sp, [ch 3, dc, ch 2, 2 dc] in same ch sp (for corner), *dc in each of next 8 sc, [2 dc, ch 2, 2 dc] in next ch-3 sp (for corner), [dc in each of next 6 sc, 3 dc in next sp] rep across to last motif, dc in next 6 sc **, [2 dc, ch 2, 2 dc] in next ch-3 sp (for corner), rep from * to **, join in 3rd ch of beg ch-3.

Rnd 3: Sl st into ch-2 sp, [ch 3, dc, ch 2, 2 dc] in corner ch-2 sp, dc in each dc to corner ch-2 sp, [{2 dc, ch 2, 2 dc} in corner ch-2 sp, dc in each dc across to next corner ch-2 sp] 3 times, join in 3rd ch of beg ch-3.

Rnd 4: Working in front lps for this rnd only, ch 1, sc in same st, ch 3, sk next st, [sc in next st, ch 3, sk next st] rep around, join in beg sc, fasten off.

Rnd 5: Working in back lps of Rnd 3, attach cameo white in first ch of ch-2 sp of any corner, ch 3, dc in same ch as beg ch, 2 dc in next ch, dc in each dc across to next ch-2 sp, [{2 dc in next ch} twice, dc in each dc across to next ch-2 sp] rep around, join in 3rd

Continued on page 38

Pretty Pillowcases

By Sue Childress

Skill Level: Beginner

Size:

Lilac lace: 1¾ inches wide

Yellow lace: 2 inches wide

Blue lace: 3½ inches wide

Materials

✓ Crochet cotton size 10: 150 yds each lilac, yellow and blue

✓ Size 7 crochet hook or size needed to obtain gauge

✓ Hemstitched-edge pillowcases

✓ 1½ yds ⅛-inch-wide satin ribbon

✓ Appliqués

Gauge

7 sts = 1 inch

Check gauge to save time.

Pattern Notes

Weave in loose ends as work progresses.

Join rnds with a sl st unless otherwise stated.

Lilac Lace

Rnd 1 (RS): Attach lilac in edge of pillowcase, ch 1, work 294 sc evenly sp around edge, join in beg sc. (294 sc)

Rnd 2: Ch 1, sc in same st, ch 3, sk next 2 sc, [sc in next sc, ch 3, sk next 2 sc] rep around, join in beg sc. (98 ch-3 sps)

Rnd 3: Sl st into ch-3 sp, ch 1, sc in same ch-3 sp, ch 3, [sc in next ch-3 sp, ch 3] rep around, join in beg sc.

Rnd 4: Sl st into ch-3 sp, ch 1, 2 sc in same ch-3 sp, 3 dc in next ch-3 sp, [2 sc in next ch-3 sp, 3 dc in next ch-3 sp] rep around, join in beg sc. (49 sc groups; 49 dc groups)

Rnd 5: Ch 1, sc in same sc, ch 3, sc in next sc, 3 dc in 2nd dc of 3-dc group, [sc in next sc, ch 3, sc in next sc, 3 dc in 2nd dc of next 3-dc group] rep around, join in beg sc.

Rnd 6: Sl st into ch-3 sp, [ch 4 (counts as first dc, ch 1), dc, {ch 1, dc} 3 times] in same ch-3 sp, *sc in 2nd dc of 3-dc group **, [dc, {ch 1, dc} 4 times] in next ch-3 sp, rep from * around, ending last rep at **, join in 3rd ch of beg ch-4.

Rnd 7: Sl st into ch-1 sp, ch 3, dc in same ch-1 sp, 2 dc in each of next 3 ch-1 sps, *2 sc in next sc **, 2 dc in each of next 4 ch-1 sps, rep from * around, ending last rep at **, join in 3rd ch of beg ch.

Rnd 8: Ch 1, sc in same st as beg ch, ch 3, [sc in next st, ch 3] rep around, join in beg sc, fasten off.

Finishing

Sew appliqués as desired on pillowcase.

Yellow Lace

Rnd 1 (RS): Attach yellow in edge of pillowcase, ch 1, work 288 sc around, join in beg sc. (288 sc)

Rnd 2: Ch 4 (counts as first dc, ch 1 throughout), sk next sc, [dc in next sc, ch 1, sk next sc] rep around, join in 3rd ch of beg ch-4. (144 ch-1 sps)

Rnd 3: Sl st into ch-1 sp, ch 1, sc in same ch-1 sp, ch 5, sk next ch-1 sp, [sc in next ch-1 sp, ch 5, sk next ch-1 sp] rep around, join in beg sc. (72 ch-5 sps)

Rnd 4: Sl st into ch-5 sp,

In summery pastels and three different lacy patterns, these beautiful pillowcases will add elegance and cheer to any bedroom or guest room.

ch 1, beg in same ch-5 sp, [5 sc in next ch-5 sp, 5 hdc in next ch-5 sp, 5 dc in next ch-5 sp, 5 hdc in next ch-5 sp, 5 sc in next ch-5 sp, {sc, ch 5, sc} in next ch-5 sp] rep around, join in beg sc.

Rnd 5: Sl st into 3rd sc, ch 1, [sc in 3rd sc, ch 5, sc in 3rd hdc, 7 dc in 3rd dc, sc in 3rd hdc, ch 5, sc in 3rd sc, 7 dc in ch-5 sp, sc] rep around, join in beg sc.

Rnd 6: Sl st into ch-5 sp,

ch 3, 6 dc in same ch-5 sp, ch 3, sc in 4th dc of 7-dc group, ch 3, [7 dc in next ch-5 sp, ch 3, sc in 4th dc of 7-dc group, ch 3] rep around, join in top of beg ch-3.

Rnd 7: Sl st to 4th dc of 7-dc group, ch 3, 6 dc in same dc, [ch 3, sc in next ch-3 sp] twice, ch 3, [7 dc in 4th dc of 7-dc group, {ch 3, sc in next ch-3 sp} twice, ch 3] rep around, join in top of beg ch-3.

Rnd 8: Sl st into 4th dc, ch 1, [sc in 4th dc of 7-dc group, ch 3, sk next ch-3 sp, 7 dc in center ch-3 sp, ch 3, sk next ch-3 sp] rep around, join in beg sc.

Rnd 9: Sl st into ch-3 sp, ch 1, [3 sc in next ch-3 sp, sc in each of next 7 dc, 3 sc in next ch-3 sp] rep around, join in beg sc, fasten off.

Finishing
Weave ribbon through Rnd 1, tie ends in a bow. Sew

appliqués as desired on pillowcase.

Blue Lace

Rnd 1: Attach blue in edge of pillowcase, ch 1, work 295 sc evenly sp around pillowcase edge, join in beg sc. (295 sc)

Rnds 2 & 3: Ch 2 (counts as first hdc throughout), hdc in each st around, join in top of beg ch-2.

Continued on page 39

Kitchen Naturals

By Katherine Eng

Skill Level: Beginner

Size:

Round hot pads: 7¾ inches

Square hot pad: 6¾ inches

Dishcloth: 7½ x 10 inches

Materials

✓ Lion Brand Kitchen Cotton: 4½ oz natural #098

✓ Sizes E/4 and F/5 crochet hooks or size needed to obtain gauge

✓ Tapestry needle

This practical kitchen set will match any decor, making it just right for gift-giving. The double-thick hot pads and sturdy dishcloth are extra-durable, and will be treasured for years to come.

Gauge

With crochet hook size F, rnds 1 and 2 of hot pad = 1½ inches

Check gauge to save time.

Pattern Notes

Weave in loose ends as work progresses.

Join rnds with a sl st unless otherwise stated.

Each hot pad or dishcloth require 1½ oz cotton.

Pattern Stitches

Sm shell: 3 dc in indicated st.

Lg shell: 5 dc in indicated st.

Round Hot Pad

(Make 2)

Rnd 1 (RS): With crochet hook size F, ch 4, sl st to join to form a ring, ch 1, 10 sc in ring, join in beg sc. (10 sc)

Rnd 2: Ch 1, 2 sc in each sc around, join in beg sc. (20 sc)

Rnd 3: Ch 1, [sc in sc, sm shell in next sc] rep around, join in beg sc. (10 sm shells; 10 sc)

Rnd 4: Ch 3 (counts as first dc throughout), 2 dc in same sc, sc in center dc of shell, [sm shell in next sc, sc in center dc of shell] rep around, join in top of beg ch-3, sl st into center dc of shell.

Rnd 5: Ch 1, sc in same dc, lg shell in next sc, [sc in center dc of shell, lg shell in next sc] rep around, join in beg sc.

Rnd 6: Ch 3, 4 dc in same sc, sc in center dc of next shell, [lg shell in next sc, sc in center dc of next shell] rep around, join in top of beg ch-3.

Rnd 7: Ch 1, sc in each st around, working [sc, ch 2, sc] in center dc of each lg shell, join in beg sc, fasten off.

Border

Note: If hanging lp is desired, at any ch-2 sp of a shell work [sc, ch 10, sl st in first ch, sc] in ch-2 sp.

Rnd 1: With WS of hot pads tog, with crochet hook size E, draw up a lp in center sc between 2 shells, ch 1, [sc, ch 2, sc] in same sc, *ch 1, sk 1 sc, sc in next sc, ch 1, sk 1 sc, [sc, ch 3, sc] in next ch-2 sp, ch 1, sk 1 sc, sc in next sc, ch 1, sk 1 sc **, [sc, ch 2, sc] in next sc, rep from * around, ending last rep at **, join in beg sc, fasten off.

Square Hot Pad

Rnds 1 & 2: Rep Rnds 1 and 2 of round hot pad. (20 sc)

Rnd 3: Ch 1, [sc in each of next 4 sc, 2 sc in next sc] rep around, join in beg sc. (24 sc)

Rnd 4: Ch 1, sc in sc, *sm shell in next sc, sc in next sc, sk 1 sc, lg shell in next sc, sk 1 sc **sc in next sc, rep from * around, ending last rep at **, join in beg sc. (4 lg shells; 4 sm shells; 8 sc)

Rnd 5: Ch 3 (counts as first dc throughout), 2 dc in same sc, *sc in center dc of next shell, sm shell in next sc, [sk next dc, sc in next dc, lg shell in next dc (center corner), sc in next dc, sk next dc] for corner pattern **, sm shell in next sc, rep from * around, ending last rep at **, join in top of beg ch-3, sl st into center dc of same shell. (4 lg shells; 8 sm shells; 12 sc)

Rnd 6: Ch 1, sc in same dc, *sm shell in next sc, sc in center dc of next shell, sm shell in next sc, rep corner pattern of Rnd 5, sm shell in next sc **, sc in center dc of next shell, rep from * around, ending last rep at **, join in beg sc. (4 lg shells; 12 sm shells; 16 sc)

Rnd 7: Rep Rnd 7 of round hot pad, working [sc, ch 2, sc] in center dc of each shell.

Border

Note: If hanging lp is desired, at any corner ch-2 sp work [sc, ch 10, sl st in first ch, sc] in corner ch-2 sp.

Rnd 1: With WS of hot

pads tog, with crochet hook size E, draw up a lp in 4th sc to the left of any corner ch-2 sp, ch 1, sc in same sc, *[ch 1, sk next 2 sc, {sc, ch 2, sc} in next ch-2 sp, ch 1, sk next 2 sc, sc in next sc] 3 times, working across corner, ch 1, sk 1 sc, [sc, ch 2, sc] in next sc, ch

1, sk 1 sc, [sc, ch 3, sc] in next corner ch-2 sp, ch 1, sk 1 sc, [sc, ch 2, sc] in next sc, ch 1, sk 1 sc, sc in next sc, rep from * around, join in beg sc, fasten off.

Dishcloth

Row 1 (RS): With crochet hook size F, ch 34, sc in

2nd ch from hook, [ch 3, sk 3 chs, sc in next ch] rep across, turn.

Rows 2–37: Ch 1, sc in first sc, [ch 3, sk next ch-3 sp, sc in next sc] rep across, turn.

At the end of Row 37, fasten off. ❀

Sunflower Jewelry

By Sandy Abbate

Skill Level: Beginner

Size:

Hat: 5½ inches in diameter

Barrette: 4 inches

Earrings: 2¼ inches in diameter

Button covers: 1½ inches in diameter

Materials

- ✓ J.&P. Coats Knit-Cro-Sheen crochet cotton size 10 (225 yds per ball): cream #42
- ✓ DMC embroidery floss: 3 skeins each yellow #743 and brown #898, 2 skeins hunter green #895
- ✓ Size 6 steel crochet hook or size needed to obtain gauge
- ✓ 42 inches ½-inch-wide red ribbon
- ✓ 3 (½-inch) buttons
- ✓ 3 button-cover backs
- ✓ 2½-inch barrette back
- ✓ 2 pierced-earring studs with disk and earring backs
- ✓ 7 (½-inch) red ribbon roses
- ✓ Sewing needle and thread
- ✓ Tacky glue
- ✓ Small amount fiberfill
- ✓ Scented oil

Gauge

4 dc rnds = 1 inches; large sunflower = 1¼ inches; small sunflower = 1 inch

Check gauge to save time.

Pattern Notes

Weave in loose ends as work progresses.

Join rnds with a sl st unless otherwise stated.

Work with 6 strands embroidery floss throughout.

Pattern Stitches

Shell: [2 dc, ch 1, 2 dc] in indicated st.

Beg shell: [Ch 3, dc, ch 1, 2 dc] in indicated st.

Sunflower Hat Jewelry Holder

Hat

Rnd 1: With cream, ch 4, sl st to join to form a ring, ch 3 (counts as first dc throughout), 11 dc in ring, join in top of beg ch-3. (12 dc)

Rnd 2: Ch 3, dc in same st as beg ch-3, 2 dc in each rem st around, join in top of beg ch-3. (24 dc)

Rnd 3: Ch 3, 2 dc in next st, [dc in next st, 2 dc in next st] rep around, join in top of beg ch-3. (36 dc)

Rnd 4: Ch 3, dc in next st, 2 dc in next st, [dc in each of next 2 sts, 2 dc in next st] rep around, join in top of beg ch-3. (48 dc)

Rnd 5: Ch 3, dc in each of next 2 sts, 2 dc in next st, [dc in each of next 3 sts, 2 dc in next st] rep around, join in top of beg ch-3. (60 dc)

Rnds 6–10: Ch 3, dc in each st around, join in top of beg ch-3.

Rnd 11: Working in back lps for this rnd only, ch 3, dc in each of next 2 sts, dec 1 dc over next 2 sts, [dc in each of next 3 sts, dec 1 dc over next 2 sts] rep around, join in top of beg ch-3. (48 dc)

Rnd 12: Ch 3, dc in next st, dec 1 dc over next 2 sts, [dc in each of next 2 sts, dec 1 dc over next 2 sts] rep around, join in top of beg ch-3. (36 dc)

Rnd 13: Ch 3, dec 1 dc over next 2 sts, [dc in next st, dec 1 dc over next 2 sts] rep around, join in top of beg ch-3. (24 dc)

Stuff hat lightly with fiberfill and add scented oil to fiberfill.

Rnd 14: Ch 2, dc in next

dd a ray of sunshine to your life when you wear these beautiful sunflower accessories! The perky sunflower hat makes a cheerfully decorative jewelry holder or pincushion.

st, [dec 1 dc over next 2 sts] rep around, join in top of beg ch-3. (12 dc)

Rnd 15: Ch 1, [dec 1 sc over next 2 sts] 6 times, join in beg sc, fasten off.

Brim

Rnd 1: Working in rem free lps of Rnd 11, with top of hat facing, attach cream, ch 1, sc in same st as beg ch, ch 3, sk 1 st, [sc in next st, ch 3, sk 1 st] rep around, join in beg sc. (30 ch-3 sps)

Rnd 2: Sl st into ch-3 sp, beg shell in same ch-3 sp, shell in each ch-3 sp around, join in top of beg ch-3. (30 shells)

Rnds 3–5: Sl st into ch-1 sp of shell, beg shell in same ch-1 sp, shell in each ch-1 sp of shell around, join in top of beg ch-3. At the end of Rnd 5, fasten off.

Finishing

Sew buttons to center of brim approximately 2 inches apart. Sew 1 ribbon rose to center top of hat. Cut a 24-inch length of red ribbon, place around base of crown and tie ends in a bow.

Sunflower Earrings

Large Sunflower

(Make 2)

Center

Rnd 1: With brown embroidery floss, ch 2, 6 sc in 2nd ch from hook, do not join. (6 sc)

Rnd 2: Work 2 sc in each sc around, do not join. (12 sc)

Rnd 3: [Sc in next sc, 2 sc in next sc] 6 times, sl st in next st, fasten off. (18 sc)

Petals

Rnd 4: Attach yellow in any sc of previous rnd, ch 1, sc in same st as beg ch, ch 3, [sc in next sc, ch 3] rep around, join in beg sc, fasten off. (18 ch-3 sps)

Small Sunflower

(Make 2)

Rnds 1 & 2: Rep Rnds 1 and 2 of large sunflower. (12 sc)

At the end of Rnd 2, sl st in next sc, fasten off.

Rnd 3: Rep Rnd 4 of large sunflower. (12 ch-3 sps)

Leaf

(Make 4)

Row 1: With hunter green, ch 4, 5 dc in 4th ch from hook, turn. (6 dc)

Row 2: Ch 3, dc in each st across, turn.

Row 3: Ch 2, [yo, insert hook in next st, yo, draw up a lp, yo, draw through 2 lps on hook] 5 times, yo, draw through all 6 lps on hook, fasten off.

Finishing

Glue 1 each large and small sunflowers and 2 leaves tog as shown, using care to glue side leaves on opposite sides. Glue 1 rose next to side leaf. Glue whole piece to earring stud.

Sunflower Button Covers

(Make 3)

Make 3 each large and small sunflowers. Make 3 leaves. For each button cover, glue 1 each large and small sunflowers and 1 leaf tog in different configurations. Glue 1 rose to each. Glue each to button back.

Sunflower Barrette

Make 2 each large and small sunflowers. Make 4 leaves. Glue 2 large sunflowers tog at center, with small sunflowers at each side. Glue 1 leaf at each end and 2 at center bottom. Glue rose centered between 2 bottom leaves. Tie 18-inch length of red ribbon into a bow and glue to back of bottom leaves. Glue whole piece to barrette back.

Finishing

Hook barrette through lps of Rnd 1 of brim of hat near bow.

Put button covers on buttons sew to hat brim. Push earrings through empty sps on brim and attach earring backs. ❁

Straw Hat Pin

By Nazanin Fard

Skill Level: Beginner

Size: 3 inches in diameter

Materials

- ✓ DMC Traditions crochet cotton size 10: 50 yds cream #712, small amount pink #818
- ✓ Size 7 steel crochet hook or size needed to obtain gauge
- ✓ 3 green leaf beads
- ✓ Beacon Fabri-Tac
- ✓ Sparkle Stiffen Stuff
- ✓ 1½-inch pin back
- ✓ Sewing needle and thread

Gauge

10 dc = 1 inch

Check gauge to save time.

Pattern Notes

Weave in loose ends as work progresses.

Join rnds with a sl st unless otherwise stated.

Hat

Rnd 1: With cream, ch 5, sl st to join to form a ring, ch 1, 10 dc in ring, join in beg sc. (10 sc)

Rnd 2: Ch 1, [2 sc in next sc, sc in next sc] rep around, join in beg sc. (15 sc)

Rnd 3: Ch 1, sc around, inc 9 sc evenly sp around, join in beg sc. (24 sc)

Rnd 4: Ch 1, sc in each sc around, join in beg sc.

Rnds 5–9: Rep Rnd 4.

Rnd 10: Rep Rnd 2. (36 sc)

Rnd 11: Rep Rnd 4.

Rnd 12: Rep Rnd 2. (54 sc)

Rnd 13: Rep Rnd 4.

Rnd 14: Ch 4 (counts as first dc, ch 1), sk next sc, [dc in next sc, ch 1, sk next sc] rep around, join in 3rd ch of beg ch-4.

Rnd 15: Ch 1, sc in same st as joining, 2 sc in next ch-1 sp, [sc in next dc, 2 sc in next ch-1 sp] rep around, join in beg sc.

Rnd 16: Rep Rnd 4.

Rnd 17: Ch 1, [2 sc in next sc, sc in each of next 2 sc] rep around, join in beg sc.

Rnd 18: Rep Rnd 4.

Rnd 19: Ch 1, [sc in each of next 2 sc, ch 3, sl st in first ch] rep around, join in beg sc, fasten off.

Rosette

(Make 2)

Row 1: With pink, ch 13, 2 dc in 4th ch from hook, 3 dc in each rem ch across, leaving a length of cotton, fasten off.

Finishing

Roll rosette into a spiral and sew to hat. Spray hat and rosettes with stiffener and allow to dry completely. Sew leaves to hat. Glue pin back to center back of hat. ❀

Accent your warm-weather wardrobe with this sweet straw hat pin. The tiny roses adorning the brim can be made in your choice of colors to coordinate with any outfit.

Crocheted Wire Earrings

By JoHanna Dzikowski

Skill Level: Beginner

Size:

Oval earrings: ¾ x 1¼ inches plus wires

Round earrings: 1 inch in diameter plus earring wires

Materials

- ✔ Silver beading wire (32 gauge): 24 yds
- ✔ Size B/1 crochet hook or size needed to obtain gauge
- ✔ 16 (5mm) beads (8 per pair)
- ✔ Sterling silver earring wires
- ✔ Tweezers
- ✔ Wire cutters

Gauge

Row 1 of beaded section of oval earrings = ⅞ inch; Rnds 1 and 2 of round earrings = ½ inch

Check gauge to save time.

Pattern Notes

Weave in loose ends as work progresses.

Do not join rnds unless otherwise stated.

Thread 4 beads onto wire before beg each earring.

Oval Earrings
(Make 2)

Rnd 1: Ch 7, sc in 2nd ch from hook, [slide 1 bead up next to work, sc in next ch] 4 times, ch 1, working on opposite side of foundation ch, sc in each of next 6 chs. (12 sc; 4 beads)

If you've not yet tried crocheting with wire, this fascinating earring set is a wonderful place to start. Simple and elegant, this pretty pair is sure to please one and all.

Row 2: Sc in each of next 6 sc on first half of Rnd 1.

Rnd 3: Sc in each of next 12 sc around piece, leaving a 3-inch length of wire, cut wire.

Round Earrings
(Make 2)

Rnd 1: Ch 4, sl st to join to form a ring, ch 1, work 8 sc in ring. (8 sc)

Rnd 2: [Sc in next sc, slide 1 bead up next to work, sc in next sc] 4 times. (8 sc; 4 beads)

Rnd 3: Sc in each of next 8 sc.

Rnd 4: [Sc in next sc, 2 sc in next sc] 4 times, leaving a 3-inch length of wire, cut wire.

Finishing

With the 3-inch length of wire, make 2 small lps, cut off excess wire, tuck in ends. You may have to shape the wire making a few adjustments so both earrings turn out exactly the same shape. Attach to earring wire. ✿

Window Soap Bags

By Roberta Maier

Skill Level: Intermediate

Size: 2½ x 4¼ inches

Materials

- ✓ Coats & Clark Aunt Lydia's bedspread crochet cotton size 10: 100 yds white #201
- ✓ Size 8 steel crochet hook or size needed to obtain gauge
- ✓ 1¾ x 3-inch bars soap with decorative centers
- ✓ ½ yd ⅟₁₆-inch-wide red satin ribbon
- ✓ 1 yd ⅛-inch-wide peach satin ribbon
- ✓ 1 small peach appliqué
- ✓ 1 small red ribbon rose
- ✓ Glue
- ✓ Tapestry needle

Gauge

5 mesh sps and 3 mesh rows = 1 inch

Check gauge to save time.

Pattern Notes

Weave in loose ends as work progresses.

Join rnds with a sl st

These decorative soap sachets make a lovely bridal shower or house warming gift. Stitch a couple for a special occasion, or a dozen for that upcoming church bazaar!

unless otherwise stated.

Back

Row 1 (RS): Ch 32, dc in 8th ch from hook, [ch 2, sk 2 chs, dc in next ch] 8 times, turn. (9 sps)

Row 2: Ch 5 (counts as first dc, ch 2 throughout), dc in next dc, [ch 2, dc in next dc] 7 times, ch 2, sk 2 chs, dc in next ch, turn.

Rows 3–13: Ch 5, dc in next dc, [ch 2, dc in next dc] 7 times, ch 2, sk 2 chs, dc in next ch, turn.

At the end of Row 13, fasten off.

Front

Rows 1 & 2: Rep Rows 1 and 2 of back.

First edge

Row 3 (RS): Ch 5, dc in next dc, ch 2, dc in next dc, leaving rem sts unworked, turn. (2 sps)

Rows 4–9: Ch 5, dc in next dc, ch 2, sk next 2 chs, dc in next ch, turn.

At the end of Row 9, ch 14, remove hook from lp, leaving a 7-inch length, fasten off.

Second edge

Row 3 (RS): With finished edge to the right, sk next 5 ch-2 sps, attach cotton in next dc, ch 5, dc in next dc, ch 2, sk next 2 chs, dc in next ch, turn. (2 sps)

Rows 4–9: Ch 5, dc in next dc, ch 2, sk next 2 chs, dc in next ch, turn.

At the end of Row 9, drop lp off hook, pick up lp from first edge, sl st in 3rd ch of beg ch-5 of Row 9 of 2nd edge, fasten off rem length from first half.

Row 10: Pick up dropped lp from 2nd edge, ch 5, dc in next dc, ch 2, dc in next dc, [ch 2, sk next 2 chs, dc in next ch] 4 times, [ch 2, sk next 2 chs, dc in next dc] twice, ch 2, sk next 2 chs, dc in next ch, turn. (9 sps)

Rows 11–13: Ch 5, dc in next dc, [ch 2, dc in next

Continued on page 39

Gauge

2 dc rows = ⅜ inch

Check gauge to save time.

Pattern Notes

Weave in loose ends as work progresses.

You might want to thread a few extra beads into cotton in case a bead breaks during the process of pushing along cotton.

Pattern Stitches

Bead sc (bsc): Slide bead close to hook, insert hook in indicated st, yo, draw up a lp, keeping bead on RS, yo, draw through both lps on hook.

Bead ch (bch): Slide bead close to hook, yo, draw lp through keeping bead on RS.

Bottle Collar

Row 1 (RS): With white, ch 34, sc in 2nd ch from hook, sc in each rem ch across, turn. (33 sc)

Row 2: Ch 1, sc in first sc, [ch 1, sk 1 sc, sc in next sc] 16 times, turn. (16 ch-1 sps)

Row 3: Sl st into ch-1 sp, ch 3 (counts as first dc throughout), 3 dc in same ch-1 sp as beg ch, 4 dc in each rem ch-1 sp across, turn. (64 dc)

Row 4: Ch 4 (counts as first dc, ch 1 throughout), dc in next dc, [ch 1, dc in next dc] rep across, turn.

Row 5: Ch 4, dc in next dc, [dc, ch 2, dc] in ch-1 sp, dc in next dc, ch 1, dc in next dc, *[ch 1, dc in next dc] twice, [dc, ch 2, dc] in next ch-1 sp, dc in next dc, ch 1, dc in next dc, rep from * across, fasten off.

Row 6: String 33 pearl beads onto purple cotton, attach purple to first dc, ch 1, sc in same st, bsc in next sp, *sc in next dc, [2 dc, 1 bch, ch 1, 2 dc] in next ch-2 sp, sk 1 dc, sc in next dc **, sc in next sp, sc in next dc, bsc in next sp, sc in next dc, sc in next sp, rep from * across, ending last rep at **, bsc in next sp, sc in next dc, fasten off.

Finishing

Fill shaker with bath powder; place cover on top and cover hole openings of shaker with transparent tape. Weave ribbon through ch-1 sps of Row 2. Place collar around neck of shaker and sew ends of Row 1 tog. Tie ribbon ends in a bow. Knot ends of ribbon or trim as desired. Glue ribbon rose over center of bow. Remove transparent tape unless you are making this for a gift, then leave holes covered so that powder will not leak from shaker. ❀

Bath Powder Bottle Collar

By Margaret Nobles

Skill Level: Beginner

Size: 1⅜ inches wide

Materials

✓ Crochet cotton size 10: Small amount each white and purple

✓ Size 8 steel crochet hook or size needed to obtain gauge

✓ 12mm purple ribbon rose

✓ 12 inches ⅛-inch-wide purple ribbon

✓ 33 (3mm) pearl beads

✓ Bead needle

✓ Bath powder

✓ Transparent tape

✓ Glue

✓ Glass salt or pepper shaker 4½–5 inches in diameter around neck of bottle

With this beautiful bottle collar you can turn ordinary household necessities into decorative works of art.

Shoe Bag & Toe Sachets

By Laura Gebhardt

Skill Level: Beginner

Size:

Bag: 12 x 17 inches

Toe sachets: 3 x 4 inches

Materials

- ✓ Worsted weight yarn: 6 oz soft navy, 3 oz grape ivy
- ✓ Size H/8 crochet hook or size needed to obtain gauge
- ✓ 2 scented dryer sheets
- ✓ Small amount fiberfill
- ✓ Tapestry needle

Gauge

4 groups of 3 sts = 3½ inches; 6 rows = 2 inches
Check gauge to save time.

Pattern Notes

Weave in loose ends as work progresses.

Join rnds with a sl st unless otherwise stated.

Pattern Stitch

3-st group: [Sc, hdc, dc] in indicated st.

Shoe Bag Sides

(Make 2)

Row 1 (RS): Beg at bottom with soft navy, ch 44, 3-st group in 2nd ch from hook, sk next 2 chs, [3-st group in next ch, sk next 2 chs] 13 times, sc in last ch, turn. (14 sets of 3-st groups)

Rows 2–37: Ch 1, 3-st group in first sc, [3-st group in next sc] 13 times, sc in last sc, turn. (14 sets of 3-st group)

Row 38 (WS): Ch 3 (counts as first dc), dc in each st across, turn. (43 dc)

Row 39: Ch 3 (counts as first hdc, ch 1), [sk next dc, hdc in each of next 2 dc, ch 1] 13 times, sk next dc, hdc in each of next 2 dc, turn. (29 hdc; 14 ch-1 sps)

Row 40: Ch 3, dc in each hdc and in each ch-1 sp across, fasten off. (43 dc)

Joining

Row 1: With WS of sides tog, attach soft navy in dc at end of Row 40, ch 1, working through both thicknesses, sc evenly sp down side, across bottom and up opposite side edge, do not work across sts of Row 40.

Row 2: Ch 1, reverse sc in each st of Row 1, fasten off.

Edging

Rnd 1: Attach grape ivy in first dc of Row 40, ch 3, 2 dc in same st as beg ch-3, 3 dc in each dc of Row 40 on both sides, join in 3rd ch of beg ch-3. (258 dc)

Rnd 2: Ch 1, sc in same st, [ch 2, hdc in last sc made, sk next 2 dc, sc in next dc] rep around, join in beg sc, fasten off.

Ties

(Make 2)

With grape ivy, ch 151, sl st in 2nd ch from hook, sl st in each rem ch across, fasten off.

Weave first tie through ch-1 sps of Row 39 first side; weave 2nd ch through ch-1 sps of Row 39 of 2nd side. Knot ends tog at each side of bag.

Toe Sachets

(Make 2)

Row 1: With grape ivy, leaving a 10-inch length at beg, ch 3, sc in 2nd ch from hook, sc in next ch, turn. (2 sc)

Row 2: Ch 1, 2 sc in each sc across, turn. (4 sc)

Rows 3–8: Ch 1, 2 sc in first sc, sc in each sc across to last sc, 2 sc in last sc, turn. (16 sc at end of Row 8)

Rows 9–18: Ch 1, sc in each sc across, turn.

Rows 19–24: Ch 1, dec sc over next 2 sc, sc in each sc across to last 2 sc, dec sc over next 2 sc, turn. (4 sc at end of Row 24.

Row 25: Ch 1, [dec sc over next 2 sc] twice, turn. (2 sc)

Row 26: Ch 1, dec sc over next 2 sc, fasten off.

Fold Row 1 to Row 26, sew first side seam. Stuff with fabric dryer sheet and fiberfill as needed, sew 2nd side closed. ✿

hile packing your luggage, tuck your shoes into this handsome travel bag. A pair of toe sachets will keep your shoes nicely shaped and fragrant!

Garnet Purse

By Dawn Goodan

Skill Level: Beginner

Size: 5½ x 6½ inches

Materials

✓ DMC Cebelia crochet cotton size 10 (282 yd balls): 2 balls garnet #816

✓ Size 7 steel crochet hook or size needed to obtain gauge

✓ 7½ x 12-inch garnet material

✓ Sewing needle and thread

✓ Straight pins

✓ Tapestry needle

The next time you want an evening on the town, stitch this attractive jewel-toned purse. Petite and demure, it will be a fine companion on any social occasion.

Gauge

8 rows = 1½ inches; 5 patterns = 2 inches

Check gauge to save time.

Pattern Notes

Weave in loose ends as work progresses.

Ch 3 counts as first dc throughout.

Purse

(Make 2)

Row 1 (RS): Ch 70, sc in 2nd ch from hook, sc in each rem ch across, turn. (69 sc)

Row 2 (WS): Ch 3, 2 dc in same st as beg ch-3, [sk 3 sts, {sc, ch 3, 3 dc} in next st] rep across to last st, dc in last st, turn.

Row 3 (RS): Ch 3, [fpdc around each of next 3 dc, ch 3, sc in next ch sp] rep across to last 3 dc sts, fpdc around each of next 2 dc, dc in last dc, turn.

Row 4 (WS): Ch 3, 2 dc in same st as beg ch-3, [{sc, ch 3, 3 dc} in next ch sp] rep across to last st, sc in last st, turn.

Rows 5–30: Rep Rows 3 and 4. At the end of Row 30, fasten off.

With tapestry needle and length of garnet, sew across opposite sides of foundation chs and sew sides of purse tog, leaving Row 30 of each side open.

Handle

(Make 2)

Ch 2, sc in 2nd ch from hook, turn last sc made to your left, sc in strand on left side of st, [turn last sc just made to your left, sc in both strands on left side of st] rep until piece measures 12½ inches, fasten off.

Lining

Cut material on fold, 7½ x 6 inches. Sew ¼ inch hem down each side of material, fold in half and sew sides tog, sewing a ¼ inch hem down each side. Sew a ½-inch hem around top opening of lining. Place lining inside of purse and sew in place around top and down each side seam.

Finishing

Pin ¼ inch of handle to Row 25 approximately 2 inches in from edge, rep the same on opposite edge of purse with opposite end of same handle, sew ¼ inch of handle to purse. Rep on opposite side of purse with 2nd handle. ❀

Bouclé Shrug

By Laura Gebhardt

Skill Level: Beginner

Size: 22 x 60 inches

Materials

✓ Bernat Soft Bouclé fashion weight yarn: 16 oz natural #6703

✓ Sizes G/6 and H/8 crochet hooks or size needed to obtain gauge

✓ Tapestry needle

This soft and bountiful shrug is a unique winter warmer for all ages. Stitched in one piece, it works up quickly and easily into an elegant, perfectly-fitting garment.

Gauge

9½ rows and 13 sts = 4 inches

Check gauge to save time.

Pattern Note

Weave in loose ends as work progresses.

Shrug

Row 1 (RS): With crochet hook size H, ch 72, hdc in 3rd ch from hook, hdc in each rem ch across, turn. (71 hdc)

Row 2: Ch 2 (counts as first hdc throughout), hdc in each hdc across, turn.

Rep Row 2 until piece measures 52 inches from beg, ending with a WS row. Do not fasten off.

Cuff

(Make 2)

Row 1: With crochet hook size G, ch 3, [dec 1 dc over next 2 sts] rep across, turn. (36 sts)

Row 2: Ch 2, *fpdc around next dc, bpdc around next dc] rep across, ending with hdc in last st, turn.

Rows 3–7: Ch 2, [fpdc around fpdc, bpdc around bpdc] rep across, ending with hdc in last st. At the end of Row 7, fasten off.

With RS facing, working in opposite side of foundation ch, attach yarn in first ch, ch 3, [dec 1 dc over next 2 sts] rep across, turn. (36 sts)

Rep Rows 2–7 of cuff.

Finishing

Sew sleeve seam 16 inches from bottom of cuff upward. ❋

Ruffled Sachets

By Janet Giese

Skill Level: Intermediate

Size:

Square sachet: 4¾ inches

Round sachet: 4¾ inches

Heart sachet: 5¼ inches

Materials

✓ DMC Traditions crochet cotton size 10: 360 yds cream #746, 50 yds each peach #754, pistachio green #369, pink #818 and 10 yds yellow #745

✓ Size 7 steel crochet hook or size needed to obtain gauge

✓ 1 yd ¼-inch-wide cream satin ribbon

✓ Potpourri

Gauge

Rnds 1 and 2 = 1¼ inches

Check gauge to save time.

Pattern Notes

Weave in loose ends as work progresses.

Join rnds with a sl st unless otherwise stated.

Leaving a 3-inch tail at beg of Rnd 1, work sts over ring and tail, every few sts, pull tail to tighten sts on ring.

Each sachet requires 120 yds cream, 50 yds peach, pistachio green or pink, small amount yellow and 12 inches of ribbon.

Pattern Stitches

Popcorn (pc): 5 dtr in indicated st or sp, draw up a lp, remove hook, insert hook in first st of group, pick up dropped lp and draw through st on hook.

Beg popcorn (beg pc): Ch 4, 4 dtr in indicated st or sp, draw up a lp, remove hook, insert hook in top of beg ch-5, pick up dropped lp and draw through st on hook.

2-dtr cl: Holding back on hook last lp of each st, dtr in first indicated st and in 2nd indicated st, yo, draw through all 3 lps on hook.

Square Sachet

Motif

(Make 2)

Rnd 1 (RS): With green, ch 6, sl st to join to form a ring, beg pc in ring, ch 7, [pc in ring, ch 7] 3 times, join in top of beg pc. (4 pc; 4 ch-7 sps)

Rnd 2: Sl st into ch-7 sp, ch 1, [{3 sc, ch 2, 3 sc} in next ch-7 sp] 4 times, join in beg sc.

Rnd 3: *Ch 7, pc in ch-2 sp, ch 7, sl st in 3rd sc, sl st in next sc, rep from * around, sl st last ch 7 in 3rd sc, do not join. (4 pc; 8 ch-7 sps)

Rnd 4: Ch 1, [9 sc in ch-7 sp, ch 1] rep around, join in beg sc, fasten off. (72 sc; 8 ch-1 sps)

Rnd 5: Attach cream with sc in back lps of ch-1 sp over corner pc, *ch 5, tr in back lp of next ch-1, p, [ch 1, tr in same sp, p] 3 times, ch 5, [2 sc, p, sc] in back lp of next ch-1, rep from * around, ending with 2 sc, p in same sp as beg sc, sl st to join in beg sc, sl st in next 2 chs.

Rnd 6: Ch 11, tr in same ch as beg ch, *ch 2, sk next 2 chs, tr in next ch, [ch 2, tr in next ch-1 sp] 3 times, ch 2, tr in first ch past p, ch 2, sk 2 chs, tr in next ch, ch 5, 2-dtr cl in same ch as tr and in 2nd ch past p, ch 5, tr in same ch as dtr, rep from * around, ending with ch 5, dtr in same ch as tr, sl st in 6th ch of beg ch-11.

Rnd 7: Ch 9, *sk next 2 chs, tr in next ch, ch 2, [2 tr in next tr, ch 2, 1 tr in next tr, ch 2] 3 times, 2 tr in next tr, ch 2, sk next 2 chs, tr in next ch, ch 3, 2 dtr in top of cl (corner), ch 3, rep from * around, ending with ch 3, dtr in top of cl, sl st in 6th ch of beg ch-9.

Rnd 8: Sc in sp, ch 5, *[dtr, ch 1] 7 times in same sp, [dtr, ch 1] 5 times in each ch-2 sp, [dtr, ch 1] 8 times in each ch-3 sp on corners, join, fasten off.

Rnd 9: Attach green in any ch-1 sp, [ch 3, sl st in next ch-1 sp] rep around, fasten off.

Center trim

Working in back lps of Rnd 4 only, attach yellow in 3rd sc past ch-1 sp on side edge, *[ch 3, sk 1 sc, sl st in next sc] 3 times, sl st in sp, sl st in next sc,

Flowers and ruffles abound in these three charming sachets. Adorned with dainty ribbons, they make a truly elegant gift. Pick your favorite shape or crochet all three!

[ch 3, sk 1 sc, sl st in next sc] 3 times, ch 1, sl st in sp, ch 1, sl st in 3rd sc, rep from * around, join in first sl st, fasten off.

Finishing

Cut a 12-inch length of ribbon. Holding motifs tog and matching center pc and outer corners weaving ribbon through Rnd 7, weave ribbon under 2nd group of 2-tr left of corner, [weave over single tr, under 2-tr] rep around filling with potpourri before closing, tie ends in a bow.

Round Sachet

Motifs

(Make 2)

Rnd 1 (RS): With peach, ch 6, sl st to join to form a ring, beg pc in ring, ch 7, [pc, ch 7] 5 times in ring, join in top of beg pc. (6 pc; 6 ch-7 sps)

Rnd 2: Ch 1, [9 sc in next ch-7 sp] rep around, join in beg sc, fasten off. (54 sc)

Rnd 3: Attach cream in 3rd sc of any 9-sc group, ch 4, dtr in 4th sc, p, ch 3, *tr in same sc as dtr, p, ch 3, 2-dtr cl in same sc as tr and in 5th sc, p, ch 3, tr in same sc as last dtr, p, ch 3, 2-dtr cl in same sc as tr and 4th sc, p, ch 3, rep from * around, work last dtr and tr in same st as beg ch, join with ch 1, dc under p.

Rnd 4: Ch 10, *sc in 2nd ch of ch 3, ch 9, rep from * around to last p, ch 3, tr in first ch of beg ch, sc over tr.

Rnd 5: Ch 5, *sc in 5th ch in next sp, ch 5, rep from * around, join in first sc, sl st into next sp.

Rnd 6: Ch 6, [dtr, ch 1] 6 times in same sp, *[dtr, ch 1] 7 times in next sp, rep from * around, join last ch 1 in 5th ch of beg ch, fasten off.

Rnd 7: Attach peach with sl st in any ch-1 sp of previous rnd, [ch 3, sl st in next ch-1 sp] rep around, fasten off.

Center trim

Working in back lps of Rnd 2 only, attach yellow to first sc in group of 4 above pc, sl st in next 3 sc, *ch 3, sl st in first sc past cl, ch 3, sl st in sc past cl, sl st in next 3 sc, rep from * around, fasten off.

Finishing

Cut a 12-inch length of ribbon. Holding motifs tog and matching pc, weave ribbon through ch-9 sps of Rnd 4 over and under each ch-9 group, filling with potpourri before closing, tie ends in a bow.

Heart Sachet

Motifs

(Make 2)

Rnd 1: With pink, ch 6, sl st to join to form a ring, beg pc in ring, ch 5, sc in ring, ch 5, [pc in ring, ch 5, tr, ch 3, tr, ch 5] twice in ring, join in top of beg pc. (3 pc)

Rnd 2: Ch 1, 5 sc in sp, sl st in center sc, [5 sc in next sp, ch 1] twice, 3 sc in next sp, ch 1, 5 sc in next sp, ch 5, 5 sc in next sp, ch 1, 3 sc in next sp, ch 1, 5 sc in next sp, ch 1, join in beg sc, fasten off.

Rnd 3: Working in back lps for this rnd only, attach cream with sc in sl st in center of heart, [ch 3, tr, ch 3, tr in 3rd sc, ch 3, sc in ch-1 sp] twice, ch 3, sc in ch-1 sp, ch 3, [tr, ch 3, tr] in 3rd sc, ch 3, 2 tr in 3rd ch of ch-5, ch 3, [tr, ch 3, tr] in 3rd sc, [ch 3, sc in next ch-1 sp] twice, ch 3, [tr, ch 3, tr] in 3rd sc, ch 3, sc in ch-1 sp, ch 3, [tr, ch 3, tr] in 3rd sc, ch 3, join in beg sc.

Rnd 4: Ch 1, 3 sc in next sp, ch 1, 5 sc in next sp, ch 1, [3 sc in next sp, ch 1] twice, 5 sc in next sp, ch 1, [3 sc in next sp, ch 1] 3 times, 5 sc in next sp, ch 1, 3 sc in next sp, ch 2, 3 sc in next sp, ch 1, 5 sc in next sp, ch 1, [3 sc in next sp, ch 1] 3 times, 5 sc in next sp, ch 1, [3 sc in next sp, ch 1] twice, 5 sc in next sp, ch 1, 3 sc in next sp, sl st in joining.

Rnd 5: Sl st in next 3 sc, sc in ch-1 sp, ch 5, tr in next ch-1 sp, ch 2, [dtr ch 2] 4 times in next ch-1 sp, tr in next ch-1 sp, ch 5, sc in next ch-1 sp, [ch 3, sc in next ch-1 sp] 3 times, *ch 5, tr in next ch-1 sp, ch 2, [dtr, ch 2] 4 times in next ch-1 sp, tr in next ch-1 sp, ch 5, sc in next ch-1 sp *, [ch 3, sc in next ch-1 sp] 3 times, rep from * to *, sl st in next 3 sc and in joining.

Rnd 6: Ch 4, hdc in sc, [ch 5, dc in next tr, {ch 3, dc in next dtr} 4 times, ch 3, dc in next tr, ch 5, sc in next sc, ch 5, sk next sc, sc in 2nd ch of ch-3, ch 5, sk next sc, sc in next sc] twice, ch 5, dc in next tr, [ch 3, dc in next dtr] 4 times, ch 3, dc in next tr, ch 5, hdc in next sc, ch 3, join in first ch of beg ch-4, sl st in next 3 chs and in hdc.

Rnd 7A: Ch 14, sc in next dc, [ch 13, sk next dc, sc in next dc] twice, [ch 13, sc in 3rd ch of ch-5] 4 times, ch 13, sk next dc, sc in next dc, ch 13, sk next dc, sc in 2nd ch of next ch-3, ch 13, sk next dc, sc in next dc, [ch 13, sc in 3rd ch of ch-5] 4 times, [ch 13, sk next dc, sc in next dc] 3 times, ch 13, sc in hdc, ch 7, join in first ch of beg ch, fasten off.

Rnd 7B: Holding previous rnd of lps to back, attach cream with sc in 3rd ch left of joining, [ch 13, sk next dc, sc in next dc] 3 times, [ch 13, sc in next sc] 3 times, ch 13, sc in next dc, ch 13, sk next dc, sc in next dc, ch 13, sc in next dc, ch 13, sk next dc, sc in next dc, [ch 13, sc in next sc] 3 times, ch 13, sc in next dc, [ch 13, sk next dc, sc in next dc] twice, ch 13, sk next dc, sc in 3rd ch of ch-5, ch 7, sc in center

joining, ch 7, join in beg sc, fasten off.

Rnd 8: Attach cream with sc to first ch-13 lp in back row left of ch-7 lp, ch 5, [dtr, ch 1] 6 times in same sp, *[dtr, ch 1] 7 times in next front lp, rep from * around alternating back and front lps for ruffle, sk the 3 ch-7 lps, sl st last dtr in 4th ch of beg ch-5, fasten off.

Rnd 9: Attach pink in any ch-1 sp, [ch 3, sl st in next ch-1 sp] rep around, after sl st between last 2 dtr, sl st in beg sl st to join ruffle trim, fasten off.

Center trim

Working in back lps of Rnd 2 only, attach yellow in first sc left of center st, sl st in next sc, [ch 3, sk next used sc, sl st in next 2 sc] rep around, join in beg sl st, fasten off.

Finishing

Cut a 12-inch length of ribbon. Holding motifs tog and matching the 3 ch-7 sps of both pieces, in ch-7 left of center, weave ribbon under sc, *sk next sc, weave under next sc, rep from * around, ending with ribbon coming up under sc in ch-7 sp right of center, fill with potpourri, tie ends in a bow. ❦

Handy Eyeglasses Holder Pin

By Ruth Shepherd

Skill Level: Beginner

Size: 2¼ x 2¾ inches

Materials

✓ DMC Baroque crochet cotton size 10: Small amount ecru and red

✓ Size 9 steel crochet hook or size needed to obtain gauge

✓ 1-inch plastic ring

✓ 9 (3mm) gold beads

✓ ¾-inch pin back

✓ Sewing needle and thread

More than just a decoration, this innovative pin is ideal for holding reading glasses when not in use, or your eyeglasses when you want a little catnap! Of course, it looks wonderful as an accent pin, too!

Gauge

9 sts = 1 inch

Check gauge to save time.

Pattern Notes

Weave in loose ends as work progresses.

Join rnds with a sl st unless otherwise stated.

Head

Rnd 1 (RS): Attach ecru to plastic ring, ch 1, sc over ring until ring is covered, join in beg sc, turn.

Collar

Row 2: Ch 1, sc in each of next 12 sc, turn. (12 sc)

Row 3: Ch 1, 2 sc in first sc, sc in each sc across to last sc, 2 sc in last sc, turn. (14 sc)

Rows 4 & 5: Rep Row 3. (18 sc)

Row 6: Ch 3 (counts as first hdc, ch 1), hdc in next st, [ch 1, hdc in next st] rep across, turn.

Row 7: Ch 3, sl st in first hdc, [ch 3, sl st in next hdc] rep across, fasten off.

Row 8 (RS): Attach red around vertical bar of first hdc of Row 6, ch 1, 3 sc over same hdc, [3 sc over next vertical bar of next hdc] rep across, fasten off.

Hair

Row 1 (RS): With ecru, ch 8, 3 sc in 2nd ch from hook, 3 sc in each of next 6 chs, sl st in 2nd free sc of ring, [ch 3, sl st in next sc] rep around ring to last unused sc, ch 8, 3 sc in 2nd ch from hook, 3 sc in each of next 6 chs, sl st in same sc on ring, fasten off.

Eyeglasses Hanger

Row 1: Attach red with sl st in 5th ch-3 sp of Row 7, ch 24, sl st in 5th ch-3 sp from opposite end of Row 7, turn.

Row 2: Ch 1, sc in each ch across, fasten off.

Finishing

Sew gold beads evenly sp across glasses hanger. Sew pin back to WS over Rows 3 and 4. ✿

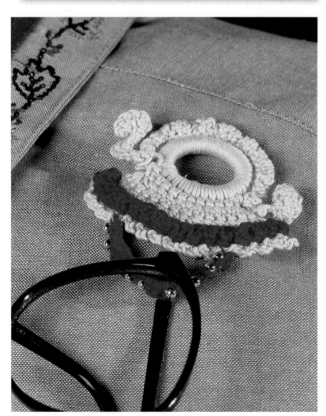

Elegant Christmas Cardigan

Continued from page 16

ch, sc in next ch, leaving last ch unworked, rep from * 7 times, leaving a 24-inch length of yarn, fasten off. (8 petals)

Small

(Make 2)

With crochet hook size G and scarlet, *ch 8, sl st in 2nd ch from hook, sc in next ch, hdc in next ch, 2 dc in next ch, hdc in next ch, sc in next ch, leaving last ch unworked, rep from * 7 times, leaving a 24-inch length of yarn, fasten off. (8 petals)

Attaching Flowers & Sequins

Using photo as a placement guide, sew 3 large poinsettias to each sweater front and 1 small poinsettia to each sleeve, curving tips of petals as desired and leaving an open circle in center of each flower.

Thread beading needle with black thread, randomly attach gold sequins to each flower center opening by bringing needle up through back of sweater front, inserting needle through center of gold sequin, inserting needle through gold rocaille bead, bring needle back through center of sequin to back of front and pulling thread gently until sequin fits snugly against front of sweater.

Cut a 12-inch length of green threaded sequins. Pull sequins off each end of strand, leaving a 1-inch piece of thread. Using photo as a guide for attaching sequin strand, pull 1 thread end of strand through to back of sweater. Use tapestry needle and black thread to sew sequin strand end to WS of sweater. Couch strand down on front of sweater in a nice swirl using green sewing thread. Bring rem thread end to back of sweater and sew in place. Rep with as many strands of green sequins as desired.

Randomly attach gold sequins to yoke area of sweater fronts and to bottom of each sleeve.

Assembly

With yarn needle and black yarn, sew shoulder seams. Sew sleeve seams, insert sleeve into armhole and sew sleeve in place.

Sweater Edging

Rnd 1 (RS): With crochet hook size I, attach black with a sc in bottom left corner of sweater, sc in rem lp of each ch across bottom of sweater, 3 sc in right corner of sweater bottom, sc in each st along edge of right side of sweater, sc evenly sp around neck edge, dec 1 st at inside curve of neck where dec is made, sc in each st along edge of left front of sweater to last st, 3 sc in last st, join in beg sc, turn.

Rnds 2–4: Ch 1, sc in same st as joining, sc in each st around, making 3 sc in center of each 3-sc group at bottom corner of sweater, join in beg sc, turn.

Rnd 5: With crochet hook size G, ch 1, sc in same st as joining, ch 3, sk next sc, [sc in next sc, ch 3, sk next sc] rep around, join in beg sc, fasten off.

Sleeve Edging

Rnd 1 (RS): With crochet hook size I, attach black at sleeve seam, ch 1, sc evenly sp around sleeve opening, join in beg sc, turn.

Rnds 2–4: Ch 1, sc in each sc around, join in beg sc, turn.

Rnd 5: Rep Rnd 5 of sweater edging. ❀

Summer Afternoon Afghan

Continued from page 18

ch of beg ch-3, fasten off.

Rnd 6: Adjusting sts as necessary to allow 7-dc groups to fall in 2nd dc of first 2-dc group of each corner, attach pale antique rose in 2nd dc of first 2-dc group at any corner, ch 3, 6 dc in same st, sk next st, sc in next st, sk next st, [3 dc in next st, sk next st, sc in next st, sk next st] rep across to next corner, *7 dc in 2nd dc of first 2-dc of next corner, sk next st, sc in next st, sk next st, [3 dc in next st, sk next st, sc in next st, sk next st] rep across to next corner, rep from * twice, join in top of beg ch-3, fasten off.

Rnd 7: Attach cameo white with a sl st in any sc, ch 1, sc in same st as beg ch, ch 3, sk next st, [sc in next st, ch 3, sk next st] rep around, join in beg sc, fasten off.

Second–Sixth Strips

Work as for first strip, substituting joining ch-3 for the ch-3 on long side to be joined to previous strip. ❀

Pretty Pillowcases

Continued from page 21

Rnd 4: Sl st in next hdc, [ch 4, 2 tr, ch 2, 3 tr] in same hdc, sk next 4 hdc, [{3 tr, ch 2, 3 tr} in next hdc, sk next 4 hdc] rep around, join in top of beg ch-4. (59 shells)

Rnd 5: Sl st into ch-2 sp, ch 1, [sc, ch 5, 4 tr] in same ch-2 sp, [{sc, ch 5, 4 tr} in next ch-2 sp] rep in each

ch-2 sp around, join in beg sc.

Rnds 6–8: Sl st into ch-5 sp, ch 1, [{sc, ch 5, 4 tr} in next ch-5 sp] rep around, join in beg sc.

Rnd 9: Sl st into ch-5 sp, ch 1, [2 sc in ch-5 sp, sc in each of next 4 tr] rep around, join in beg sc, fasten off.

Finishing

Sew appliqués as desired on pillowcase. ❀

Window Soap Bags

Continued from page 28

dc] 7 times, ch 2, sk next 2 chs, dc in next ch, turn. At the end of Row 13, do not turn.

Edging

Note: Hold back and front WS tog and working through matching sps of both thicknesses at the same time to join.

Row 1: Ch 1, sc in end of Row 13, 2 sc in each sp across side edge to corner, 5 sc in corner sp, 2 sc in ch sp across bottom to next corner, 5 sc in corner sp, 2 sc in each sp across side edge, sc in end of Row 13.

Rnd 2: Working around top opening of bag, ch 1, sc in last joining st, ch 1, [{dc, ch 1} 5 times in next dc, sc in next dc, ch 1] rep around top opening, join in beg sc.

Rnd 3: Ch 1, [sc in next ch-1 sp, ch 3] rep around, join in beg sc, fasten off.

Window opening edging

Rnd 1 (RS): Attach thread with sc in any ch-2 sp, sc in same sp, [2 sc in next sp] rep in each sp around opening, join in beg sc, fasten off.

Finishing

Note: Double peach ribbon before weaving.

Insert bar of soap in bag so that design on soap shows through window.

Beg at side joining edge, weave ribbon in and out of Row 13, cross ends as if tying a bow, pull ends tightly to close opening, then wrap one end of ribbon around bag one way and other end around the other way to meet where ribbons first cross; knot ribbons securely, allowing ends to flow down side of sachet. If desired, tie ribbon in a bow after wrapping; secure bow with dot of glue and allow ends of ribbon to flow down side.

Glue appliqué or ribbon rose in place to cover knots; allow to dry completely. ❀

Crochet Tips & Techniques

Drawstring Alternative

Whenever a pattern calls for a drawstring or crocheted tie, substitute a long shoestring in a coordinated color. You'll be able to move onto your next crochet project even faster!

Display Seasonal Designs

Many of the seasonal designs and dolls such as scarecrows, Valentine's Day, etc., can be made into attractive door decorations by sewing a plastic curtain ring on the back. Smaller designs, such as ornaments and fridgies, look great hanging in the window.

Eliminating Spaces

To eliminate the space between ch 3 and first dc, after joining previous row, ch 2 and work dc in same st as joining. When joining this round, join in top of first dc, skipping ch 2. Be sure and count ch 2 and first dc as one dc. The ch 2 fills the open sp. This works with thread and yarn, and cannot be noticed unless you're counting the stitches.

Stiffening Inserts

An inexpensive way to stiffen crocheted items that call for cardboard inserts is to use sections cut from plastic milk cartons. This makes the item completely washable. Remember to round off any sharp corners.

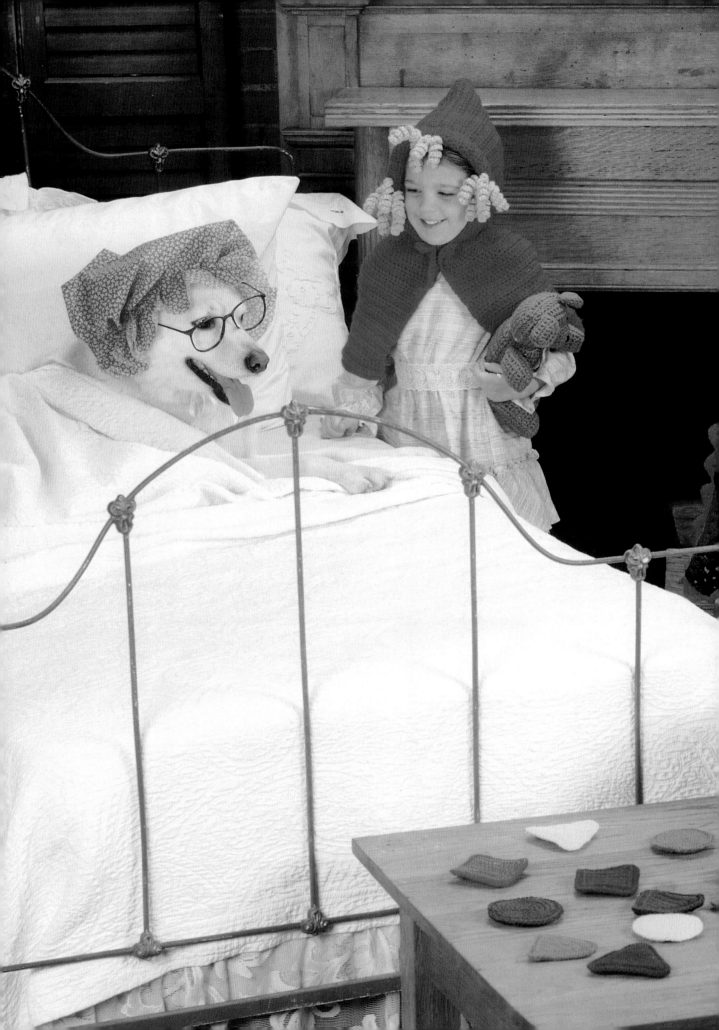

Kid-Pleasing Presents

Here's a colorful collection of gifts for that hard-to-please kid! From comfy sweaters and animal puppets, to sweet dolls and dresses, these gifts are as much fun to crochet as they are to wear and play with!

Caitlin Victorian Doll

By Brenda Stratton
for Crochet Trends and Traditions

Skill Level: Intermediate

Size: Fits 13–15-inch cloth-body doll

Materials

✓ Bernat Berella "4" worsted weight yarn: 6 oz #8846

✓ Size G/6 crochet hook or size needed to obtain gauge

✓ 13-inch cloth-body doll by Wang's

✓ 6-inch opening ivory lace umbrella by Wang's #XM1676

✓ 12 eggshell 1-inch satin ribbon bows with pearl centers

✓ 1 bow-shaped filigree craft backing

✓ ¾-inch pearl cameo button with gold edging

✓ 1 yd ⅜-inch-wide ivory satin ribbon

✓ 4½ yds 1½-inch-wide ruffled ivory lace

✓ 4 sets size 4/0 snap fasteners

✓ Hot-glue gun

✓ Sewing needle and thread

✓ Darning needle

✓ Yarn needle

Gauge

4 sc rows, 2 dc rows and 4½ sts = 1 inch

Check gauge to save time.

Pattern Notes

Weave in loose ends as work progresses.

Join rnds with a sl st unless otherwise stated.

Ch 3 counts as first dc throughout.

D**emure blue-green and palest ivory complement Caitlin's pretty face as she dons her hat and parasol for an afternoon outing.**

Dress

Bodice

Row 1: Beg at neckline, ch 27, sc in 2nd ch from hook, [sc in each of next 2 chs, 2 sc in next ch] 4 times, [2 sc in next ch, sc in each of next 2 chs] 4 times, sc in last ch, turn. (34 sc)

Row 2: Ch 1, [sc in next 11 sts, 2 sc in next st] twice, sc in next 10 sts, turn. (36 sc)

Row 3: Ch 1, sc in each st across, turn.

Row 4: Ch 1, [sc in next 11 sts, 2 sc in next st] twice, sc in next 12 sts, turn. (38 sc)

Row 5: Ch 1, [sc in each of next 12 sts, 2 sc in next st] twice, sc in next 12 sts, turn. (40 sc)

Row 6: Ch 1, sc in each of next 4 sts, 2 sc in next st, sc in each of next 14 sts, 2 sc in next st, sc in each of next 15 sts, 2 sc in next st, sc in each of next 4 sts, turn. (43 sc)

Row 7: Ch 1, sc in each of next 3 sts, 2 sc in next st, sc in each of next 4 sts, ch 9 loosely, sk next 6 sts (arm-hole opening), 2 sc in next st, [sc in each of next 4 sts, 2 sc in next st] twice, sc in next 3 sts, 2 sc in next st, ch 9 loosely, sk next 6 sts (arm-hole opening), sc in next 4 sts, 2 sc in next st, sc in each of next 3 sts, turn. (55 sts)

Row 8: Ch 2 (counts as first hdc throughout), hdc in next 7 sts, hdc dec over next 2 sts, sc in each of next 9 chs, sc in each of next 2 sts, [sc in each of next 4 sts, 2 sc in next st] 3 times, sc in next 2 sts, sc in each of next 9 chs, hdc dec over next 2 sts, hdc in each of next 7 sts, turn. (56 sts)

Row 9: Ch 2, hdc in each of next 7 sts, hdc dec over next 2 sts, sc in each of next 8 sts, sc dec over next 2 sts, [sc in each of next 2 sts, sc dec over next 2 sts] 5 times, sc in each of next 8 sts, hdc dec over next 2 sts, hdc in each of next 7 sts, turn. (48 sts)

Row 10: Ch 1, sc in each of next 4 sts, sc dec over next 2 sts, sc in each of next 3 sts, sc dec over next 2 sts, [sc in each of next 5 sts, sc dec over next 2 sts] 4 times, sc in each of next 3 sts, sc dec over next 2 sts, sc in next 4 sts, turn. (41 sts)

Row 11: Ch 2, hdc in each of next 4 sts, hdc dec over next 2 sts, hdc in each of next 2 sts, sc in next st, [sc in each of next 3 sts, sc dec over next 2 sts] 4 times, sc in next 4 sts, hdc in each of next 2 sts, hdc dec over next 2 sts, hdc in next 4 sts, turn. (34 sts)

Rows 12 & 13: Rep Row 3.

Row 14: Ch 1, sc in each st across, sl st to join.

Skirt

Rnd 1: Working in back lps for this rnd only, ch 3, dc in same st, 2 dc in each

st around, join in top of beg ch-3. (68 dc)

Rnd 2: Ch 3, dc in each of next 15 sts, 2 dc in next st, [dc in each of next 16 sts, 2 dc in next st] 7 times, join in top of beg ch-3. (72 dc)

Rnd 3: Ch 3, dc in each of next 7 sts, 2 dc in next st, [dc in each of next 8 sts, 2 dc in next st] 7 times, join in top of beg ch-3. (80 dc)

Rnd 4: Ch 3, dc in each st around, join in top of beg ch-3.

Rnd 5: Rep Rnd 4.

Rnd 6: Ch 3, dc in next 8 sts, 2 dc in next st, [dc in each of next 9 sts, 2 dc in next st] 7 times, join in top of beg ch-3. (88 dc)

Rnd 7: Rep Rnd 4.

Rnd 8: Ch 3, dc in each of next 9 sts, 2 dc in next st, [dc in each of next 10 sts, 2 dc in next st] 7 times, join in top of beg ch-3. (96 dc)

Rnd 9: Rep Rnd 4.

Rnd 10: Ch 3, dc in each of next 10 sts, 2 dc in next st, [dc in each of next 11 sts, 2 dc in next st] 7 times, join in top of beg ch-3. (104 dc)

Rnds 11–15: Rep Rnd 4. At the end of Rnd 15, fasten off.

Overskirt

Rnd 1: Working in rem free lps of Row 14 of bodice, attach yarn, ch 1, sc in same st, [ch 3, sk 1 st, sc in next st] rep around, ending with ch 3, sk last st, join in beg sc. (18 lps)

Rnd 2: Ch 3, 5 dc in same ch sp, sc in next ch sp, [shell of 5 dc in next ch sp, sc in next ch sp] rep around, join in top of beg ch-3, sl st in last sc worked. (9 groups of 5-dc shells)

Rnd 3: Ch 3, [7 dc in center of next shell, dc in next sc]

rep around, join in top of beg ch-3. (9 groups of 7-dc shells)

Rnd 4: Ch 3, [9 dc in center st of next shell, dc in single dc between shells] rep around, join in top of beg ch-3. (9 groups 9-dc shells)

Rnd 5: Ch 3, [11 dc in center st of next shell, dc in single dc between shells] rep around, join in top of beg ch-3. (9 groups of 11-dc shells)

Rnd 6: Ch 3, [13 dc in center st of next shell, dc in single dc between shells] rep around, join in top of beg ch-3. (9 groups 13-dc shells)

Rnd 7: [Ch 1, sl st in next st] rep around, fasten off.

Sleeve

(Make 2)

Rnd 1: Attach yarn at center underarm, ch 1, sc in same st, sc in each of next 4 sts, sc in side edge of next sc row, 2 hdc in each of next 6 sc, sc in side edge of next sc row, sc in each of next 4 sts, do not join. (23 sts)

Rnd 2: Sc in each of next 6 sts, [dc in next st, 2 dc in next st] 6 times, sc in next 4 sts, 2 sc in next st, do not join. (30 sts)

Rnds 3 & 4: [Sc in each sc, dc in each dc] rep around, do not join.

Rnd 5: [Sc dec over next 2 sts] 3 times, dc in each of next 18 sts, [sc dec over next 2 sts] 3 times, join in beg sc. (24 sts)

Rnd 6: Ch 3, dc in each st around, join in top of beg ch-3.

Rnd 7: Ch 3, dc in next st, dc dec over next 2 sts, [dc in each of next 2 sts, dc dec over next 2 sts] rep

around, join in top of beg ch-3. (18 dc)

Rnd 8: Rep Rnd 6, fasten off.

Back opening & collar

Row 1: Attach yarn at bottom left edge of back opening, ch 1, sc evenly in ends of rows to neckline, 2 sc in corner of neckline, sc in each st across neckline, do not work down right back edge, fasten off.

Cut a 14-inch length of lace, gather top edge of lace to fit neckline opening; sew in place.

Finishing

Sew snap fasteners evenly sp down back opening.

Sew lace to underside of bottom edge of overskirt scallops as shown. Sew lace around bottom edge of each sleeve.

Sew 3 rows of lace around bottom of skirt as shown. Place dress on doll from bottom and fasten snaps.

Glue a 1-inch satin bow to each upward point of scallops on overskirt. Glue a bow to each sleeve.

Belt

Cut a 12-inch length of ivory ribbon; place around waist, overlap ends at back and sew or glue in place.

Brooch

Glue the pearl cameo button to center of bow-shaped filigree craft backing; glue brooch at front center of neck.

Bonnet

Note: Bonnet is oval, with length fitting between the doll's ears at back.

Rnd 1: Ch 6, 3 sc in 2nd ch from hook, sc in next 3 chs, 3 sc in next ch,

working on opposite side of foundation ch, sc in next 3 chs, join in beg sc. (12 sc)

Rnd 2: Ch 3, dc in same st as beg ch-3, 2 dc in each of next 2 sts, dc in next 3 sts, 2 dc in each of next 3 sts, dc in each of next 3 sts, join in top of beg ch-3. (18 dc)

Rnd 3: Ch 3, dc in same st as beg ch-3, [dc in next st, 2 dc in next st] twice, sc in next 3 dc, [dc in next st, 2 dc in next st] twice, dc in each of next 4 sts, join in top of beg ch-3. (24 dc)

Rnd 4: Ch 3, dc in same st, 2 dc in each st around, join in top of beg ch-3. (48 dc)

Rnd 5: Ch 3, dc in each of next 2 sts, 2 dc in next st, [dc in each of next 3 sts, 2 dc in next st] rep around, join in top of beg ch-3. (60 dc)

Rnd 6: Ch 1, sc in same as beg ch-1, [sc in next st, ch 1] rep around, join in beg sc, fasten off.

Cut a 24-inch length of ivory lace; gather to measure 10 inches; sew lace to base of Rnd 4 on underside of bonnet.

For bonnet ties, cut 2 lengths of ribbon each 10 inches long; sew in place on underside of bonnet at sides. Place bonnet on doll and tie in a bow under chin. Glue a 1-inch satin ribbon bow to center back of bonnet.

Finishing

Cut 2 lengths of yarn each 10 inches long. Starting at back underside of sleeve, weave through top of Rnd 14 of sleeve; pull tightly, tie in a small bow, hide ends under sleeve and trim. Place closed umbrella under sleeve of doll's dress, catching a few sts at back to hold umbrella in place. ❦

Mini Purse Necklace

By Sandy Abbate

Skill Level: Beginner

Size: 4¼ inches square

Materials

✓ Coats & Clark Red Heart Super Saver worsted weight yarn: Small amounts of hot red #390, amethyst #356, paddy green #368 and mexicana #950

✓ Size H/8 crochet hook or size needed to obtain gauge

✓ ⅝-inch heart buttons: 1 each royal blue, yellow, purple and orange

✓ Sewing needle and matching threads

✓ Yarn needle

Gauge

4 sc rows and 4 sc sts = 1 inch

Check gauge to save time.

Pattern Notes

Weave in loose ends as work progresses.

Join rnds with a sl st unless otherwise stated.

Back

Row 1 (WS): With hot red, ch 17, sc in 2nd ch from hook, sc in each rem ch across, turn. (16 sc)

Row 2 (RS): Ch 1, sc in each sc across, turn.

Rows 3–16: Rep Row 2. At the end of Row 16, fasten off.

Place a marker in first and last st of Row 16.

Flap

Row 1 (RS): Working in back lps for this row only, attach amethyst in 2nd st of Row 16, ch 1, sc in same st, sc in each of next 13 sts, turn. (14 sc)

Rows 2 & 3: Ch 1, sc dec over next 2 sc, sc in each sc across to last 2 sc, sc dec over next 2 sc, turn. (10 sc)

Row 4: Ch 1, sc in each of next 4 sc, ch 2, sk 2 sc (buttonhole), sc in next 4 sc, turn.

Row 5: Ch 1, sc dec over next 2 sc, sc in next 2 sc, 2 sc over ch-2 sp, sc in next 2 sc, sc dec over next 2 sc, fasten off. (8 sc)

Front

Rows 1–16: Rep Rows 1–16 of back.

Place a marker in first and last sc of Row 16.

Use photo as a guide.

With sewing needle and matching threads, sew yellow button centered on Row 9 of front and royal

---

This sweet little purse, with its cheerful heart flowers and rainbow colors, will delight any little girl. It's super-simple and fun to make!

blue and purple on Row 7 at each side of yellow at a slight outward angle. With yarn needle and length of paddy green, sew stems with straight sts and leaves with lazy-daisy sts at the base of each button.

Assembly

With WS facing, place front and back tog; working through both thicknesses, attach mexicana in side edge of Row 16, ch 1, sc in same st as beg ch, sc evenly sp around purse to marker, sl st in st with marker, ch 100 (for strap), sl st in st with 2nd marker at opposite edge, join in beg sc, fasten off.

Flap Trim

With RS of flap facing, attach mexicana in same st on back where marker was placed, ch 1, sc in same st, sc evenly sp around flap, sc in same st on back where marker was placed, fasten off.

Sew orange button to center of Row 15 of front corresponding to buttonhole on flap. ✿

Baby Bunny in Bunting

By Michele Wilcox

Skill Level: Beginner

Size:

Bunny: 9 inches

Bunting: 6½ x 8 inches

Materials

✓ Bernat Berella worsted weight yarn by Spinrite: 3-oz pearl gray #8912, 1½-oz pale tapestry gold #8887, 1-oz winter white #8941

✓ Size F/5 crochet hook or size needed to obtain gauge

✓ 12 inches ¼-inch-wide light blue ribbon

✓ Crochet cotton size 5: 1 yd each blue and coral

✓ Fiberfill

✓ 2-inch piece cardboard

✓ Tapestry needle

Gauge

7 sc rnds and 7 sc sts = 1½ inches

Check gauge to save time.

Pattern Notes

Weave in loose ends as work progresses.

Do not join rnds unless otherwise stated; use a scrap of CC yarn to mark rnds.

Bunny

Head & Body

Rnd 1: Starting at top of head, with pearl gray, ch 2, 6 sc in 2nd ch from hook. (6 sc)

Rnd 2: Work 2 sc in each sc around. (12 sc)

Rnd 3: [Sc in next sc, 2 sc in next sc] rep around. (18 sc)

Rnd 4: [Sc in each of next 2 sc, 2 sc in next sc] rep around. (24 sc)

Rnd 5: Sc in each sc around.

Rnd 6: [Sc in each of next 3 sc, 2 sc in next sc] rep around. (30 sc)

Rnds 7–14: Rep Rnd 5.

Rnd 15: [Sc dec over next 2 sc] rep around. (15 sc)

Rnd 16: Rep Rnd 5.

Rnd 17: Rep Rnd 2. (30 sc) Stuff head with fiberfill.

Rnd 18: [Sc in each of next 4 sc, 2 sc in next sc] rep around. (36 sc)

Rnds 19–30: Rep Rnd 5.

Rnd 31: [Sc in each of next 4 sc, sc dec over next 2 sc] rep around. (30 sc)

Rnd 32: [Sc in each of next 3 sc, sc dec over next 2 sc] rep around. (24 sc)

Rnd 33: [Sc in each of next 2 sc, sc dec over next 2 sc] rep around. (18 sc) Stuff body with fiberfill.

Rnd 34: [Sc in next sc, sc dec over next 2 sc] rep around, sl st in next sc, leaving a length of yarn, fasten off. (12 sc)

Weave rem length through sts of Rnd 34, pull to close opening, secure and fasten off.

Ear

(Make 2)

Rnds 1 & 2: Rep Rnds 1 and 2 of head and body. (12 sc)

Rnd 3: Sc in each sc around.

Rnd 4: [Sc in each of next 3 sc, 2 sc in next sc] rep around. (15 sc)

Rnds 5–10: Rep Rnd 3. At the end of Rnd 10, leaving a length of yarn, fasten off.

Fold Rnd 10, flat across, fold Rnd 10 in half again, working through all 4 thicknesses, sew across edge; sew to top of head.

Arm

(Make 2)

Rnds 1 & 2: Rep Rnds 1 and 2 of head and body. (12 sc)

Rnds 3–10: Sc in each sc around.

Stuff arm with fiberfill.

Rnd 11: [Sc dec over next 2 sc] 6 times, sl st in next st, leaving a length of yarn, fasten off.

Sew arm to side of body.

Leg

(Make 2)

Rnds 1–3: Rep Rnds 1–3 of head and body. (18 sc)

Rnd 4: Sc in each sc around.

This sweet, cuddly little bunny will delight any little girl. She can play with him by day, then tuck him into his cozy bunting at night. He's just the right size for snuggling!

Rnds 5 & 6: Rep Rnd 4.

Rnd 7: [Sc dec over next 2 sc] 4 times, sc in each of next 10 sc. (14 sc)

Rnd 8: Rep Rnd 4.

Rnd 9: Work 2 sc in each of next 4 sc, sc in next 10 sc. (18 sc)

Rnds 10–16: Rep Rnd 4.

Rnd 17: [Sc in next sc, sc dec over next 2 sc] rep around. (12 sc)

Stuff leg with fiberfill.

Rnd 18: [Sc dec over next 2 sc] rep around, sl st in next st, leaving a length of yarn, fasten off. (6 sc)

Weave rem length through sts; sew leg to bottom of body.

Tail

Wrap winter white around 2-inch piece of cardboard 75 times. Slip bundle off

cardboard and with another length of winter white tie tightly around center of bundle; cut all lps; fluff and trim to 1 inch. Attach tail to back center bottom of body.

Facial features

With blue cotton, embroider eyes over Rnd 9 of head in satin st.

With coral, embroider nose in satin st, centered over

Rnd 10 between eyes; embroider mouth directly below nose.

Place ribbon around neckline; tie ends in a bow.

Bunting

Row 1: With pale tapestry gold, ch 53, sc in 4th ch from hook, dc in next ch, [sc in next ch, dc in next ch] rep across, turn.

Row 2: Ch 1, [sc in each dc, dc in each sc] rep across, turn.

Row 3: Ch 3 (counts as first dc throughout), [sc in each dc, dc in each sc] rep across, turn.

Rows 4–22: Rep Rows 2 and 3. At the end of Row 22, fasten off.

Place piece on a flat surface with foundation ch facing; fold each outer edge of rows to center (so that opening of bunting is at center); working through both thicknesses, sew across foundation ch. At center front opening, sew up center Rows 1–12.

Top trim

Rnd 1: With WS facing, attach winter white with sl st at center front in Row 12, ch 1, sc in same st as beg ch-1, work 12 sc evenly sp across side edge, 3 sc in corner, 51 sc across Row 22, 3 sc in corner, 12 sc across rem edge, join in beg sc.

Rnd 2: Ch 3, [dc, hdc] in same st as joining, [sk 1 sc, {sc, ch 3, dc, hdc} in next sc] rep around, join in base of beg ch-3, fasten off.

Insert bunny into bunting. ❦

Little Red Riding Hood Costume

By Michele Wilcox

Skill Level: Beginner

Size:

Hood: 9½ x 15 inches

Attached cape: 10 inches long

Materials

✓ Bernat Berella worsted weight yarn by Spinrite: 3 skeins geranium #8929, 2 oz light tapestry gold #8886

✓ Size G/6 crochet hook or size needed to obtain gauge

✓ Yarn needle

This whimsical costume is quick, easy and fun to make. You'll love the way it transforms your toddler into a curly-haired, adventurous Red Riding Hood.

Gauge

5 hdc rows and 8 hdc sts = 2 inches

Check gauge to save time.

Pattern Notes

Weave in loose ends as work progresses.

Costume can be made larger of smaller with a change in hook size.

Curls

(Make 14)

Row 1: Beg at neckline, with light tapestry gold, ch 15, 3 sc in 2nd ch from hook, 3 sc in each rem ch across, fasten off.

Hood

Row 1: With geranium, ch 45, hdc in 2nd ch from hook, hdc in each rem ch across, turn. (44 hdc)

Row 2: Ch 1, hdc in each of next 19 hdc, [2 hdc in next hdc] 6 times, hdc in each of next 19 hdc, turn. (50 hdc)

Row 3: Ch 1, hdc in each hdc across, turn.

Row 4: Ch 1, hdc in each of next 22 hdc, [2 hdc in next hdc] 6 times, hdc in each of next 22 hdc, turn. (56 hdc)

Row 5: Rep Row 3.

Row 6: Ch 1, hdc in each of next 25 hdc, [2 hdc in next hdc] 6 times, hdc in each of next 25 hdc, turn. (62 hdc)

Rows 7–24: Rep Row 3. At the end of Row 24, leaving a length of yarn, fasten off.

Fold Row 24 in half and sew across edge.

Cape

Row 1: Holding hood upside down and working in opposite side of foundation ch, sk first 4 chs, attach geranium in next ch, ch 1, sc in same ch as beg ch-1, sc in each of next 35 chs, leaving rem 4 chs unworked, turn. (36 sc)

Row 2: Ch 1, 2 hdc in each sc across, turn. (72 hdc)

Row 3: Ch 1, [hdc in next hdc, 2 hdc in next hdc] rep across, turn. (108 hdc)

Rows 4–28: Ch 1, hdc in each hdc across, turn.

At the end of Row 28, fasten off.

Drawstring

Row 1: With geranium, ch 130, sl st in 2nd ch from hook, sl st in each rem ch across, fasten off.

Finishing

To form casing for drawstring, fold first 4 skipped sts of front of hood back; sew edge in place along hook. Pass drawstring through casing.

Sew 4 curls at center top front of hood; sew 5 curls at each front edge of hood. ❧

Fourth of July Picnic Dress

By Beverly Mewhorter

Skill Level: Beginner

Size: Fits 4½-inch fashion doll

Materials

- ✓ Crochet cotton size 10: 50 yds each red, white and blue
- ✓ Size 7 steel crochet hook or size needed to obtain gauge
- ✓ 19 (5mm) white sequin stars
- ✓ 3 size 4/0 snap fasteners
- ✓ Sewing needle and thread
- ✓ Hot-glue gun
- ✓ Tapestry needle

Gauge

7 sc sts = 1 inch

Check gauge to save time.

Pattern Notes

Weave in loose ends as work progresses.

Join rnds with a sl st unless otherwise stated.

Petticoat

Row 1: With white, ch 19, sc in 2nd ch from hook, sc in each rem ch across, turn. (18 sc)

Row 2: Ch 1, 3 sc in each sc across, turn. (54 sc)

Rows 3–8: Ch 1, sc in each sc across, turn.

Row 9: Ch 1, 4 sc in each sc across, fasten off.

Sew Rows 5–9 closed.

Row 10: Attach white in side edge of Row 1, ch 1, sc evenly sp around back opening, fasten off.

Sew 1 snap fastener to top edge of back opening. Place petticoat on doll.

Dress

Bodice

Row 1: With blue, ch 19, sc in 2nd ch from hook, sc in each rem ch across, turn. (18 sc)

Row 2: Ch 1, sc in each of next 4 sc, ch 8, sk next 2 sc (armhole opening), sc in next 6 sc, ch 8, sk next 2 sc (armhole opening), sc in each of next 4 sc, turn.

Row 3: Ch 1, sc in each of next 4 sc, sc in each of next 8 chs, sc in each of next 6 sc, sc in each of next 8 chs, sc in next 4 sc, turn. (30 sc)

Row 4: Ch 1, sc in next sc, sc dec over next 2 sc, [sc in next sc, sc dec over next 2 sc] rep around, turn. (20 sc)

Row 5: Ch 1, [draw up a lp in each of next 3 sc, yo, draw through all 4 lps on hook] 6 times, sc in each of next 2 sc, turn. (8 sc)

Row 6: Ch 1, 3 sc in each sc across, fasten off. (24 sc)

Sleeve

(Make 2)

Rnd 1: Attach blue at underarm, ch 1, 10 sc evenly sp around armhole opening, join in beg sc. (10 sc)

Rnds 2 & 3: Ch 1, sc in each sc around, join in beg sc. At the end of Rnd 3, fasten off.

Skirt

Rnd 1: Attach red in opposite side of foundation ch of bodice, ch 1, 3 sc in same ch, 3 sc in each ch, join in beg sc, fasten off. (54 sc)

Rnd 2: Attach white, ch 1, sc in each sc around, join in beg sc, fasten off.

Rnd 3: Attach red, ch 1, sc in each sc around, join in beg sc, fasten off.

Rnds 4–9: Rep Rnds 2 and 3.

Back opening trim

Attach blue at back right neckline opening, ch 1, sc evenly sp down back opening and up opposite side, fasten off. Sew 2 snap fasteners evenly sp down back opening. Place dress on doll.

Hat

Rnd 1: With red, ch 2, 10 sc in 2nd ch from hook, join in beg sc, fasten off. (10 sc)

Rnd 2: Attach white, ch 1, 2 sc in each sc around, join in beg sc. (20 sc)

Rnd 3: Attach red, ch 1, [sc in next sc, 2 sc in next sc] rep around, join in beg sc, fasten off. (30 sc)

Rnd 4: Attach white, ch 1, [sc in each of next 2 sc, 2 sc in next sc] rep around,

Star-spangled and red, white and blue, this little girl is ready to celebrate! Take her to the park for fireworks, or add her to a holiday doll collection.

TIPS

Rustproof Pins
Truly rustproof pins are a necessity for any project that requires stiffening and pinning. Any pin that is not made of 100 percent stainless steel is eventually going to leave rust spots on your work. Some manufacturers incorporate other metals into their steel to cut the cost. This is fine for many projects when the pins don't come in contact with water.

Brighten Neutral Colors
Breathe new life into neutral-colored scrap yarns for use in fashion projects. Check the needlework department of your local craft store for eye-catching metallic thread. These threads come on various size spools in gold, silver, copper, bronze, and a whole spectrum of colored metallics as well.

Work with one strand each of yarn and thread combined, or just add touches of the metallic thread, a row or two here and there, for accents.

—*Dawn Thompson*

join in beg sc, fasten off. (40 sc)

Rnd 5: Working in back lps for this rnd only, attach red, ch 1, sc in each st around, join in beg sc, fasten off.

Rnd 6: Attach white, ch 1, sc in each sc around, join in beg sc, fasten off.

Rnd 7: Attach red, ch 1, sc in each sc around, join in beg sc, fasten off.

Rnds 8 & 9: Rep Rnds 6 and 7.

Rnd 10: Attach white, ch 1, [sc in each of next 2 sc, sc dec over next 2 sc] rep around, join in beg sc, fasten off. (30 sc)

Rnd 11: Attach blue, ch 1, sc in each sc around, join in beg sc.

Rnds 12 & 13: Ch 1, sc in each sc around, join in beg sc.

Rnd 14: Working in front lps for this rnd only, ch 1, [sc in next sc, 2 sc in next sc] rep around, join in beg sc.

Rnd 15: Ch 1, [sc in each of next 2 sc, 2 sc in next sc] rep around, join in beg sc, fasten off. Place hat on doll.

Finishing
Glue 2 stars on each sleeve; glue 3 stars to front bodice. Glue 12 stars evenly sp around Rnds 12 and 13 of hatband. 🐚

Baby's Spring Outfit

By Beverly Mewhorter

Skill Level: Beginner

Size: Fits 16-inch baby doll

Materials

✓ Coats & Clark Red Heart Super Saver worsted weight yarn: 6 oz cottage garden #398, 4 oz rose pink #372

✓ Size G/6 crochet hook or size needed to obtain gauge

✓ 16-inch cloth-body baby doll

✓ 2⅝ yds ¼-inch-wide white ribbon

✓ 12 pink lace/ribbon flowers with rose bud centers

✓ Hot-glue gun

✓ Tapestry needle

Gauge

4 sc sts = 1 inch

Check gauge to save time.

Pattern Notes

Weave in loose ends as work progresses.

Join rnds with a sl st unless otherwise stated.

Ch 3 counts as first dc throughout.

Dress

Bodice

Row 1: With cottage garden, ch 48, sc in 2nd ch from hook, sc in each rem ch across, turn. (47 sc)

Row 2: Ch 1, sc in each of next 10 sts, ch 14, sk next 6 sts (armhole opening), sc in each of next 15 sts, ch 14, sk next 6 sts (armhole opening), sc in next 10 sts, turn. (35 sc; 2 ch-14 sps)

Row 3: Ch 1, sc in each sc and each ch across, fasten off. (63 sc)

Row 4: Working in back lps for this row only, attach rose pink, ch 1, sc in each

A pretty baby, all dressed up in her sweet ruffled dress, is ready for her first spring outing. Shoes, headband and matching pantaloons complete this adorable set.

st across, turn. (63 sc)

Row 5: Ch 1, sc in each of next 2 sc, [sc dec next 2 sc tog, sc in each of next 2 sc] 15 times, sc in last sc, turn. (48 sc)

Row 6: Ch 1, [sc dec over next 2 sc] rep across, turn. (24 sc)

Row 7: Ch 1, sc in next 2 sc, [sc dec over next 2 sc, sc in each of next 2 sc] rep across, turn. (18 sc)

Row 8: Ch 1, sc in each sc across, turn.

Row 9: Ch 3, 3 dc in same st as beg ch-3, sc in next st, [4 dc in next st, sc in next st] rep across, fasten off.

Sleeve

(Make 2)

Rnd 1: With rose pink, ch 20, join to form a ring, ch 1, sc in each ch around, join in beg sc. (20 sc)

Rnds 2–12: Ch 1, sc in each st around, join.

Rnd 13: Ch 1, sc in same st, [4 dc in next st, sc in next st] rep around, join in beg sc, fasten off.

Sew sleeve to armhole opening.

Bodice ruffle

Row 1: Working in rem free lps of Row 3 of bodice, attach cottage

garden, ch 1, 2 sc in each st across, turn.

Row 2: Ch 1, sc in each sc across, turn.

Row 3: Ch 1, sc in same st as beg ch, [4 dc in next sc, sc in next sc] rep across, fasten off.

Skirt

Row 1: Attach cottage garden in opposite side of foundation ch of bodice, ch 1, 4 sc in same st as beg ch-1, work 4 sc in each st across, turn.

Row 2: Ch 1, sc in first sc, [ch 2, sk next sc, sc in next sc] rep across, turn.

Rows 3–24: Ch 1, sc in sc, [ch 2, sk next ch-2 sp, sc in next sc] rep across, fasten off.

Row 25: Attach rose pink, ch 1, sc in same sc, [4 dc in next ch-2 sp, sc in next sc] rep across, fasten off.

With length of cottage garden, sew back skirt opening matching end of Rows 7–25.

Place dress on doll. Starting at back neckline, weave a 30-inch length of ribbon through sps of Row 9 of bodice; tie ends in a bow. Cut a 14-inch length of ribbon, pass through back opening at Row 3 on each

side; tie ends in a bow. Glue 7 flowers evenly sp across front bodice over rose pink section.

Booties

(Make 2)

Rnd 1: With rose pink, ch 2, 8 sc in 2nd ch from hook, join in beg sc. (8 sc)

Rnd 2: Ch 1, 2 sc in each sc around, join in beg sc. (16 sc)

Rnd 3: Ch 1, [sc in next sc, ch 2, sk next sc] rep around, join in beg sc. (8 sc; 8 ch-2 sps)

Rnds 4–10: Ch 1, [sc in next sc, ch 2, sk next ch-2 sp] rep around, join in beg sc. At the end of Rnd 10, fasten off.

Rnd 11: Attach cottage garden in any sc, ch 1, [sc in next sc, 4 dc in next ch-2 sp] rep around, join in beg sc, fasten off.

Weave a 14-inch length of ribbon through ch-2 sps of Rnd 10. Place bootie on doll; tie ends in a bow at center front.

Glue 1 flower to top of each bootie.

Headband

Rnd 1: With cottage garden, ch 50, join to form a ring, ch 1, sc in same ch as beg ch-1, [ch 2, sk 1 ch, sc in next ch] rep around, join in beg sc, fasten off.

Rnd 2: Working on opposite side of foundation ch, attach cottage garden in beg ch, ch 1, sc in same ch, [ch 2, sk next ch, sc in next ch] rep around, join in beg sc, fasten off.

Glue 3 flowers to headband.

Pants

Rnd 1: With rose pink, ch 50, join to form a ring, ch 1, sc in each ch around, join in beg sc. (50 sc)

Rnd 2: Ch 1, sc in each sc around, join in beg sc.

Rnds 3–10: Rep Rnd 2.

First leg

Rnd 11: Sk next 24 sts, sl st in next st, ch 1, sc in same st, sc in each of next 24 sc, join in beg sc. (25 sc)

Rnds 12–18: Rep Rnd 2. At the end of Rnd 18, fasten off.

Rnd 19: Attach cottage garden, ch 1, sc in same st as beg ch, [sk next sc, 4 dc in next sc, sk next sc, sc in next sc] rep around, join in beg sc, fasten off.

Second leg

Rnd 11: Attach rose pink in first sk sc of Rnd 10, ch 1, sc in same sc, sc in each of next 24 sc, join in beg sc. (25 sc)

Rnds 12–19: Rep Rnds 12–19 of first leg.

Waistband

Rnd 1: Attach cottage garden in opposite side of foundation ch, ch 1, sc in same st, [sk next 2 chs, ch 2, sc in next ch] rep around, join in beg sc.

Rnd 2: Ch 1, sc in sc, [4 sc in next ch-2 sp, sc in next sc] rep around, join in beg sc, fasten off.

Weave 30 inches of ribbon through ch-2 sps of Rnd 1 of waistband; with ribbon ends at front, place pants on doll; tie ribbon ends in a bow. ❦

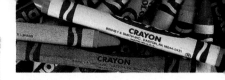

Flower Power Child's Afghan

By Sandy Abbate

Skill Level: Intermediate

Size: 44 inches square

Materials

✓ Coats & Clark Red Heart Super Saver worsted weight yarn: 8-oz skein each paddy green #368, hot red #390, cherry red #319 and bright yellow #324, 2 oz each amethyst #356, royal #385 and mexicana #950

✓ Size I/9 crochet hook or size needed to obtain gauge

✓ Yarn needle

Gauge

2 rows and 4 sc sts = 1 inch

Check gauge to save time.

Pattern Notes

Weave in loose ends as work progresses.

Join rnds with a sl st in top of beg ch-3 unless otherwise stated.

Ch 3 counts as first dc throughout.

Use afghan diagram as a guide.

Pattern Stitch

Tr cluster (tr cl): [Yo hook twice, insert hook in next st, yo, draw up a lp, {yo, draw through 2 lps on hook} twice] 3 times in same st, yo, draw through all 4 lps on hook.

Center Square

Rnd 1 (RS): With hot red, ch 3, sl st to join to form a ring, ch 3, 2 dc in ring, ch 1, [3 dc in ring, ch 1] 3 times, join.

Rnd 2: Sl st into ch-1 sp, [ch 3, 2 dc, ch 1, 3 dc] in same corner ch-1 sp, [{3 dc, ch 1, 3 dc} in next corner ch-1 sp] 3 times, join.

Rnd 3: Sl st in corner ch-1 sp, [ch 3, 2 dc, ch 1, 3 dc] in corner sp, *ch 1, sk next 3 dc, 3 dc in sp before next 3-dc group, ch 1 **, [3 dc, ch 1, 3 dc] in next corner ch-1 sp, rep from * around, ending last rep at **, join.

Rnd 4: Sl st in corner ch-1 sp, [ch 3, 2 dc, ch 1, 3 dc] in corner sp, *ch 1, [3 dc in next ch-1 sp, ch 1] rep across edge to next corner ch-1 sp **, [3 dc, ch 1, 3 dc] in corner ch-1 sp, rep from * around, ending last rep at **, join.

Rnds 5–11: Rep Rnd 4. At the end of Rnd 11, fasten off.

First Border

Row 1 (RS): Attach amethyst in any corner ch-1 sp, ch 4 (counts as first dc, ch 1), [3 dc, ch 1] in each ch-1 sp to next corner ch-1 sp, dc in corner ch-1 sp, turn.

Row 2 (WS): Ch 3, [3 dc, ch 1] in each ch-1 sp across, dc in 3rd ch of beg ch-4, turn.

Row 3 (RS): Ch 4, [3 dc, ch 1] in each ch-1 sp across, dc in last dc, turn.

Rows 4 & 5: Rep Rows 2 and 3.

Row 6: Rep Row 2, fasten off.

Rep Rows 1–6 of first border on each rem side.

Small Corner Block

(Make 4)

Rnds 1–3: With royal, rep Rnds 1–3 of center square. At the end of Rnd 3, fasten off.

Sew a small corner block to each corner of first border.

Triangular Section

Row 1 (RS): Attach cherry red in corner ch-1 sp of corner block, ch 3, [{3 dc, ch 1} in next ch-1 sp on corner block] 3 times, [3 dc, ch 1] in sp between first dc and next 3-dc group on border, [{3 dc, ch 1} in next ch-1 sp on border] 10 times, [3 dc, ch 1] in sp between next 3-dc group and last dc on border, [{3 dc, ch 1} in next ch-1 sp on corner block] twice, 3 dc in next ch-1 sp on corner block, dc in corner ch-1 sp of corner block, turn. (18 groups 3-dc)

Row 2: Ch 3, [3 dc, ch 1] in each ch-1 sp across to last ch-1 sp, 3 dc in last ch-1 sp, dc in sp between last 3-dc group and turning ch, turn.

Rows 3–17: Rep Row 2, there will be 1 less 3-dc group on each row.

Row 18: Ch 3, [3 dc, ch 1, 3 dc] in next ch-1 sp for corner, dc in sp between last 3-dc group and turning ch, fasten off.

Rep triangular section on rem 3 sides.

Second Border

Rnd 1 (RS): Attach bright yellow in any corner ch-1 sp, [ch 3, 2 dc, ch 1, 3 dc] in same corner ch-1 sp, ch 1, working in ch-3 and dc sps on ends of rows, *[sk next 3 dc, [3 dc in next sp, ch 1, sk 1 sp] 9 times, [3 dc, ch 1] in corner ch-1 sp of royal block, sk 1 sp, 3 dc in next sp, [ch 1, sk 1 sp, 3 dc in next sp] 8 times, ch 1 **, sk next 3 dc, [3 dc, ch 1, 3 dc] in next corner ch-1 sp, ch 1, rep from * around, ending last rep at **, join.

The bold geometric design and vibrant rainbow flowers of this playful afghan will make it your child's favorite!

Rnds 2–6: Rep Rnd 4 of center square. At the end of Rnd 6, fasten off.

Third Border

Row 1: With paddy green, rep Row 1 of first border.

Rows 2–7: Rep Rows 2 and 3 of first border.

Row 8: Rep Row 2 of first border, fasten off.

Large Corner Blocks
(Make 4)

Rnds 1–4: With royal, rep Rnds 1–4 of center square. At the end of Rnd 4, fasten off.

Sew a large corner block to each corner of 3rd border.

Edging

Note: Not shown on diagram.

Rnd 1 (RS): Working in back lps for this rnd only, attach hot red in any corner ch-1 sp of large corner block, sk next 3 dc, [3 dc, ch 1, 3 dc] in next ch-1 sp, *sl st in next ch-1 sp, [3 dc, ch 1, 3 dc] in next ch-1 sp, rep from * around, sl st to join in same ch-1 sp as beg.

Rnd 2: Sl st in next dc, ch 1, sc in same dc, sc in each of next 2 dc, *[2 sc, ch 1, 2 sc] in next ch-1 sp, sc in each of next 3 dc, sl st in next sl st **, sc in each of next 3 dc, rep from * around, ending last rep at **, fasten off.

Flowers
(Make 5)

Rnd 1 (RS): With mexicana, ch 4, sl st to form a ring, ch 3, 23 dc in ring, join. (24 dc)

Rnd 2: [Ch 5, tr cl in next dc, ch 5, sl st in each of next 2 dc] 8 times, leaving a length of yarn, fasten off.

Sew 1 flower to center of center square. Sew 1 flower centered to each triangular section.

Block and place on a flat surface until completely dry. ❦

Diagram of Afghan

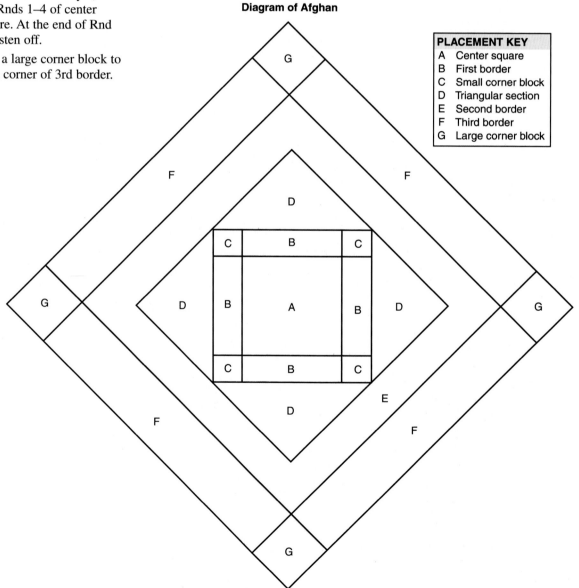

PLACEMENT KEY
A Center square
B First border
C Small corner block
D Triangular section
E Second border
F Third border
G Large corner block

Froggie Bath Mitt

By Beverly Mewhorter

Skill Level: Beginner

Size: 4½ x 8 inches

Materials

✓ 4-ply worsted weight cotton: 1½ oz shaded green, small amount of cream, scrap of black

✓ Size F/5 crochet hook or size needed to obtain gauge

✓ Tapestry needle

This quirky little frog just loves to splash in the tub. He's lovable and friendly, and turns daily scrubbing into a "ribbit"-ing good time!

Gauge

4 sc sts = 1 inch

Check gauge to save time.

Pattern Notes

Weave in loose ends as work progresses.

Join rnds with a sl st unless otherwise stated.

Mitt

(Make 2)

Row 1: Starting at bottom, with shaded green, ch 16, sc in 2nd ch from hook, sc in each rem ch across, turn. (15 sc)

Rows 2–23: Ch 1, sc in each sc across, turn.

Row 24: Ch 1, sc dec over next 2 sc, sc across to last 2 sc, sc dec over next 2 sc, turn. (13 sc)

Rows 25 & 26: Rep Row 24. (9 sc)

Joining

Rnd 1: Holding both mitt sections tog and working through both thicknesses, attach shaded green in side edge of Row 1, ch 1, sc evenly sp along side edge, 2 sc in corner st of Row 26, sc across, ending with 2 sc in last sc, sc evenly sp down side edge of rows ending in Row 1, fasten off.

Eye

(Make 2 each cream and shaded green)

Rnd 1: Ch 4, 11 dc in 4th ch from hook, join in top of beg ch-4, fasten off. (12 dc) With length of black, embroider a straight st in the center of cream sections.

Rnd 2: Holding 1 each cream and shaded green tog and working through both thicknesses, attach shaded green, ch 1, 2 sc in same st, 2 sc in each st around, join in beg sc, fasten off. (24 sc)

Sew eyes to top of mitt and sew tog at center.

Mouth

With black, ch 31, fasten off. Sew mouth to front of mitt in a squiggle design. 🐸

Teach Me Shapes & Colors

By Lori Zeller

Skill Level: Beginner

Size: Approximately 3 inches

Materials

✓ Worsted weight yarn: 2 oz each purple, blue, green, yellow, orange and red

✓ Size F/5 crochet hook or size needed to obtain gauge

✓ Magnet strips or hook-and-loop tape

✓ Tapestry needle

Gauge

5 sc rows and 5 sc sts = 1 inch

Check gauge to save time.

Pattern Notes

Weave in loose ends as work progresses.

Join rnds with a sl st unless otherwise stated.

Make 1 shape of each yarn color throughout.

These child-friendly magnets are wonderful teachers! Arrange them in any number of combinations, and play sorting games to help your child learn the basic shapes and colors.

Use magnets or hook-and-loop tape on back of shapes depending upon whether you want to use shapes on a magnetic surface or a fabric surface.

Triangle
(Make 2)

Row 1: Ch 2, sc in 2nd ch from hook, turn. (1 sc)

Row 2: Ch 1, 3 sc in the 1 sc, turn. (3 sc)

Row 3: Ch 1, 2 sc in first sc, sc in next sc, 2 sc in last sc, turn. (5 sc)

Row 4: Ch 1, sc in each sc across, turn.

Row 5: Ch 1, 2 sc in first sc, sc in each sc across to last sc, 2 sc in last sc, turn. (7 sc)

Rows 6–11: Rep Rows 4 and 5. (13 sc)

Rnd 12: Ch 1, sc evenly sp around entire outer edge, working 3 sc at each corner to keep work flat, join in beg sc, fasten off.

Rnd 13: Holding both triangles tog and working through both thicknesses, attach yarn, ch 1, sc around entire outer edge, inc at each corner to keep work flat, join in beg sc, fasten off.

Circle
(Make 2)

Note: *Do not join Rnds 1–5 of circle; use a scrap of CC yarn to mark rnds.*

Rnd 1: Ch 2, 7 sc in 2nd ch from hook. (7 sc)

Rnd 2: Work 2 sc in each sc around. (14 sc)

Rnd 3: [Sc in next sc, 2 sc in next sc] rep around. (21 sc)

Rnd 4: [Sc in each of next 2 sc, 2 sc in next sc] rep around. (28 sc)

Rnd 5: [Sc in each of next 3 sc, 2 sc in next sc] rep around. (35 sc)

Rnd 6: [Sc in each of next 4 sc, 2 sc in next sc] rep

around, join in beg sc, fasten off. (42 sc)

Rnd 7: Holding both circles tog and working through both thicknesses, attach yarn, ch 1, [sc in each of next 5 sc, 2 sc in next sc] rep around, join in beg sc, fasten off. (49 sc)

Square
(Make 2)

Row 1: Ch 11, sc in 2nd ch from hook, sc in each rem ch across, turn. (10 sc)

Rows 2–9: Ch 1, sc in each sc across, turn.

Row 10: Ch 1, sc in each sc across, sl st in side edge of last sc to position yarn for edging.

Rnd 11: Ch 1, sc evenly sp around entire outer edge, working 3 sc in each corner, join in beg sc, fasten off.

Rnd 12: Holding both squares tog and working through both thicknesses, attach yarn, ch 1, sc around entire outer edge, inc at each corner to keep work flat, join in beg sc, fasten off.

Finishing

With steam iron, press each shape lightly. Glue pieces of magnet strip or hook-and-loop tape to back of each shape. ❦

Choo-Choo Train Afghan

By Beverly Mewhorter

Skill Level: Beginner

Size: 39 x 66 inches

Materials

✓ Coats & Clark Red Heart Classic worsted weight yarn: 40 oz white #311, 2 oz each cherry red #319, grass green #687, bright yellow #324, royal #385, vibrant orange #354 and black #312

✓ Size N/15 crochet hook or size needed to obtain gauge

✓ Size J/10 crochet hook

✓ Tapestry needle

Boys and girls alike will love this playful, kid-sized afghan. Brightly colored train cars chugging across the lower edge make great "vehicles" for playing pretend, or for learning about colors.

Gauge

With 2 strands of yarn held tog and N hook, 2 dc sts = 1 inch

Check gauge to save time.

Pattern Notes

Weave in loose ends as work progresses.

Join rnds with a sl st unless otherwise stated.

Afghan

Row 1: With crochet hook size N and 2 strands of white yarn held tog, ch 106, sc in 2nd ch from hook, sc in each rem ch across, turn. (105 sc)

Rows 2–43: Ch 3 (counts as first dc throughout), dc in each st across, turn.

Row 44: Ch 1, sc in each st across, turn.

Row 45: Sl st in each st across, fasten off.

Fringe

For each fringe, cut 6 strands of white each 12 inches long. Insert hook in end of row, fold strands in half, draw fold through st on hook to form a lp, draw cut ends through lp on hook, pull gently to secure.

Rep fringe in each end of a row on each side of afghan.

Caboose

(Make 2)

Row 1: With crochet hook size J and cherry red, ch 23, sc in 2nd ch from hook, sc in each rem ch across, turn. (22 sc)

Rows 2–18: Ch 1, sc in each sc across, turn. At the end of Row 18, fasten off.

Car

(Make 2 each bright yellow, grass green and royal)

Row 1: With hook size J,

ch 23, sc in 2nd ch from hook, sc in each rem ch across, turn. (22 sc)

Rows 2–12: Ch 1, sc in each sc across, turn. At the end of Row 12, fasten off.

Engine

(Make 2)

Row 1: With hook size J and vibrant orange, ch 23, sc in 2nd ch from hook, sc in each rem ch across, turn. (22 sc)

Rows 2–12: Ch 1, sc in each sc across, turn.

Row 13: Ch 1, sc in each of next 12 sc, leaving rem sts unworked, turn. (12 sc)

Rows 14–20: Ch 1, sc in each sc across, turn. At the end of Row 20, fasten off.

Smoke stack

Row 1: With hook size J, sk next 4 sts of Row 12 of engine, attach grass green in next st, ch 1, sc in same st as beg ch, sc in each of next 2 sts, turn. (3 sc)

Rows 2 & 3: Ch 1, sc in each sc across, turn.

Row 4: Ch 3, dc in same st as beg ch-3, 2 dc in each st across, turn. (6 dc)

Row 5: Ch 1, 2 sc in first st, sc in each of next 4 sts, 2 sc in last st, fasten off. (8 sc)

Wheel

(Make 20)

Rnd 1: With hook size J and black yarn, ch 4, 13 dc in 4th ch from hook, join in top of beg ch-4, fasten off. (14 dc)

Wheel Bar

(Make 10)

With hook size J and black, ch 15, fasten off.

Window

(Make 6)

Row 1: With hook size J and white, ch 7, sc in 2nd ch from hook, sc in each rem ch across, turn. (6 sc)

Rows 2–4: Ch 1, sc in each sc across, turn.

Row 5: Sl st in each st across, fasten off.

Assembly

Using photo as a guide, sew 1 window to each engine and 2 to each caboose. Arrange and st 3 cars centered 3 inches from bottom edge of afghan; st the caboose and engine curving upward from cars toward each side. Sew 2 wheels to each car, engine and caboose; sew wheel bars to wheels. St rem train on opposite end of afghan in same manner. 🍎

Inside-Out Eggs

By Donna Collinsworth

Skill Level: Beginner

Size: 4 inches tall

Materials

- ✓ Worsted weight yarn: Small amounts of pink, blue, yellow, purple, white, lavender, peach and orange
- ✓ Size G/6 crochet hook or size needed to obtain gauge
- ✓ 7mm glue-on wiggle eyes
- ✓ 10mm white pompoms
- ✓ Hot-glue gun
- ✓ Scrap of ¼-inch-wide pink satin ribbon
- ✓ Fiberfill
- ✓ Yarn needle

Inside each of these plump, colorful eggs hides a friendly bunny or duck, ready to "hatch"! Your children will have lots of fun turning them inside out and back again.

Gauge

4 sc rows and 4 sc sts = 1 inch

Check gauge to save time.

Pattern Notes

Weave in loose ends as work progresses.

Join rnds with a sl st unless otherwise stated.

Pattern Stitches

Shell: 5 dc in indicated st.

Beg shell: Ch 3, 4 dc in same st as beg ch-3.

Beg half shell: Ch 3, 2 dc in same st as beg ch-3.

Egg

Basic Egg

Rnd 1: Ch 6, join to form a ring, ch 1, 9 sc in ring, join in beg sc, turn. (9 sc)

Rnd 2: Ch 1, sc in same st as beg ch-1, shell in next sc, sk next sc, [sc in next sc, shell in next sc, sk next sc] twice, join in beg sc, turn. (3 shells)

Row 3: Beg shell in sc, sc in 3rd dc, shell in next dc, sc in next dc, shell in next sc, sc in 3rd dc, shell in next sc, sc in next dc, sk next dc, shell in next dc, sk next dc, sc in last dc, turn. (5 shells)

Rows 4–6: Beg half shell in first sc, [sc in 3rd dc, shell in next sc] 4 times, sc in last dc, turn. (1 half shell; 4 shells)

Row 7: Beg half shell in first sc, sc in 3rd dc, shell in next sc, sk 4 dc, sc in 5th dc, shell in 3rd dc of next shell, sc in next dc, shell in next sc, sc in last dc, turn. (1 half shell; 3 shells)

Row 8: Beg half shell in first sc, [sc in 3rd dc, shell in next sc] 3 times, sc in last dc, turn.

Row 9: Beg half shell in first sc, sk 4 dc, sc in 5th dc, shell in 3rd dc of next shell, sc in next dc, shell in next sc, sc in last dc, turn. (1 half shell; 2 shells)

Rnd 10: Beg shell in first sc, [sc in 3rd dc of next shell, shell in next sc] twice, sc in last dc, join in top of beg ch-3, turn. (3 shells)

Rnd 11: Beg shell in same sc as joining, sc in 3rd dc of next shell, shell in next dc, sc in 2nd dc of next shell, join in top of beg ch-3, turn. (2 shells)

Rnd 12: Ch 1, sc in same sc as joining, sc in 3rd dc of next shell, sc in next sc, sc in 3rd dc of next shell, join in beg sc, fasten off. (4 sc)

Three-Color Egg

With 3 yarn colors, work the following color sequence of basic egg pattern.

Rnds 1 & 2: Color A.

Row 3: Color B.

Row 4: Color C.

Row 5: Color A.

Row 6: Color B.

Row 7: Color C.

Row 8: Color A.

Row 9: Color B.

Rnd 10: Color C.

Rnds 11 & 12: Color A.

Note: You can also make a 2-color striped egg, following the above sequence and only alternate 2 colors. Or alternate switching the colors every 2 rows or rnds.

Egg With Center Stripe

Follow basic egg pattern working all rows and rnds with 1 color except work Rows 5 and 6 with an alternate color.

Checkered Egg

With 2 yarn colors, work basic egg pattern working Rnd 1 in 1 color and then alternate the st sequence of [sc, shell] with the 2 colors carrying the unworked yarn at back of work.

Dotted Egg

Note: When working color B, carry color A behind sts as work progresses.

Rnd 1: With A, ch 6, join to form a ring, ch 1, 9 sc in ring, join, turn. (9 sc)

Rnd 2: Ch 1, sc in first sc, shell in next sc, sk next sc, sc in next sc, shell in next sc, sk next sc, sc in next sc, drop A, with B, shell in next sc, pick up A, fasten off B, sk next sc, sl st in beg sc, turn.

Row 3: Beg shell in same sc, sc in 3rd dc of next shell, shell in next dc, sc in next dc, shell in next sc, sc in 3rd dc, join B, drop A, shell in next sc, pick up A, fasten off B, sc in next dc, sk next dc, shell in next dc, sk next dc, sc in next dc, turn.

Row 4: Beg half shell in same sc, [sc in 3rd dc, shell in next sc] twice, sc in 3rd dc, join B, drop A, shell in next sc, pick up A, fasten off B, sc in 3rd dc, shell in next sc, sc in last dc, turn.

Row 5: Beg half shell in first sc, [sc in 3rd dc, shell in next sc] 3 times, sc in 3rd dc, join B, drop A, shell in next sc, pick up A, fasten off B, sc in last dc, turn.

Row 6: Rep Row 5.

Row 7: Beg half shell in first sc, sc in 3rd dc, shell in next sc, sk 4 dc, sc in 5th dc, join B, drop A, sk next 2 dc, shell in 3rd dc, pick up A, fasten off B, sc in 2nd dc, shell in next sc, sc in last dc, turn.

Row 8: Beg half shell in first sc, sc in 3rd dc, shell in next sc, sc in 3rd dc, join B, drop A, shell in next sc, pick up A, fasten off B, sc in 3rd dc, shell in next sc, sc in last dc, turn.

Row 9: Beg half shell in first sc, sk next 4 dc, sc in 5th dc, sk next 2 dc, shell in next dc, sc in next dc, join B, drop A, shell in

next sc, pick up A, fasten off B, sc in last dc, turn.

Rnd 10: Beg shell in first sc, sc in 3rd dc, shell in next sc, sc in 3rd dc, join B, drop A, shell in next sc, pick up A, fasten off B, sc in last dc, join in top of beg ch-3, turn.

Rnd 11: Beg shell in first sc, sc in 3rd dc, join B, drop A, shell in 2nd dc, pick up A, fasten off B, sc in 2nd dc, join in top of beg ch-3, turn.

Rnd 12: Ch 1, sc in first sc, sc in 3rd dc, sc in next sc, sc in 3rd dc, join in beg sc, fasten off.

Bunny & Duck

Basic Body

Rnd 1: Ch 4, join to form a ring, ch 1, 8 sc in ring, join in beg sc, turn. (8 sc)

Rnd 2: Ch 1, [2 sc in next sc, sc in next sc] rep around, join in beg sc, turn. (12 sc)

Rnd 3: Rep Rnd 2. (18 sc)

Rnd 4: Ch 1, [2 sc in next sc, sc in each of next 2 sc] rep around, join in beg sc, turn. (24 sc)

Row 5: Ch 1, sc in each sc across, turn.

Rows 6 & 7: Rep Row 5.

Row 8: Ch 1, [sc dec over next 2 sc, sc in each of next 4 sc] rep across, turn. (20 sc)

Rows 9 & 10: Rep Row 5.

Row 11: Ch 1, [sc dec over next 2 sc, sc in each of next 8 sc] rep across, turn. (18 sc)

Row 12: Rep Row 5.

Row 13: Ch 1, sc in each of next 3 sc, [sc dec over next 2 sc, sc in next 3 sc] rep across, turn. (15 sc)

Row 14: Rep Row 5.

Rnd 15: Ch 1, [sc dec over next 2 sts, sc in next 3 sc] rep across, join in beg sc, turn. (12 sc)

Rnd 16: Ch 1, sc in each sc around, join in top of beg sc, turn.

Rnd 17: Ch 1, [sc dec over next 2 sc, sc in next 2 sc] rep around, join in beg sc, turn. (9 sts)

Rnd 18: Sk first sc, [sc dec over next 2 sc] rep around, join in beg sc, fasten off. (4 sc)

Basic Head

Rnds 1 & 2: Rep Rnds 1 and 2 of basic body. (12 sc)

Rnds 3–6: Ch 1, sc in each sc around, join in beg sc, turn.

Rnd 7: Ch 1, [sc dec over next 2 sts, sc in next 2 sc] rep around, join in beg sc, turn. (9 sc)

Rnd 8: Ch 1, [sc dec over next 2 sc, sc in next sc] rep around, join in beg sc, fasten off. (6 sc)

Stuff head with fiberfill and sew to body towards larger end.

Bunny Ear

(Make 2)

Row 1: Ch 2, sc in 2nd ch from hook, turn. (1 sc)

Row 2: Ch 1, 2 sc in the 1 sc, turn. (2 sc)

Rows 3 & 4: Ch 1, sc in each sc across, turn.

Row 5: Ch 1, sc dec over next 2 sc, fasten off.

Sew ears to each side of head.

Bunny Tail

Rnd 1: With white, ch 2, 6 sc in 2nd ch from hook, join in beg sc, turn. (6 sc)

Rnds 2 & 3: Ch 1, sc in each sc around, join in beg

sc, turn. At the end of Rnd 3, fasten off.

Sew tail to small end of body.

Finishing

Glue eyes to head. For nose, cut a small triangle from pink ribbon and glue to face center below eyes. Glue 2 pompoms under nose.

Turn inside out and place inside egg; sew opening of both sections tog so that when you turn the egg inside out, the bunny will be right side out.

Duck Wing

(Make 2)

Row 1: Ch 2, sc in 2nd ch from hook, turn. (1 sc)

Row 2: Ch 1, 2 sc in the 1 sc, turn. (2 sc)

Row 3: Ch 1, 2 sc in first sc, sc in next sc, turn. (3 sc)

Row 4: Ch 1, 2 sc in first sc, sc in each rem sc

across, turn. (4 sc)

Rows 5 & 6: Rep Row 4. (6 sc)

Row 7: Ch 1, sc dec over next 2 sc, sc in next 2 sc, sc dec over next 2 sc, fasten off. (4 sc)

Sew wing to each side of body.

Duckbill

Row 1: With orange, ch 3, join to form a ring, ch 1, 4 sc in ring, do not join, fasten off.

Sew flat side of duck bill to head at center front.

Finishing

Glue 2 eyes centered above bill.

Turn duck inside out and place inside egg, sew opening of both sections tog so that when you turn the egg inside out, the duck will be right side out. 🐣

Louie Lizard

By Beverly Mewhorter

Skill Level: Beginner

Size: 21 inches long

Materials

✓ Coats & Clark Red Heart Classic worsted weight yarn: 3 oz light clay #275, small amounts black #12 and medium clay #280

✓ Size H/8 crochet hook or size needed to obtain gauge

✓ (12mm) black animal eyes

✓ Fiberfill

✓ Tapestry needle

Gauge

5 sc rows and 5 sc sts = 1½ inches

Check gauge to save time.

Pattern Notes

Weave in loose ends as work progresses.

Join rnds with a sl st unless otherwise stated.

Body & Head

(Make 2)

Row 1 (WS): Beg at back end of body, with light clay, ch 3, sc in 2nd ch from hook, sc in next ch, turn. (2 sc)

Row 2: Ch 1, sc in each sc across, turn.

Row 3: Ch 1, 2 sc in each sc across, turn. (4 sc)

Row 4: Rep Row 2.

Row 5: Ch 1, 2 sc in first sc, sc in each sc across to last sc, 2 sc in last sc, turn. (6 sc)

Rows 6–13: Rep Rows 2 and 5. (14 sc)

Rows 14–25: Rep Row 2.

Row 26: Ch 1, sc dec over next 2 sc, sc in each sc across to last 2 sc, sc dec over next 2 sc, turn. (12 sc)

Row 27: Rep Row 2.

Rows 28–35: Rep Rows 26 and 2. (4 sc)

Row 36: Rep Row 2.

Rows 37 & 38: Rep Row 5. (8 sc)

Row 39: Rep Row 2.

Rows 40 & 41: Rep Row 5. (12 sc)

Row 42: Rep Row 2.

Rows 43 & 44: Rep Row 26. (8 sc)

Row 45: Rep Row 2.

Rows 46 & 47: Rep Row 26. (4 sc)

Row 48: Ch 1, [sc dec over next 2 sc] twice, turn. (2 sc)

Rows 49 & 50: Rep Row 2. At the end of Row 50, fasten off.

Tail

Row 1: Attach light clay in opposite side of foundation ch at back end of body, ch

1, sc in same ch as beg ch-1, sc in next ch, turn. (2 sc)

Rows 2–22: Ch 1, sc in each of next 2 sc, turn. (2 sc)

Row 23: Ch 1, sc dec over next 2 sc, turn. (1 sc)

Row 24: Ch 1, sc in sc, fasten off.

Attach eyes to 1 side of head over Rows 46 and 47. Matching sts and ends of rows, sew 2 sides tog stuffing body and head only as work progresses.

For nose, with black embroider 2 straight sts over Row 50.

With medium clay, embroider 4 rows of zigzag design on back of lizard as desired.

Top Leg
(Make 4)

Row 1: With light clay, ch 5, sc in 2nd ch from hook, sc in each rem ch across, turn. (4 sc)

Rows 2–10: Ch 1, sc in each sc across, turn.

Row 11: Ch 1, [sc dec over next 2 sc] twice, turn.

Row 12: Ch 7, sl st in 2nd ch from hook, sl st in each of next 5 chs, sl st in same sc, ch 7, sl st in 2nd ch

from hook, sl st in each of next 5 chs, sl st in next sc, ch 7, sl st in 2nd ch from hook, sl st in each of next 5 chs, sl st in same sc, fasten off. (3 toes)

Bottom Leg
(Make 4)

Rows 1–11: Rep Rows 1–11 of top leg. At the end of Row 11, fasten off.

Matching rows, sew top and bottom leg tog. Sew legs to body. 🐾

This reptilian friend is ready to crawl atop a rock pile and bask in the sun. Lifelike and desert-colored, he'll be happy to go bug-hunting with your little boy.

Teddy Bear

By Michele Wilcox

Skill Level: Beginner

Size: 12 inches tall

Materials

✓ Worsted weight yarn: 3-oz antique gold, scrap of black

✓ Size G/6 crochet hook or size needed to obtain gauge

✓ 24 inches ¼-inch-wide blue satin ribbon

✓ Fiberfill

✓ Tapestry needle

Simple and sweet, this baby bear waits to hug his new friend. He's little enough for small children to hold, but he's stuffed full of love!

Gauge

4 sc rows and 4 sc sts = 1 inch

Check gauge to save time.

Pattern Notes

Weave in loose ends as work progresses.

Join rnds with a sl st unless otherwise stated.

Body & Head

(Make 2)

Row 1: Beg at bottom of body, with antique gold, ch 19, sc in 2nd ch from hook, sc in each rem ch across, turn. (18 sc)

Row 2: Ch 1, sc in each sc across, turn.

Rows 3–17: Rep Row 2.

Row 18: Ch 1, [sc dec over next 2 sc] 9 times, turn. (9 sc)

Row 19: Rep Row 2.

Row 20: Ch 1, [2 sc in next sc] 3 times, sc in each of next 3 sc, [2 sc in next sc] 3 times, turn. (15 sc)

Rows 21–30: Rep Row 2.

Row 31: Ch 1, [sc dec over next 2 sc] 3 times, sc in each of next 3 sc, [sc dec over next 2 sc] 3 times, turn. (9 sc)

Rnd 32: Ch 1, sc evenly sp around entire outer edge, working 3 sc in each bottom corner, join in beg sc, fasten off.

Leg

(Make 2)

Row 1: With antique gold, ch 9, sc in 2nd ch from hook, sc in each rem ch across, turn. (8 sc)

Row 2: Ch 1, sc in each sc across, turn.

Rows 3–11: Rep Row 2.

Row 12: Ch 1, [sc dec over next 2 sc] 4 times, turn. (4 sc)

Row 13: Rep Row 2.

Row 14: Ch 1, [2 sc in next sc] 4 times, turn. (8 sc)

Rows 15–25: Rep Row 2.

Rnd 26: Ch 1, sc evenly sp around entire outer edge, working 3 sc in each corner, join in beg sc, fasten off.

Arm

(Make 2)

Row 1: With antique gold, ch 7, sc in 2nd ch from hook, sc in each rem ch across, turn. (6 sc)

Row 2: Ch 1, sc in each sc across, turn.

Rows 3–9: Rep Row 2.

Row 10: Ch 1, [sc dec

over next 2 sc] 3 times, turn. (3 sc)

Row 11: Rep Row 2.

Row 12: Ch 1, [2 sc in next sc] 3 times, turn. (6 sc)

Rows 13–21: Rep Row 2.

Rnd 22: Ch 1, sc evenly sp around entire outer edge, working 3 sc in each corner, join in beg sc, fasten off.

Ear

(Make 2)

Row 1: With antique gold, ch 5, 2 sc in 2nd ch from hook, sc in each of next 2 chs, 2 sc in last ch, turn. (6 sc)

Row 2: Ch 1, sc in each sc across, turn.

Rows 3 & 4: Rep Row 2.

Row 5: Ch 1, [sc dec over next 2 sc] 3 times, turn. (3 sc)

Row 6: Rep Row 2.

Row 7: Ch 1, [2 sc in next sc] 3 times, turn. (6 sc)

Rows 8–10: Rep Row 2.

Row 11: Ch 1, sc dec over next 2 sc, sc in each of next 2 sc, sc dec over next 2 sc, fasten off. (4 sc)

Snout

Rnd 1: With antique gold, ch 2, 6 sc in 2nd ch from hook, join in beg sc. (6 sc)

Rnd 2: Ch 1, 2 sc in each sc around, join in beg sc. (12 sc)

Rnd 3: Ch 1, sc in each sc around, join in beg sc.

Rnd 4: Ch 1, [sc in next sc, 2 sc in next sc] rep around, join in beg sc. (18 sc)

Rnd 5: Rep Rnd 3, fasten off.

Finishing

Sew snout to head front between Rows 22–28, stuffing with fiberfill before closing.

With black, embroider satin st eyes above snout at each side of Row 28. Embroider satin st nose over upper end over Rnds 1 and 2; embroider mouth with straight sts directly below nose.

Whipstitch body and head sections tog, stuffing with fiberfill before closing. Do not stuff ear, fold in half and sew around outer edge; sew each ear to top of head.

Fold leg in half and sew closed, stuffing with fiberfill before closing; sew to bottom of body.

Fold arm in half and sew

closed, stuffing with fiberfill before closing; sew to side of body.

Place ribbon around neckline and tie in a bow at center front. ❦

TIPS

Afghan Tips

Work your crochet stitches over the ends of yarn as often as possible. This will save time because you will not have to weave in so many ends.

—Sandy Abbate

When working an afghan in motifs such as pentagons, octagons, etc., leave an end about 18 inches long when fastening off at the end of the last round. Use this end to sew motifs together.

—Sandy Abbate

Place a marker every 10 rows or every pattern repeat at the end of the last row worked. This will save time by making it much easier to count rows you have worked.

—Sandy Abbate

Silk Ribbon Embroidery

Silk ribbon embroidery is a beautiful technique best worked on a dense crochet fabric that can't be seen through, such as single crochet or afghan stitch. Try it on the neck and front edge of a cardigan, work a "corsage" on a blouse or jacket, or use it on a pillow or afghan block. Avoid placing the whole stitched design in an area that needs to stretch, such as the neck or hem of a blouse, as the ribbon has no give.

—Dawn Thompson

Rag-Rug Fabrics

Calicoes and solids in cotton or cotton/synthetic blends make wonderful rag rugs. For best results, use just one type of fabric for each rug. Cottons and blends wash, stretch and work up differently, and it's wise to keep fabric types as similar as possible.

—Dawn Thompson

Easier Multicolored Fringe

Instead of just tying on a new color when switching yarns for a multicolored, fringed project, leave a long tail of yarn at the edges that are as long as the desired finished fringe. Not only are you changing color, you're actually fringing your piece as you go along. No loose ends to weave in, only a lovely, multicolored fringe without the extra work. If the fringe isn't dense enough, tie in a few more strands here and there.

—Dawn Thompson

Pampered-Pet Pleasers

Pets are loyal, loving and even entertaining! Pamper your furry best friend by crocheting a comfy bed, irresistible sweater, snazzy collar or fun toy for him or her today!

Canine Comfort Dog Sweater

By Connie Folse

Skill Level: Beginner

Size:

Length: 13½ inches

Chest: 14 inches unstretched

Materials

✓ 3-ply sport weight yarn: 9 oz MC, 3 oz CC

✓ Size E/4 crochet hook or size needed to obtain gauge

✓ Tapestry needle

Gauge

5 sc rows and 5 sc sts = 1 inches

Check gauge to save time.

Pattern Notes

Weave in loose ends as work progresses.

Join rnds with a sl st unless otherwise stated.

Sweater

Collar

Rnd 1: With MC, ch 50, using care not to twist ch, sl st to join to form a ring, ch 1, sc in each ch around, join in beg sc. (50 sc)

Rnd 2: Ch 3 (counts as first dc throughout), fpdc around

ake your furry friend for a walk–in style! Your dog will look absolutely precious in his new "dog togs," plus he'll stay nice and warm!

next st, [dc in next st, fpdc around next st] rep around, join in top of beg ch-3.

Rnds 3–12: Rep Rnd 2.

Rnd 13: Ch 3, 2 dc in next st, [dc in next st, 2 dc in next st] rep around, join in top of beg ch-3.

Rnd 14: Ch 3, dc in each st around, join in top of beg ch-3.

Rnds 15 & 16: Rep Rnd 14. At the end of Rnd 16, do not fasten off.

Body

Row 1: Ch 31, sc in 2nd ch from hook, sc in each rem ch across, sl st in next 2 dc of Rnd 16, turn. (30 sc)

Row 2: Ch 1, sk 2 sl sts, sc in each sc across, turn.

Rnd 3: Ch 1, sc in each sc across, sl st in each of next 2 sts of Rnd 16, turn.

Rows 4 & 5: Rep Rows 2 and 3.

Row 6: Ch 1, sk 2 sl sts, sc in each of next 2 sc, ch 15 loosely, sk next 15 sc (leg opening), sc in each of next 13 sc, turn.

Row 7: Ch 1, sc in each of next 13 sc, sc in each of next 15 chs, sc in next 2 sc, sl st in next 2 sts of Rnd 16, turn.

Row 8: Rep Row 2.

Row 9: Ch 1, 2 sc in first sc, sc in each rem sc across, sl st in next 2 sts of Rnd 16, turn. (31 sc)

Row 10: Rep Row 2.

Rows 11–30: Rep Rows 9 and 10. (41 sc)

Row 31: Rep Row 9. (42 sc)

Rows 32–45: Rep Rows 2 and 3.

Row 46: Rep Row 2.

Row 47: Ch 1, sc dec over next 2 sc, sc in each rem sc across, sl st in next 2 sts of Rnd 16, turn. (41 sc)

Row 48: Rep Row 2.

Rows 49–68: Rep Rows 47 and 48. (31 sc)

Row 69: Rep Row 3.

Row 70: Rep Row 2.

Row 71: Ch 1, sc in each of next 13 sc, ch 15 loosely, sk next 15 sc, sc in next 2 sc, sk last sc, sl st in next 2 sts of Rnd 16, turn.

Row 72: Ch 1, sk 2 sl sts, sc in next 2 sc, sc in each of next 15 chs, sc in next 13 sc, turn. (30 sc)

Row 73: Rep Row 3.

Row 74: Rep Row 2.

Row 75: Ch 1, sc in each sc across, sl st in 3rd ch of ch-3 of Rnd 16, turn.

Row 76: Ch 1, holding Row 75 to opposite side of foundation ch of Row 1, sl st in each st across, fasten off.

Collar trim

Rnd 1: With neck opening facing away, attach CC in opposite side of foundation ch of collar, ch 1, beg in same st as beg ch-1, [sc in next st, 2 sc in each of next 3 sts, sc in next st] rep around, join in beg sc, fasten off.

Sleeve

(Make 2)

Rnd 1: Attach MC with sl st in leg opening, ch 1, work 32 sc evenly sp around, join in beg sc. (32 sc)

Rnd 2: Ch 1, [sc dec over next 2 sc, sc in next 14 sc] twice, join in beg sc. (30 sc)

Rnd 3: Ch 1, sc in each sc around, join in beg sc.

Rnds 4 & 5: Rep Rnd 3.

Rnd 6: Ch 1, [sc in next 4 sc, sc dec over next 2 sc] 5 times, join in beg sc. (25 sc)

Rnds 7–10: Rep Rnd 3. At the end of Rnd 10, fasten off.

Rnd 11: Attach CC, ch 1, sc in each st around, join in beg sc. (25 sc)

Rnd 12: Ch 1, [sc in next sc, 2 dc in each of next 3 sc, sc in next sc] 5 times, join in beg sc, fasten off.

Body trim

Rnd 1 (RS): Attach CC in side edge of Row 75 of body, ch 1, sc in same row, sc in side edge of each row around, join in beg sc. (75 sc)

Rnd 2: Ch 1, reverse sc in each sc around, join in beg sc, fasten off. ◆

Cat Play Tunnel

By Connie Folse

Skill Level: Beginner

Size: 9½ x 25 inches

Materials

- ✓ Worsted weight yarn: 9 oz each variegated and 2 matching colors
- ✓ Size J/10 crochet hook or size needed to obtain gauge
- ✓ 3 (9-inch) metal hoops
- ✓ 3-inch piece cardboard
- ✓ Tapestry needle

Fun, fun, fun! Cats will find this three-dimensional tunnel irresistible. They'll climb, crawl, hide and roll for hours on end, while keeping you entertained as well!

Gauge

4 dc rows = 3 inches; 5 dc sts = 2 inches

Check gauge to save time.

Pattern Notes

Weave in loose ends as work progresses.

Join rnds with a sl st unless otherwise stated.

Tunnel

Rnd 1: Holding 1 strand of each 3 colors tog, attach strands to first hoop, ch 1, work 76 sc evenly sp around hoop, join in beg sc. (75 sc)

Rnd 2: Ch 3 (counts as first dc throughout), dc in each st around, join in top of beg ch-3.

Rnds 3–17: Rep Rnd 2.

Rnd 18: Holding 2nd hoop next to Rnd 17, working over hoop and into sts of Rnd 17, ch 1, sc in each st around, join in beg sc.

Rnds 19–34: Rep Rnd 2.

Rnd 35: Holding 3rd hoop next to Rnd 34, working over hoop and into sts of Rnd 17, ch 1, sc in each st around, join in beg sc, fasten off.

Tassel

(Make 4)

Cut 1 strand of each of 3 colors each 10 inches long. (3 strands)

Cut an 8-inch length of variegated yarn.

Hold 10-inch strands on top edge of cardboard, with 1 strand each color, wrap 3 times around cardboard. Knot 10-inch strands tog at top; cut bottom edge of strands; remove from cardboard.

Wrap strand of variegated yarn 1-inch below knot at top; knot several times to secure. Trim bottom of tassel evenly.

Tie tassels to tunnel evenly sp around Rnd 35. Trim the rem ends of the 10-inch strands as desired. ◆

Fancy Collar

By Jamie Folse

Skill Level: Beginner

Size: 1¼ inches wide

Model fits approximately 11½-inch neckline

Materials

✓ 3-ply soft baby yarn: 1 oz MC

✓ Size H/8 crochet hook or size needed to obtain gauge

✓ 12 inches ⅛-inch-wide elastic unstretched

✓ Sewing needle and thread

✓ Tapestry needle

Show your love for your dog or cat by crocheting this fancy ruffled collar. Easy to make and easy to wear, it's the ideal gift for the truly pampered pet!

Gauge

6 dc sts of Rnd 3 = 1 inch

Check gauge to save time.

Pattern Notes

Weave in loose ends as work progresses.

Join rnds with a sl st unless otherwise stated.

For larger or smaller collar, cut elastic to fit loosely around pet's neck.

Using care to keep elastic untwisted, overlap ends ¼–½ inch, sew ends tog.

Collar

Rnd 1: Attach yarn with sl st to elastic, ch 1, work 90 sc over elastic or enough to completely cover elastic, join in beg sc.

Rnd 2: Ch 3, dc in same st as beg ch-3, 2 dc in each sc around, join in top of beg ch-3.

Rnd 3: Ch 3, dc in same st, 2 dc in each rem dc around, join in top of beg ch-3, fasten off. ◆

Hideaway Bed

By Beverly Mewhorter

Skill Level: Beginner

Size: 20 x 25 inches

Materials

✓ Coats & Clark Red Heart Classic worsted weight yarn: 12 oz grape ivy #958, 11 oz lavender #584

✓ Size J/10 crochet hook or size needed to obtain gauge

✓ Tapestry needle

This unique pet bed will fascinate your cat or small dog. Watch him or her peek into the pocket, crawl inside, and settle down with a lazy yawn!

Gauge

3 sc sts = 1 inch

Check gauge to save time.

Pattern Notes

Weave in loose ends as work progresses.

Join rnds with a sl st unless otherwise stated.

Bottom Pad

Note: Make 1 each grape ivy and lavender.

Continued on page 76

"Nip" the Mouse

By Beverly Mewhorter

Skill Level: Beginner

Size: 9½ inches long including tail

Materials

✓ Worsted weight yarn: 2½-oz light gray, scrap of black

✓ Size G/6 crochet hook or size needed to obtain gauge

✓ 8mm black animal eyes

✓ 12 inches ⅜-inch-wide pink ribbon

✓ 8-inch square white felt

✓ Hot-glue gun

✓ Tapestry needle

With frizzled whiskers and an irresistibly curly tail, this frisky mouse will keep your cat busy for many fun-filled hours.

Gauge

4 sc sts = 1 inch
Check gauge to save time.

Pattern Note

Weave in loose ends as work progresses.

Body Bottom

Row 1: With light gray, ch 3, sc in 2nd ch from hook, sc in next ch, turn. (2 sc)

Row 2: Ch 1, 2 sc in each sc across, turn. (4 sc)

Row 3: Ch 1, 2 sc in first sc, sc in each sc across to last sc, 2 sc in last sc, turn. (6 sc)

Row 4: Ch 1, sc in each sc across, turn.

Row 5: Rep Row 3. (8 sc)

Rows 6–8: Rep Row 4.

Rows 9 & 10: Rep Row 3. (12 sc)

Rows 11–18: Rep Row 4.

Row 19: Ch 1, sc dec over next 2 sc, sc across to last 2 sc, sc dec over next 2 sc, turn. (10 sc)

Continued on next page

Rows 20 & 21: Rep Row 19. At the end of Row 21, fasten off. (6 sc)

Body Top

Rows 1–9: Rep Rows 1–9 of body bottom. (10 sc)

Row 10: Ch 1, 2 sc in first sc, sc in each of next 2 sc, [2 sc in next sc] 4 times, sc in each of next 2 sc, 2 sc in last sc, turn. (16 sc)

Rows 11–20: Rep Rows 11–20 of body bottom. (12 sc)

Row 21: Ch 1, [sc dec over next 2 sc] 6 times, fasten off.

Body Finishing

Secure eyes to body top over Row 6 with ½ inch sp

between eyes.

With length of black, sew nose with satin stitch centered over Row 2.

With length of light gray, matching sts and ends of rows, sew top and bottom body tog, stuffing with fiberfill before closing.

Tail

With light gray, ch 31, 2 sc in 2nd ch from hook, 2 sc in each rem ch across, leaving a length of yarn, fasten off. Sew tail to center of body top over Row 21.

Ear

(Make 2)

Row 1: With light gray, ch

3, sc in 2nd ch from hook, sc in next ch, turn. (2 sc)

Row 2: Ch 1, 2 sc in each sc across, turn. (4 sc)

Rows 3 & 4: Ch 1, 2 sc in first sc, sc in each sc across to last sc, 2 sc in last sc, turn. (8 sc)

Row 5: Ch 1, sc in each sc across, turn.

Rows 6 & 7: Rep Row 5.

Rows 8 & 9: Ch 1, sc dec over next 2 sc, sc in each sc across to last 2 sc, sc dec over next 2 sc, turn. (4 sc)

Row 10: Rep Row 5, fasten off.

Using ear as a pattern cut 2 pieces of white felt; set aside.

Rnd 11: Attach light gray in opposite side of foundation ch, ch 1, sc in each of next 2 chs, sc in side edge of each row, 2 sc in first sc of Row 10, sc in next 2 sc, 2 sc in last sc of Row 10, sc evenly sp down side edge of rows, join in beg sc, fasten off.

Sew ears over Row 10 of top body with ¼-inch between ears; glue felt inside each ear.

For whiskers, cut a 4-inch length of black yarn; tie in a knot under nose, separate plies and trim.

Attach pink ribbon between ears and tie ends in a bow. ◆

Hideaway Bed

Continued from page 74

Row 1: Ch 71, sc in 2nd ch from hook, sc in each rem ch across, turn. (70 sc)

Row 2: Ch 1, sc in first sc, dc in next sc, [sc in next sc, dc in next sc] rep across, turn.

Row 3: Ch 1, [sc in each dc, dc in each sc] rep across, turn. (70 sts)

Rows 4–51: Rep Row 3.

Row 52: Ch 1, sc in each st across, fasten off. (70 sc)

Rnd 53: Holding both sections of bottom pad tog and working through both thicknesses, attach grape ivy, ch 1, sc evenly sp around entire outer edge, working 3 sc in each corner and stuffing not too firmly with fiberfill before closing, join in beg sc, fasten off.

Top Cover

Row 1: With grape ivy, ch 51, sc in 2nd ch from hook, sc in each rem ch across, turn. (50 sc)

Rows 2–42: Rep Rows 2–42 of bottom pad. (50 sts)

Row 43: Ch 1, sc in each st across, fasten off.

Rnd 44: Attach lavender in first sc of Row 43, ch 1, 3 sc in same sc as beg ch-1, sc evenly sp around entire outer edge, working 3 sc in each rem corner, join in beg sc.

Rnds 45 & 46: Ch 1, sc in each sc around, 3 sc in each center corner sc, join in beg sc. At the end of Rnd 3, fasten off.

Sew 1 short end to short end of bottom pad; sew both sides to pillow pad, leaving opening on top of pillow.

Paw Print

(Make 1)

Rnd 1: With lavender, ch 4, 9 dc in 4th ch from hook, join in top of beg ch-4. (10 dc)

Rnd 2: Ch 3 (counts as first dc throughout), dc in same st as beg ch, 2 dc in each rem st around, join in top of beg ch-3. (20 dc)

Rnd 3: Ch 3, dc in same st as beg ch-3, dc in next st, [2 dc in next st, dc in next st] rep around, join in top of beg ch-3. (30 dc)

Rnd 4: Ch 3, dc in same st as beg ch-3, dc in each of next 2 sts, [2 dc in next st, dc in each of next 2 sts] rep around, join in top of beg ch-3, fasten off. (40 dc)

Toes

(Make 4)

Rnds 1 & 2: Rep Rnds 1 and 2 of paw print. (20 dc)

At the end of Rnd 2, fasten off.

Using photo as a guide, sew paw print to top cover and toes across upper side, evenly spaced. ◆

Cozy Pet Bed

By Connie Folse

Skill Level: Beginner

Size: 19 x 20 inches

Materials

- ✓ Coats & Clark Red Heart Super Saver worsted weight yarn: 18 oz each pale green #363 and gray heather #400
- ✓ Size J/10 crochet hook or size needed to obtain gauge
- ✓ Tapestry needle

Gauge

5 dc sts = 2 inches

Check gauge to save time.

Pattern Notes

Weave in loose ends as work progresses.

Join rnds with a sl st unless otherwise stated.

Bed

(Make 2)

Row 1: Holding 1 strand each pale green and gray heather tog, ch 53, dc in 4th ch from hook, dc in each rem ch across, turn. (51 dc)

Row 2: Ch 3, dc in next st, [fpdc around next dc, bpdc around next dc] rep across to last 3 sts, bpdc around next dc, dc in each of next 2 dc, turn.

Rows 3–28: Ch 3, dc in next dc, [fpdc around each fpdc, bpdc around each bpdc] rep across to last 2 sts, dc in each of next 2 dc, turn.

At the end of Row 28, fasten off.

Border

Rnd 1: Holding bed section tog and working through both thicknesses, attach 1 strand each of pale green and gray heather tog in first st of Row 28, ch 1, [sc in each st across edge, 2 sc in end of each row across] twice, join in beg sc.

Rnd 2: Working in back lps only, ch 1, hdc in each st around, join in top of beg hdc.

Rnd 3: Ch 1, [fpdc around next hdc, bpdc around next hdc] rep around, join in top of beg fpdc.

Rnd 4: Ch 1, [fpdc around fpdc, bpdc around bpdc] rep around, join in top of beg fpdc.

Rnd 5: Rep Rnd 4.

Rnd 6: Working in back lps only, ch 1, hdc in each st around, join in top of beg hdc.

Rnd 7: Rep Rnd 3.

Rnd 8: Rep Rnd 4, fasten off.

Finishing

Thread tapestry needle with 1 strand each pale green and gray heather, sew Rnd 8 to rem free lps of Rnd 1 of border. ◆

Extra-cushioned and double-thick, this cozy pet pad is just perfect for a midafternoon nap. Dogs and cats alike will appreciate its simple comfort.

Kitty's Pup Tent

By Darla Fanton

Skill Level: Intermediate

Size: 15 x 19 inches tall

Materials

- ✓ Coats & Clark Red Heart Super Saver worsted weight yarn: 18 oz buff #334, 19 oz light periwinkle #347
- ✓ Size K/10½ double ended crochet hook or size needed to obtain gauge
- ✓ Size H/8 crochet hook
- ✓ 1⅛ yds 24-inch-wide 1-inch thick Poly-fil® Nu-Foam®
- ✓ Tapestry needle
- ✓ Safety pin

Gauge

6 rows = 1 inch; 9 stitches = 2 inches

Check gauge to save time.

Pattern Notes

Weave in loose ends as work progresses.

Use crochet hook size K unless otherwise stated.

When picking up a lp in horizontal st, insert hook under top lp only unless otherwise instructed, yo and draw through keeping lp on hook.

Poly-fil products can be found at your local fabric, quilt and chain stores. To locate a store near you, call (800) 243-0989.

Base

(Make 2)

Row 1: With double ended hook and light periwinkle, ch 67, insert hook in 2nd ch from hook, [yo, draw through ch forming a lp on hook, keeping lps on hook] rep across foundation ch; slide all sts to opposite end of hook, turn. (67 lps on hook)

Row 2: Place buff on hook with a sl knot, draw through first lp, [yo, draw through 2 lps (1 lp each color)] rep across until 1 lp remains on hook, do not turn.

Row 3: With buff, ch 1, sk first vertical bar, [pick up lp in next horizontal st] rep across; slide all sts to opposite end of hook, turn.

Row 4: Pick up light periwinkle, yo and draw through 1 lp, [yo, draw through 2 lps] rep across until 1 lp remains on hook, do not turn.

Row 5: With light periwinkle, rep Row 3.

Row 6: With buff, rep Row 4.

Rows 7–92: Rep Rows 3–6, ending with a Row 4.

Row 93: With light periwinkle, ch 1, sk first vertical bar, [insert hook in next horizontal st, yo and draw through st and lp on hook] rep across, fasten off.

Sides & Back Panel

(Make 6)

Rows 1–58: Rep Rows 1–58 of base.

Row 59: With buff, ch 1, sk first horizontal st (dec made), [draw up lp in next horizontal st] rep across to last horizontal st, sk last st (dec made); slide all sts to opposite end of hook, turn. (65 lps on hook)

Row 60: Rep Row 4.

Row 61: With light periwinkle, rep Row 59. (63 lps on hook)

Row 62: Rep Row 6.

Rows 63–122: Rep Rows 59–62. At the end of Row 122, fasten off.

Front Panel

(Make 2)

Side A

Row 1: With double ended hook and light periwinkle, ch 19, insert hook in 2nd ch from hook, [yo and draw through ch forming a lp on hook, keeping all lps on hook] rep across foundation ch; slide all sts to opposite end of hook, turn. (19 lps on hook)

Rows 2–44: Work as for base evenly on 19 sts.

Row 45: With light periwinkle, ch 1, sk first vertical bar, [draw up lp in next horizontal st] rep across to last horizontal st, yo, draw up lp in last horizontal st, draw up lp under last vertical bar; slide all sts to opposite end of hook and turn. (21 lps on hook)

Row 46: Rep Row 6.

Row 47: With buff, ch 1, yo, draw up lp under first vertical bar, [draw up lp in next horizontal st] rep across; slide all sts to opposite end of hook, turn. (23 lps on hook)

Row 48: Rep Row 4.

Rows 49–58: Rep Rows 45–48. (33 lps on hook at the end of Row 57)

At the end of Row 58, break off yarn, placing rem lp from hook on safety pin.

Side B

Rows 1–44: Rep Rows 1–44 of Side A. (19 sts)

Row 45: With light periwinkle, ch 1, yo, draw up lp under first vertical bar, [draw up lp in next horizontal st going under top lp only] rep across; slide all sts to opposite end of hook, turn. (21 lps on hook)

Your cat is special—and now you can crochet a special place all his own. He'll purr with gratitude when you introduce him to this comfy, cozy hideaway home.

Row 46: Rep Row 6.

Row 47: With buff, ch 1, sk first vertical bar, [draw up lp in next horizontal st] rep across to last horizontal st, yo, draw up lp in last horizontal st, draw up lp under last vertical bar; slide all sts to opposite end of hook, turn. (23 lps on hook)

Row 48: Rep Row 4.

Rows 49–58: Rep Rows 45–48. (33 lps on hook at end of Row 57)

Row 59: With buff, ch 1, sk first horizontal st (dec made), *draw up lp in next horizontal st] rep across sts on Side B, yo, place lp from stitch holder on Side A on hook; rep from * across Side A to last horizontal st, which you will sk. (65 lps on hook)

Row 60: Rep Row 4.

Row 61: With light periwinkle, ch 1, sk first horizontal st, [draw up lp in next horizontal st] rep across to last horizontal st, sk last st; slide all sts to opposite end of hook and turn. (63 lps on hook)

Row 62: Rep Row 6.

Row 63: With buff, rep Row 61. (61 lps on hook)

Rows 64–122: Rep Rows 60–63, decreasing 2 sts on each odd numbered row, at the end of Row 122, fasten off.

Assembly

From foam, cut 15-inch square for base. Following diagrams, from foam, cut 3 side/back pieces and 1 front piece.

Place the base foam piece between the base crochet sections, having the predominantly light periwinkle side out on 1 piece and the buff out on the other. With crochet hook size H and light periwinkle, working through both thicknesses, sc around entire outer edge with 3 sc in each corner, sl st to join in beg sc, fasten off. Rep joining in same manner for sides, front and back. With tapestry needle and light periwinkle yarn, working through both lps of sc edging, sew sections tog. ◆

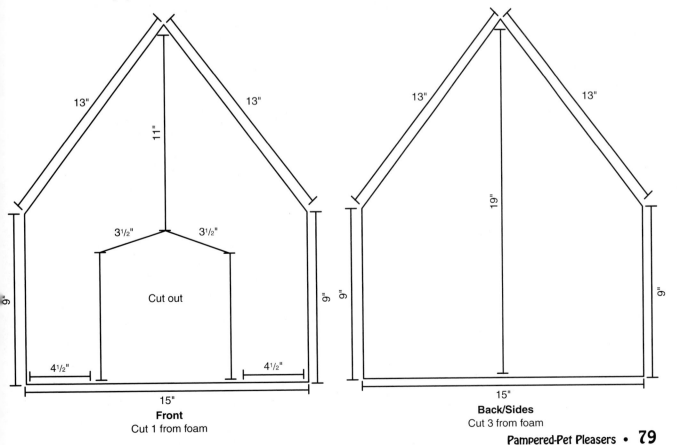

Front
Cut 1 from foam

Back/Sides
Cut 3 from foam

Dapper Dog Sweater

By Connie Folse

Skill Level: Beginner

Size:

Length: 11 inches

Chest: 13 inches

Materials

- ✓ 4-ply worsted weight yarn: 3 oz MC, small amount CC
- ✓ Size G/6 crochet hook or size needed to obtain gauge
- ✓ Tapestry needle

The smallest of your canine companions will be glad for some extra warmth on those brisk autumn strolls. Crochet this cute sweater and let him show his fashionable side!

Rnd 11: Ch 1, hdc in each st around, join in top of beg hdc.

Rnd 12: Rep Rnd 11.

Rnd 13: Ch 1, sc in each of next 11 sts, hdc in each

Gauge

4 sc rnds and 4 sc sts = 1 inch

Check gauge to save time.

Pattern Notes

Weave in loose ends as work progresses.

Join rnds with a sl st unless otherwise stated.

Sweater

Collar

Rnd 1: With MC, ch 35, using care not to twist, sl st to join in beg ch to form a ring, ch 1, sc in each ch around, join. (35 sc)

Rnds 2–9: Ch 1, sc in each sc around, join in beg sc. At the end of Rnd 9, fasten off.

Rnd 10: Attach CC with sl st in first sc of Rnd 9, ch 1, reverse sc in each st around, join, fasten off.

Turn collar inside out. Fold last 4 rnds over first 6 rnds.

Body

Rnd 1: Attach MC in opposite side of foundation ch of Rnd 1 of collar, ch 1, [sc in each of next 4 sc, 2 sc in next sc] rep around, join in beg sc. (42 sc)

Rnd 2: Ch 1, sc in each sc around, join in beg sc.

Rnd 3: Rep Rnd 2.

Rnd 4: Ch 1, [sc in each of next 5 sc, 2 sc in next sc] rep around, join in beg sc. (49 sc)

Rnds 5–7: Rep Rnd 2.

Rnd 8: Ch 1, [sc in each of next 6 sc, 2 sc in next sc] rep around, join in beg sc. (56 sc)

Rnd 9: Ch 1, hdc in each of next 10 sts, ch 8, sk next 8 sts (leg opening), hdc in each of next 30 sts, ch 8, sk next 8 sts (leg opening), join in top of beg hdc.

Rnd 10: Ch 1, hdc in each of next 10 sts, hdc in each of next 8 chs, hdc in next 30 hdc, hdc in each of next 8 chs, join in top of beg hdc. (56 hdc)

of next 45 sts, join in beg sc. (56 sts)

Rnd 14: Ch 1, hdc in first st, sc in next 11 sts, hdc in each of next 44 sts, join in top of beg hdc.

Rnd 15: Ch 1, hdc in each of next 2 sts, sc in next 11 sts, hdc in each of next 43 sts, join in top of beg hdc.

Rnd 16: Ch 1, hdc in each of next 3 sts, sc in next 11 sts, hdc in next 42 sts, join in top of beg hdc.

Row 17: Ch 1, sc in next 5 sts, hdc in each of next 32 sts, sc in next 5 sts, turn. (42 sts)

Row 18: Ch 1, [sc dec over next 2 sts] twice, sc in next 3 sts, hdc in next 28 sts, sc in next 3 sts, [sc dec over next 2 sts] twice, turn. (38 sts)

Row 19: Ch 1, [sc dec over next 2 sts] twice, sc in each of next 3 sts, hdc in each of next 24 sts, sc in each of next 3 sts, [sc dec over next 2 sts] twice, turn. (34 sts)

Row 20: Ch 1, [sc dec over next 2 sts] twice, sc in next 3 sc, hdc in next 20 sts, sc in next 3 sts, [sc dec over next 2 sts] twice, turn. (30 sts)

Row 21: Ch 1, [sc dec over next 2 sts] twice, sc in next 3 sts, hdc in next 16 sts, sc in next 3 sts, [sc dec over next 2 sts] twice, turn. (26 sts)

Row 22: Ch 1, [sc dec over next 2 sts] twice, sc in next 3 sts, hdc in next 12 sts, sc in next 3 sts, [sc dec over next 2 sts] twice, turn. (22 sts)

Row 23: Ch 1, [sc dec over next 2 sts] twice, sc in next 3 sts, hdc in next 8 sts, sc in next 3 sts, [sc dec over next 2 sts] twice, turn. (18 sts)

Row 24: Ch 1, [sc dec over next 2 sts] twice, sc in next 3 sts, hdc in next 4 sts, sc in next 3 sts, [sc dec over next 2 sts] twice, turn, fasten off. (14 sts)

Rnd 25: Attach CC in any st of Row 24, ch 1, sc evenly sp around, join.

Sleeve
(Make 2)

Rnd 1: Attach MC in any st of arm opening, ch 1, work 20 sc evenly sp around opening, join in beg sc. (20 sc)

Rnds 2–4: Ch 1, sc in each

sc around, join in beg sc. At the end of Rnd 4, fasten off.

Rnd 5: Attach CC, ch 1, reverse sc in each st around, join in beg sc, fasten off. ◆

"Catch Me!" Mouse

By Stacey Graham

Skill Level: Beginner

Size: 3 inches long plus tail

Materials

- ✓ Craft cord: 10-yd skein
- ✓ Size H/8 crochet hook or size needed to obtain gauge
- ✓ Rocaille beads: 2 blue and 1 orange
- ✓ Sewing needle and thread
- ✓ Fiberfill
- ✓ Dried catnip
- ✓ Tapestry needle

Your cat will pounce at the opportunity to play with this shiny, life-sized mouse. Make several more if your cat is especially playful!

Gauge

4 sc rnds and 4 sts = 1 inch
Check gauge to save time.

Pattern Notes

Weave in loose ends as work progresses.

Join rnds with a sl st unless otherwise stated.

Mouse Body

Rnd 1 (RS): Beg at tail, leaving a 3-inch length of cord at beg, ch 2, 6 sc in 2nd ch from hook, join in beg sc. (6 sc)

Rnd 2: Ch 1, 2 sc in each sc around, join in beg sc. (12 sc)

Draw rem beg length from WS to RS through center of Rnd 1, pull to close opening; knot ½ inch from end and separate plies of cord.

Rnd 3: Ch 1, sc in each sc around, do not join.

Rnds 4–10: Sc in each sc around.

Stuff body with fiberfill and catnip.

Rnd 11: [Sc dec over next 2 sc, sc in next sc] 4 times, join in beg sc, leaving a length of cord, fasten off. (8 sc)

Weave rem length through sts of Rnd 11, pull tightly to close opening, secure, fasten off.

Ear

(Make 2)

Row 1: Ch 3, 5 hdc in 3rd ch from hook, fasten off. (6 hdc)

Finishing

Sew ears to top of mouse between Rnds 8 and 9.

Sew blue beads ½-inch apart over Rnd 10. Sew orange bead for nose at center point of weave of Rnd 11. ◆

Diamond Dog Collar

By Stacey Graham

Skill Level: Beginner

Size: 1½ x 16 inches

Materials

- ✓ J.&P. Coats crochet nylon: 22 yds country blue #22, 10 yds natural #16
- ✓ Size D/3 crochet hook or size needed to obtain gauge
- ✓ Heavy duty slide lock for 1-inch strapping
- ✓ Tapestry needle

Gauge

Scallop and 1 sc = 1¼ inches
Check gauge to save time.

Pattern Notes

Weave in loose ends as work progresses.

Larger dogs often need a collar that reflects their size and build. This bold, broadbanded collar will make your dog look quite handsome.

Join rnds with a sl st unless otherwise stated.

Collar length can be inc or dec by adding or subtracting multiples of 6 chs from beg foundation ch.

Pattern Stitch

Scallop: 5 dc in indicated st.

Collar

Rnd 1 (RS): With country blue, ch 98, sc in 2nd ch from hook, *sk next 2 chs, scallop in next ch, sk next 2 chs, sc in next ch *, rep from * to * 15 times; working on opposite side of foundation ch, sc in same ch as last sc, rep from * to * 16 times, join in beg sc, fasten off.

Row 2 (RS): Position half of slide lock between first and 2nd scallop, attach natural in center dc of 2nd scallop and center dc of first scallop, ch 1, sc in same dc, [3 dc in next sc, sc in center dc of next scallop] 12 times, 3 dc in next sc; position other half of slide lock between last 2 scallops, working through both thicknesses, sc in center dc of scallop, fasten off.

Row 3 (RS): Working on opposite side of Rnd 1, attach natural in center dc of scallops folded over slide lock, ch 1, working through both thicknesses of end scallops, sc in same dc, [3 dc in next sc, sc in center dc of next scallop] 12 times, 3 dc in next sc, working through both thicknesses, sc in center dc of scallops folded over slide lock, fasten off.

With WS facing, thread tapestry needle with a length of country blue, sew under side scallop at center to next scallop of collar, fasten off. Rep on opposite end of collar. ◆

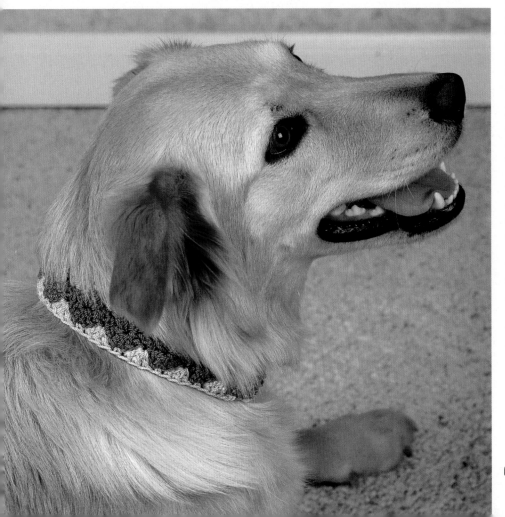

Domed Pet Bed

By Connie Folse

Skill Level: Beginner

Size: 12 x 18 inches

Materials

- ✓ 4-ply worsted weight yarn: 18 oz variegated, 9 oz each 2 solid colors
- ✓ Size J/10 crochet hook or size needed to obtain gauge
- ✓ Tapestry needle

Gauge

7 sc sts = 4 inches
Check gauge to save time.

Pattern Notes

Weave in loose ends as work progresses.

Join rnds with a sl st unless otherwise stated.

Work with 2 strands of variegated and 1 strand each of 2 solid colors held tog throughout pattern.

Bottom

(Make 2)

Rnd 1 (RS): Holding 4 strands of yarn tog, ch 2, 6 sc in 2nd ch from hook, join in beg sc. (6 sc)

Rnd 2: Ch 1, 2 hdc in each st around, join in top of beg hdc. (12 hdc)

Rnd 3: Ch 1, [hdc in next st, 2 hdc in next st] rep around, join in top of beg hdc. (18 hdc)

Rnd 4: Ch 1, [hdc in each of next 2 sts, 2 hdc in next st] rep around, join in top of beg hdc. (24 hdc)

Rnd 5: Ch 1, [hdc in each of next 3 sts, 2 hdc in next

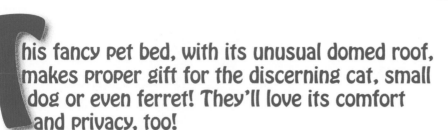

*T*his fancy pet bed, with its unusual domed roof, makes proper gift for the discerning cat, small dog or even ferret! They'll love its comfort and privacy, too!

st] rep around, join in top of beg hdc. (30 hdc)

Rnd 6: Rep Rnd 4. (40 hdc)

Rnd 7: Rep Rnd 5. (50 hdc)

Rnd 8: Ch 1, [hdc in each of next 4 sts, 2 hdc in next st] rep around, join in beg hdc. (60 hdc)

Rnd 9: Ch 1, [hdc in each of next 5 sts, 2 hdc in next st] rep around, join in top of beg hdc. (70 hdc)

Rnd 10: Ch 1, [hdc in each of next 6 sts, 2 hdc in next st] rep around, join in top of beg hdc. (80 hdc)

Rnd 11: Ch 1, [hdc in each of next 3 sts, 2 hdc in next st] rep around, join in top of beg hdc. (100 hdc)

Rnd 12: Ch 1, hdc in each st around, join in top of beg hdc, fasten off.

Sides

Rnd 1: With WS facing, holding both bottoms tog, attach 4 strands of yarn in any sc, ch 1, working through both thicknesses, sc in each st around, join in beg sc, turn. (100 sc)

Rnd 2: Ch 1, working in back lps only, sc in each st around, join in beg sc.

Rnd 3: Ch 1, sc in each sc around, join in beg sc.

Rnds 4 & 5: Rep Rnd 3.

Rnd 6: Rep Rnd 3, turn.

Rnd 7: Ch 1, working in back lps only, sc around, join in beg sc.

Rnds 8–10: Rep Rnd 3.

Rnd 11: Ch 1, holding Rnd 10 to Rnd 1 of side and working through both thicknesses, sc in each st around, join in beg sc, fasten off.

Dome

Row 1: Holding 4 strands of yarn tog, attach yarn in rem free lp of Rnd 6 of sides, ch 1, sc in same st, sc in each of next 84 sts, leaving rem 15 sts unworked for opening, turn. (85 sc)

Row 2: Ch 1, sc in each sc, turn.

Rows 3–5: Rep Row 2.

Row 6: Ch 1, [sc in each of next 13 sc, sc dec over next 2 sc] twice, sc in next 12 sc, sk next sc, sc in next 12 sc, [sc dec over next 2 sc, sc in next 13 sc] twice, turn. (80 sc)

Row 7: Rep Row 2.

Row 8: Ch 1, [sc in each of next 6 sc, sc dec over next 2 sc] 5 times, [sc dec over next 2 sc, sc in next 6 sc] 5 times, turn. (70 sc)

Rows 9 & 10: Rep Row 2.

Row 11: Ch 1, [sc in each of next 5 sc, sc dec over next 2 sc] 5 times, [sc dec over next 2 sc, sc in each of next 5 sc] 5 times, turn. (60 sc)

Rows 12 & 13: Rep Row 2.

Row 14: Ch 1, [sc in each of next 4 sc, sc dec over next 2 sc] 5 times, [sc dec over next 2 sc, sc in next 4 sc] 5 times, turn. (50 sc)

Rows 15 & 16: Rep Row 2.

Row 17: Ch 1, [sc in next 3 sc, sc dec over next 2 sc] 5 times, [sc dec over next 2 sc, sc in next 3 sc] 5 times, turn. (40 sc)

Rows 18 & 19: Rep Row 2.

Row 20: Ch 1, [sc in each of next 2 sc, sc dec over next 2 sc] 5 times, [sc dec over next 2 sc, sc in each of next 2 sc] 5 times, turn. (30 sc)

Rows 21 & 22: Rep Row 2.

Row 23: Ch 1, [sc in each of next 3 sc, sc dec over next 2 sc] 3 times, [sc dec over next 2 sc, sc in each of next 3 sc] 3 times, do not turn. (24 sc)

Rnd 24: Sc in first sc of Row 23, sc in each of next 23 sc, join in beg sc. (24 sc)

Rnd 25: Ch 1, [sc in next sc, sc dec over next 2 sc] rep around, join in beg sc. (16 sc)

Rnd 26: Working in back lps for this rnd only, [sc dec over next 2 sts] rep around, join in beg sc, fasten off. (8 sc)

Weave a length of yarn through Rnd 26; pull ends to close opening, knot ends to secure.

Opening Trim

Row 1: Holding 4 strands tog, attach with sc in first rem free lp of Rnd 25, sc around post of each first st across side edge of Rows 24–1, sl st in first unworked st of Rnd 6 of sides, fasten off.

Rep Row 1 on opposite edge of opening. ◆

Crawly Critters

By Lori Zeller

Skill Level: Beginner

Size:

Snake: 19 inches long

Caterpillar: 13½ inches long

Materials

- ✓ Worsted weight yarn: 2 oz green, 1 oz each light blue, royal blue and navy blue
- ✓ Size F/5 crochet hook or size needed to obtain gauge
- ✓ Black and red dimensional fabric paint
- ✓ Fiberfill
- ✓ Tapestry needle

Gauge

5 sc rnds and 5 sc sts = 1 inch

Check gauge to save time.

Pattern Notes

Weave in loose ends as work progresses.

Do not join rnd unless otherwise stated.

W

hen your dog spies these wiggly creatures, he'll be ready to play tug-of-war! They make great throw-and-fetch toys too.

Snake

Rnd 1: Starting at head, with green, ch 2, 5 sc in 2nd ch from hook. (5 sc)

Rnd 2: Work 2 sc in each sc around. (10 sc)

Rnd 3: [Sc in next sc, 2 sc in next sc] rep around. (15 sc)

Rnd 4: [Sc in each of next 2 sc, 2 sc in next sc] rep around. (20 sc)

Rnd 5: Sc in each sc around.

Rnds 6–11: Rep Rnd 5.

Rnd 12: Sc in each sc around, sl st in next st, fasten off.

Row 13: Stuff head with fiberfill and flatten last rnd; working through both thicknesses, attach royal blue, ch 1, work 10 sc across, turn. (10 sc)

Rnd 14: Working in front lps only, sc across, turn, working in back lps only, sc across. (20 sc)

Rnds 15–20: Rep Rnd 5.

Rnd 21: [Sc dec over next 2 sc, sc in each of next 8 sc] twice. (18 sc)

Rnd 22: Rep Rnd 12.

Row 23: Stuff section just made with fiberfill and

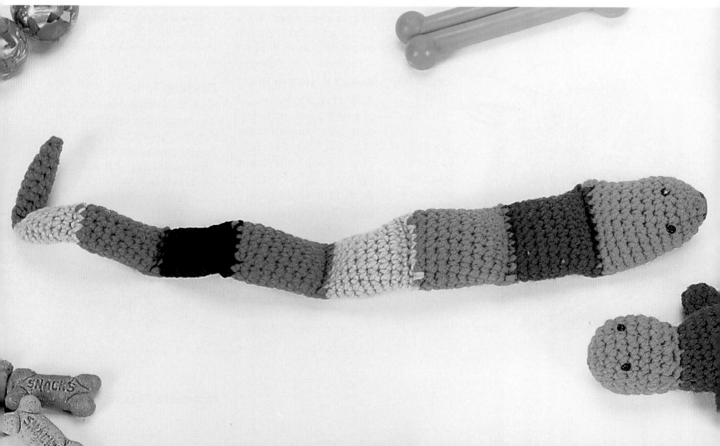

flatten, working through both thicknesses, attach green, ch 1, sc across, turn. (9 sc)

Rnd 24: Rep Rnd 14. (18 sc)

Rnds 25–30: Rep Rnd 5.

Rnd 31: [Sc dec over next 2 sc, sc in each of next 7 sc] twice. (16 sc)

Rnd 32: Rep Rnd 12.

Row 33: With light blue, rep Row 23. (8 sc)

Rnd 34: Rep Rnd 14. (16 sc)

Rnds 35–40: Rep Rnd 5.

Rnd 41: [Sc dec over next 2 sc, sc in each of next 6 sc] twice. (14 sc)

Rnd 42: Rep Rnd 12.

Row 43: With green, rep Row 23. (7 sc)

Rnd 44: Rep Rnd 14. (14 sc)

Rnds 45–50: Rep Rnd 5.

Rnd 51: [Sc dec over next 2 sc, sc in next 5 sc] twice. [12 sc)

Rnd 52: Rep Rnd 12.

Row 53: With navy blue, rep Row 23. (6 sc)

Rnd 54: Rep Rnd 14. (12 sc)

Rnds 55–60: Rep Rnd 5.

Rnd 61: [Sc dec over next 2 sc, sc in each of next 4 sc] twice. (10 sc)

Rnd 62: Rep Rnd 12.

Row 63: With green, rep Row 23. (5 sc)

Rnd 64: Rep Rnd 14. (10 sc)

Rnd 65–70: Rep Rnd 5.

Rnd 71: [Sc dec over next 2 sc, sc in next 3 sc] twice. (8 sc)

Rnd 72: Rep Rnd 12.

Row 73: With light blue, rep Row 23. (4 sc)

Rnd 74: Rep Rnd 14. (8 sc)

Rnds 75–80: Rep Rnd 5.

Rnd 81: [Sc dec over next 2 sc, sc in next 2 sc] twice. (6 sc)

Rnd 82: Rep Rnd 12.

Row 83: With green, rep Row 23. (3 sc)

Rnd 84: Rep Rnd 14. (6 sc)

Rnds 85–90: Rep Rnd 5.

Rnd 91: [Sc dec over next 2 sc, sc in next sc] twice. (4 sc)

Rnd 92: Sc in each sc around, leaving a length of yarn, fasten off.

Stuff last section with fiberfill; sew opening closed.

For eyes, paint 2 small black dots on top of head. For mouth, with red paint a smile centered below eyes.

Caterpillar

Rnd 1: Starting at top of head, with green, ch 2, 5 sc in 2nd ch from hook. (5 sc)

Rnd 2: Work 2 sc in each sc around. (10 sc)

Rnd 3: [Sc in next sc, 2 sc in next sc] rep around. (15 sc)

Rnd 4: [Sc in each of next 2 sc, 2 sc in next sc] rep around. (20 sc)

Rnd 5: Sc in each sc around.

Rnds 6–8: Rep Rnd 5.

Rnd 9: [Sc dec over next 2 sc] rep around, stuff section with fiberfill. (10 sc)

Rnd 10: Rep Rnd 5, fasten off.

Rnd 11: Attach royal blue in any sc, 2 sc in each sc around. (20 sc)

Rnds 12–17: Rep Rnd 5.

Rnd 18: Rep Rnd 9. (10 sc)

Rnd 19: Rep Rnd 5, fasten off.

Rnd 20: With green, rep Rnd 11. (20 sc)

Rnds 21–26: Rep Rnd 5.

Rnd 27: Rep Rnd 9. (10 sc)

Rnd 28: Rep Rnd 5, fasten off.

Rnd 29: With light blue, rep Rnd 11. (20 sc)

Rnds 30–46: Rep Rnds 12–28.

Rnd 47: With navy blue, rep Rnd 11. (20 sc)

Rnds 48–59: Rep Rnds 12–23.

Rnd 60: [Sc in each of next 2 sc, sc dec over next 2 sc] rep around. (15 sc)

Rnds 61 & 62: Rep Rnd 5.

Rnd 63: [Sc in next sc, dec 1 sc over next 2 sc] rep around. (10 sc)

Rnd 64: Rep Rnd 5.

Rnd 65: [Sc dec over next 2 sc] rep around, leaving a length of yarn, fasten off. (5 sc)

Sew opening closed.

Legs

Note: Make 2 each royal blue, navy blue and light blue and 4 green.

Rnd 1: Ch 2, 8 sc in 2nd ch from hook. (8 sc)

Rnds 2–4: Sc in each sc around.

Rnd 5: Sc in each of next 2 sc, [sc dec over next 2 sc] twice, sc in each of next 2 sc, leaving a length of yarn, fasten off.

Stuff legs with fiberfill. Sew on opposite sides of body to sections matching leg colors.

For eyes, paint 2 small black dots on top of head. With red, paint a smile centered below eyes. ◆

Tennis Ball Snake

By Stacey Graham

Skill Level: Beginner

Size: 20 inches long

Materials

✓ Lion Brand Homespun yarn: 1 skein sierra #318

✓ Worsted weight yarn: scrap of red

✓ Size J/10 crochet hook or size needed to obtain gauge

✓ Small amount red and white felt

✓ Craft glue

✓ Fiberfill

✓ Tennis ball

✓ Yarn needle

Gauge

2 hdc rnds and 3 hdc sts = 1 inch

Check gauge to save time.

Pattern Notes

Weave in loose ends as work progresses.

Join rnds with a sl st unless otherwise stated.

Snake

Rnd 1 (RS): With sierra,

Fuzzy, fun-shaped, and ready to play, this perky snake toy will give your dog plenty of exercise and entertainment.

ch 3, 7 hdc in 3rd ch from hook, join in top of beg ch-3. (8 hdc)

Rnd 2: Ch 2 (counts as first hdc throughout), hdc in same st, 2 hdc in each rem st around, join in top of beg ch-2. (16 hdc)

Rnd 3: Rep Rnd 2.

Rnd 4: Ch 2, hdc in next st, hdc dec over next 2 sts, [hdc in each of next 2 sts, hdc dec over next 2 sts] rep around, join in top of beg ch-2. (24 hdc)

Rnd 5: Ch 2, hdc in each st around, join in top of beg ch-2.

Rnd 6: Rep Rnd 5.

Rnd 7: Rep Rnd 4. (18 hdc)

Draw up a lp remove hook.

Fold a 6-inch length of red yarn in half; knot ½-inch from fold; insert folded end RS to WS through center of Rnd 1; sew at inside of snake head over Rnd 1.

Rnd 8: Pick up dropped lp, ch 2, hdc in each of next 3 sts, hdc dec over next 2 sts, [hdc in each of next 4 sts, hdc dec over next 2 sts] rep around, join in top of beg ch-2. (15 hdc)

Insert tennis ball into head.

Rnd 9: Hdc in each hdc around, do not join.

Rep Rnd 9 until snake measures 18 inches, stuffing with fiberfill as work progresses.

Rnd 10: [Hdc dec over next 2 sts, hdc in each of next 6 sts] continue to rep around for several rnds until only 6 hdc rem; leaving a length of yarn, fasten off.

With yarn needle, weave rem length through sts of last rnd, pull to close opening, secure.

Eyes

From white felt, cut 2 circles 1-inch in diameter. From red felt, cut 2 circles ½-inch in diameter. Glue white eyes to snake with red pupils to eye. ◆

Flying Disk Toy

By Stacey Graham

Skill Level: Beginner

Size: 10 inches in diameter

Materials

✓ Worsted weight yarn: 2 oz each MC and CC

✓ Size H/8 crochet hook or size needed to obtain gauge

✓ Fiberfill

✓ Tapestry needle

Here's a toss-and-catch toy your dog can really sink his teeth into! If he doesn't yet know how to play fetch, this soft and colorful saucer will make him eager to learn.

Gauge

4 hdc rnds and 5 hdc sts = 1½ inches

Check gauge to save time.

Pattern Notes

Weave in loose ends as work progresses.

Join rnds with a sl st unless otherwise stated.

Pattern Stitch

Long tr: Yo hook twice, sk rnd below, insert hook in indicated st, yo, draw up a lp, [yo, draw through 2 lps on hook] 3 times.

Disk Sides

(Make 2)

Rnd 1 (RS): With MC, ch 3, 9 hdc in 3rd ch from hook, join in top of beg ch-3. (10 hdc)

Rnd 2: Ch 2 (counts as first hdc throughout), hdc in same st, 2 hdc in each rem st around, join in top of beg ch-2. (20 hdc)

Rnd 3: Ch 2, hdc in same st, hdc in next st, [2 hdc in next st, hdc in next st] rep around, join in top of beg ch-2, fasten off. (30 hdc)

Rnd 4: Attach CC with sl st in any st, ch 2, hdc in same st, sk next st, long tr in st of Rnd 2 directly below skipped st, [2 hdc in next st, sk next st, long tr in st of Rnd 2 directly below skipped st] rep around, join in top of beg

Continued on page 92

Doggie Barrettes

By Stacey Graham

Dogbone Barrettes

Skill Level: Beginner

Size: 1 inch x 2 inches

Materials

✓ Crochet cotton size 10: 25 yds camel

✓ Size B/1 crochet hook or size needed to obtain gauge

✓ 2 white 1¼-inch barrettes

✓ 66 (4mm) flat-back rhinestones

✓ Gem adhesive

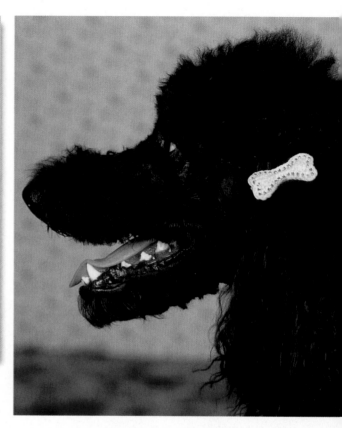

These adorable barrettes will keep wayward fur out of your dog's eyes, and make her look as cute as can be!

Gauge

4 sc sts = ½ inch

Check gauge to save time.

Pattern Notes

Weave in loose ends as work progresses.

Join rnds with a sl st unless otherwise stated.

Dog Bone

(Make 2)

Rnd 1 (RS): Ch 12, 4 dc in 4th ch from hook, sc in next 7 chs, 5 dc in next ch, working on opposite side of foundation ch, sc in next 7 chs, join in top of beg ch. (24 sts)

Rnd 2: Ch 2 (counts as first hdc), dc in same st, *[2 dc, hdc] in next dc, sl st in next dc, [hdc, 2 dc] in next dc, [dc, hdc] in next dc, sc in next sc, sl st in next 5 sc, sc in next sc **, [hdc, dc] in next dc, rep from * to ** join in top of beg ch-2, fasten off.

Finishing

Center bone on barrette front and glue in place. Glue 33 rhinestones around entire edge 1/16-inch from outer edge of bone.

Floral Barrettes

Skill Level: Beginner

Size: 1¼ inch x 2 inches

Materials

✓ Crochet cotton size 10: 50 yds light green, small amounts of blue, yellow and pink

✓ Sizes 7 and 9 steel crochet hooks or size needed to obtain gauge

✓ 54 large crystal rocaille beads

✓ Gem adhesive

Gauge

Flower = ¾ inch

Check gauge to save time.

Pattern Notes

Weave in loose ends as work progresses.

Join rnds with a sl st unless otherwise stated.

Base

(Make 2)

Row 1: String 48 beads onto green cotton, with steel hook size 9, ch 14, sc in 2nd ch from hook, sc in each of next 12 chs, turn. (13 sc)

Continued on page 92

Doggie Barrettes

Continued from page 90

Rows 2–4: Ch 1, sc in each sc across, turn.

Row 5: Ch 1, sc in first sc, [ch 3, slide 1 bead up next to lp on hook, ch 3, sc in next sc] 12 times; sl st across ends of sc rows, sl st in first ch of opposite side of foundation ch, ch 1, sc in same ch as beg ch-1, [ch 3, push up 1 bead next to lp on hook, ch 3, sc in next ch] 12 times, fasten off.

Flowers
(Make 2 each blue, yellow and pink)

Rnd 1 (RS): With steel hook size 7, ch 2, 7 sc in 2nd ch from hook, join in beg sc. (7 sc)

Rnd 2: Ch 1, [sc, hdc, 2 dc, hdc, sc] in each sc around, join in beg sc, fasten off.

Finishing

Center base on barrette and glue in place. Glue 1 of each color of flowers to base with center flower overlapping others. Glue 1 bead to the center of each flower. ◆

Flying Disk Toy

Continued from page 89

ch-2. (30 hdc; 15 long tr)

Rnd 5: Ch 2, hdc in same st, hdc in each of next 8 sts, [2 hdc in next st, hdc in each of next 8 sts] rep around, join in top of beg ch-2. (50 hdc)

Rnd 6: Ch 2, hdc in same st, hdc in each of next 9 sts, [2 hdc in next st, hdc in each of next 9 sts] rep around, join in top of beg ch-2, fasten off. (55 hdc)

Rnd 7: Attach MC with sl st in any hdc, ch 2, hdc in each of next 3 sts, sk next st, long tr in st of Rnd 5 directly below skipped st, [hdc in each of next 4 sts, sk next st, long tr in st of Rnd 5 directly below skipped st] rep around, join in top of beg ch-2. (44 hdc; 11 long tr)

Rnd 8: Ch 2, hdc in same st, hdc in each of next 10 sts, [2 hdc in next st, hdc in each of next 10 sts] rep around, join in top of beg ch-2. (60 hdc)

Rnd 9: Ch 2, hdc in same st as beg ch, hdc in each of next 5 sts, [2 hdc in next st, hdc in each of next 5 sts] rep around, join in top of beg ch-2. (70 hdc)

Rnd 10: Ch 2, hdc in same st, hdc in each of next 4 sts, [2 hdc in next st, hdc in each of next 4 sts] rep around, join in top of beg ch-2, fasten off. (84 hdc)

Rnd 11: Attach CC with sl st in any hdc, ch 2, hdc in same st, hdc in next 2 sts, sk next st, long tr in next st of Rnd 9, [2 hdc in next st, hdc in each of next 2 sts, sk next st, long tr in next st of Rnd 9] rep around, join in top of beg ch-2, fasten off. (84 hdc; 21 long tr)

Rnd 12: Ch 2, hdc in same st, hdc in each of next 6 sts, [2 hdc in next st, hdc in each of next 6 sts] rep around, join in top of beg ch-2, fasten off. (120 hdc)

Joining

Rnd 13: With WS of disk sides tog and working through both thicknesses, attach CC, ch 1, sc in each st around, stuffing with fiberfill before closing, join in beg sc, fasten off. ◆

Kitty's Favorite Mouse

By Darla Fanton

Skill Level: Beginner

Size: 2½ x 4 inches excluding tail

Materials

✓ Coats & Clark Red Heart Super Saver worsted weight yarn: ½ oz each light gray #341, gray heather #400 and small amount light raspberry #774

✓ Size K/10½ double ended crochet hook or size needed to obtain gauge

✓ Small amount fiberfill

✓ Catnip (optional)

✓ ½-inch pink pompom

✓ Aleene's OK To Wash-It glue

✓ Presto self-adhesive felt by Kunin Felt: 2-inch square each white and blue, scrap of black

✓ Tapestry needle

Gauge

6 rows = 1 inch; 9 stitches = 2 inches

Check gauge to save time.

Pattern Notes

Weave in loose ends as work progresses.

When picking up a lp in horizontal st, insert hook under top lp only unless otherwise instructed, yo and draw through keeping lp on hook.

Go get 'im, kitty! Your cat will love playing with this two-toned, long-tailed mouse. Make one for every cat in the family!

Body

Row 1: With gray heather, ch 19, insert hook in 2nd ch from hook, [yo and draw through ch forming a lp on hook] keeping all lps on hook rep across length of foundation ch; slide all sts to opposite end of hook, turn. (19 lps on hook)

Row 2: Place light gray on hook with a sl knot, draw through first lp, [yo, draw through 2 lps (1 lp of each color)] rep across until 1 lp rem on hook, do not turn.

Row 3: With light gray, ch 1, sk first vertical bar, [pick up a lp in next horizontal st] rep across skipping last horizontal st (dec made); slide all sts to opposite end of hook, turn. (18 lps on hook)

Row 4: Pick up gray heather, yo, draw through 1 lp, [yo, draw through 2 lps] rep across until 1 lp remains on hook, do not turn.

Row 5: With gray heather, ch 1, sk first vertical bar and first horizontal st (dec made), [pick up a lp in next horizontal st] rep across; slide all sts to opposite end of hook and turn. (17 lps on hook)

Row 6: With light gray, rep Row 4.

Row 7: With light gray, rep Row 5. (15 lps on hook)

Row 8: Rep Row 4.

Row 9: With gray heather,

Eye
Cut 2 from white felt

Iris
Cut 2 from blue felt

Pupil
Cut 2 from black felt

ch 1, sk first 2 horizontal sts, [draw up a lp in next horizontal st] rep across, skipping last horizontal st; slide all sts to opposite end of hook and turn. (12 lps on hook)

Row 10: Rep Row 6.

Row 11: With light gray, ch 1, sk first horizontal st, [draw up a lp in next horizontal st] rep across skipping last 2 horizontal sts; slide all sts to opposite end of hook and turn. (9 lps on hook)

Row 12: Rep Row 4.

Row 13: With gray heather, ch 1, [draw up a lp in next horizontal st] rep across. (9 lps on hook)

Row 14: Rep Row 6.

Row 15: With light gray, ch 1, draw up a lp under first vertical bar (inc made), [pick up a lp in next horizontal st] rep across, yo, draw up a lp under last vertical bar (double inc made); slide all sts to opposite end of hook and turn. (12 lps)

Row 16: Rep Row 4.

Row 17: With gray heather, ch 1, yo, pick up a lp under first vertical bar, [draw up a lp in next horizontal st] rep across, pick up a lp under last vertical bar; slide all sts to opposite end of hook, turn. (15 lps)

Row 18: Rep Row 6.

Row 19: With light gray, ch 1, draw up a lp under first vertical bar, [draw up a lp in next horizontal st] rep across, draw up a lp under last vertical bar; slide all sts to opposite end of hook, turn. (17 lps)

Row 20: Rep Row 4.

Row 21: With gray

heather, ch 1, draw up a lp under first vertical bar, [draw up a lp in next horizontal st] rep across; slide all sts to opposite end of hook, turn. (18 lps)

Row 22: Rep Row 6.

Row 23: With light gray, ch 1, [draw up lp in next horizontal st] rep across, draw up lp under last vertical bar; slide all sts to opposite end of hook, turn. (19 lps)

Row 24: Rep Row 4.

Row 25: To bind off sts; with gray heather, ch 1, [insert hook in first horizontal st, yo, draw through st and lp on hook] rep across, leaving a length of gray heather, fasten off.

Bottom & Tail

Row 1: With gray heather, ch 2, insert hook in 2nd ch from hook, yo and draw through ch forming a lp on hook; slide all sts to opposite end of hook, turn. (2 lps on hook)

Row 2: Place light gray on hook with a sl knot, draw through first lp, yo, draw through 2 lps (1 lp of each color), do not turn.

Row 3: With light gray, ch 1, draw up a lp under first vertical bar, [draw up a lp in next horizontal st] rep across, draw up a lp under last vertical bar; slide all sts to opposite end of hook, turn. (4 lps on hook)

Row 4: With gray heather, yo and draw through 1 lp, [yo, draw through 2 lps (1 of each color)] rep across until 1 lp remains on hook, do not turn.

Row 5: With gray heather, ch 1, draw up a lp in first

vertical bar, [draw up a lp in next horizontal st] rep across, draw up a lp in last vertical bar; slide all sts to opposite end of hook, turn. (6 lps on hook)

Row 6: With light gray, rep Row 4.

Rows 7–10: Rep Rows 3–6. (10 lps on hook)

Row 11: With light gray, ch 1, [draw up a lp in next horizontal st] rep across; slide all sts to opposite end of hook, turn. (10 lps)

Row 12: Rep Row 4.

Row 13: With gray heather, rep Row 11.

Row 14: Rep Row 6.

Rows 15–20: Rep Rows 11–14.

Row 21: With gray heather, ch 1, sk first horizontal st, [draw up a lp in next horizontal st] rep across, skipping last horizontal st. (8 lps)

Row 22: Rep Row 6.

Row 23: With light gray, ch 1, [insert hook in next horizontal st, yo, draw through st and lp on hook] 3 times, draw up lp in next horizontal st; slide all sts to opposite end of hook, turn. (2 lps on hook for tail)

Row 24: Rep Row 4.

Row 25: With gray heather, ch 1, draw up a lp in next horizontal st; slide all sts to opposite end of hook, turn. (2 lps)

Row 26: Rep Row 6.

Row 27: With light gray, rep Row 25.

Rows 28–48: Rep Rows 24–27. At the end of Row 48, leaving a 3-inch length of yarn, fasten off.

Cut 2 additional 6 inch strands of both light gray

and gray heather, fold strands in half, insert hook in end of tail, draw strands through at fold, including rem lengths, draw all ends through lp on hook. Cut ends to measure 2 inches.

Ear
(Make 2)

Row 1: With gray heather, ch 3, insert hook in 2nd ch from hook, [yo, draw through ch forming a lp on hook] twice; slide all sts to opposite end of hook, turn. (3 lps on hook)

Row 2: Place light raspberry on hook with sl knot, draw through first lp, [yo, draw through 2 lps (1 lp of each color)] rep across until 1 lp remains on hook, do not turn.

Row 3: With light raspberry, ch 1, draw up a lp under first vertical bar (inc made), [draw up a lp in next horizontal st] rep across, inc under last vertical bar; slide all sts to opposite end of hook, turn. (5 lps on hook)

Row 4: With gray heather, yo, draw through 1 lp, [yo, draw through 2 lps] rep across until 1 lp remains on hook, do not turn.

Row 5: With gray heather, ch 1, [draw up a lp in first horizontal st] rep across; slide all sts to opposite end of hook, turn. (5 lps on hook)

Row 6: With light raspberry, rep Row 4.

Row 7: With light raspberry, ch 1, sk first horizontal st (dec made), [draw up a lp in next horizontal st] rep across, skipping last horizontal st. (3 lps on hook)

Leaving an 8-inch tail of gray

heather, fasten off. With tapestry needle run gray heather through light raspberry lps left on hook, slide lps off hook pulling raspberry snug, fasten off. Leaving rem length gray heather for sewing ears to body.

Assembly

With tapestry needle and gray heather, sew curved edges of body sections tog. Using photo as a guide, sew ears to mouse. Stuff body with fiberfill, adding catnip if desired. With gray heather, attach base to straight edges of body leaving tail to extend beyond body. Glue pom-pom nose in place. Using diagrams as a guide, draw eyes, irises and pupils on felt paper backing, cut out features. Peel backing from felt, assemble eyes and adhere to body. ◆

Crocheting With the Double-Ended Hook

By Darla J. Fanton

Practice Swatch

Row 1: With dark shade, ch 12, working through back lps only, insert hook in 2nd ch from hook, yo and draw through, *insert hook in next ch, yo and draw through, rep from * across, leaving all lps on hook (Fig. 1), slide all sts to opposite end of hook, turn. (12 lps on hook)

Fig. 1

Row 2: To work lps off hook, place light shade on hook with a sl knot (Fig. 2), working from left to right, draw through first lp (Fig. 3), *yo, draw through 2 lps (1 lp of each color), rep from * across until there is 1 lp left on hook (Fig. 4), do not turn.

Fig. 2

Fig. 3

Fig. 4

Fig. 5

Row 3: With light shade, working right to left, ch 1, sk first vertical bar, *insert hook under top lp of next

horizontal st, yo and draw through (Fig. 5), rep from * across (Fig. 6), slide all sts to opposite end of hook, turn. (12 lps on hook)

Fig. 6

Row 4: Pick up dark shade, yo and draw through 1 lp, *yo and draw through 2 lps (1 of each color; Fig. 7), rep from * until 1 lp rem on hook, do not turn.

Fig. 7

Row 5: With dark shade, rep Row 3.

Note: Fig. 8 shows Row 5 after sliding sts to opposite end of hook and turning, ready to be Row 6.

Fig. 8

Row 6: With light shade, rep Row 4.

Rep Rows 3–6 consecutively until desired length, ending after a Row 4.

Last Row (Bind-Off Row): Ch 1, sk first vertical bar, *insert hook under top lp of next horizontal st, yo and draw through st and lp on hook (sl st made; Fig. 9), rep from * across (Fig. 10), fasten off.

Weave in yarn ends.

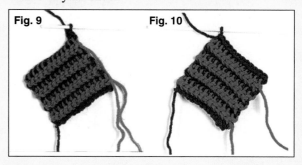

Fig. 9   **Fig. 10**

Hugs & Kisses for Baby

With their tiny fingers and toes, and innocent faces, babies are one of life's most precious treasures! Celebrate the arrival of a new baby by giving him or her a sweet blanket, cuddly toy or soft layette to use now, and treasure as a keepsake in years to come!

Bouncing Baby Jackets

By Sue Childress

Skill Level: Beginner

Size: Newborn–3 months

Materials

✓ Sport weight baby cotton:

   Boy: 200 yds MC

   Girl: 350 yds MC

✓ Size E/4 crochet hook or size needed to obtain gauge

✓ 3 pink decorative buttons

✓ 4 blue decorative buttons

✓ Sewing needle and thread

✓ Yarn needle

Gauge

5 sts = 1 inch

Check gauge to save time.

Pattern Notes

Weave in loose ends as work progresses.

Join rnds with a sl st unless otherwise stated.

Ch 3 counts as first dc throughout.

Ch 2 counts as first hdc throughout.

Pattern Stitches

Cross-st: Sk next st, dc in next st, dc in skipped st.

V-st: [Dc, ch 1, dc] in indicated st.

3-dc cl: [Yo hook, insert hook in indicated st, yo, draw up a lp, yo, draw through 2 lps on hook] 3 times in same st, yo, draw through all 4 lps on hook.

Beg 3-dc cl: Ch 2 (counts as first dc), [yo hook, insert hook in indicated st, yo, draw up a lp, yo, draw through 2 lps on hook] twice in same st, yo, draw through all 3 lps on hook.

Boy's Jacket

Row 1: With MC, ch 84, dc in 4th ch from hook, dc in next 13 chs, V-st in next ch, dc in each of next 10 chs, V-st in next ch, dc in each of next 28 chs, V-st in next ch, dc in each of next 10 chs, V-st in next ch, dc in each of next 15 chs, turn. (78 dc; 4 V-sts)

Row 2: Ch 3, dc in each of next 5 sts, [cross-st over next 2 sts] twice, dc in each of next 6 dc, V-st in ch-1 sp of V-st, dc in each of next 12 dc, V-st in next ch-1 sp of V-st, dc in each of next 10 dc, [cross-st over next 2 sts] 5 times, dc in next 10 dc, V-st in next ch-1 sp of V-st, dc in next 12 dc, V-st in next ch-1 sp of V-st, dc in next 6 sts, [cross-st over next 2 sts] twice, dc in next 6 sts, turn. (86 dc; 4 V-sts)

Rows 3–6: Ch 3, dc in each dc, V-st in each V-st, cross-st in each cross-st, turn. (118 dc; 4 V-sts)

Row 7: Ch 3, [cross-st over next 2 sts] 10 times, dc in ch-1 sp of V-st, ch 4, sk next 22 dc (armhole opening), dc in next ch-1 sp of V-st, [cross-st over next 2 sts] 20 times, dc in ch-1 sp of V-st, ch 4, sk next 22 dc (armhole opening), dc in next ch-1 sp of V-st, [cross-st over next 2 sts] 10 times, dc in last st, turn (86 dc; 2 ch-4 sps)

Row 8: Ch 3, [cross-st over next 2 sts] 10 times, dc in next dc, dc in each of next 4 chs, dc in next dc, [cross-st over next 2 sts] 20 times, dc in next dc, dc in each of next 4 chs, dc in next dc, [cross-st over next 2 sts] 10 times, dc in next dc, turn. (94 dc)

Rows 9–13: Ch 3, [cross-st over next 2 sts] 46 times, dc in last dc, turn. (94 dc)

Rows 14–16: Ch 3, dc in each st across, turn. (94 dc)

Rows 17–20: Ch 3, dc in next 7 sts, [cross-st over next 2 sts] 4 times, dc in each of next 26 sts, [cross-st over next 2 sts] 5 times, dc in each of next 26 sts, [cross-st over next 2 sts] 4 times, dc in next 8 sts, turn. (94 sts)

At the end of Row 20, do not turn.

Rnd 21: Ch 1, working up right front, work 2 sc over side edge of each row,

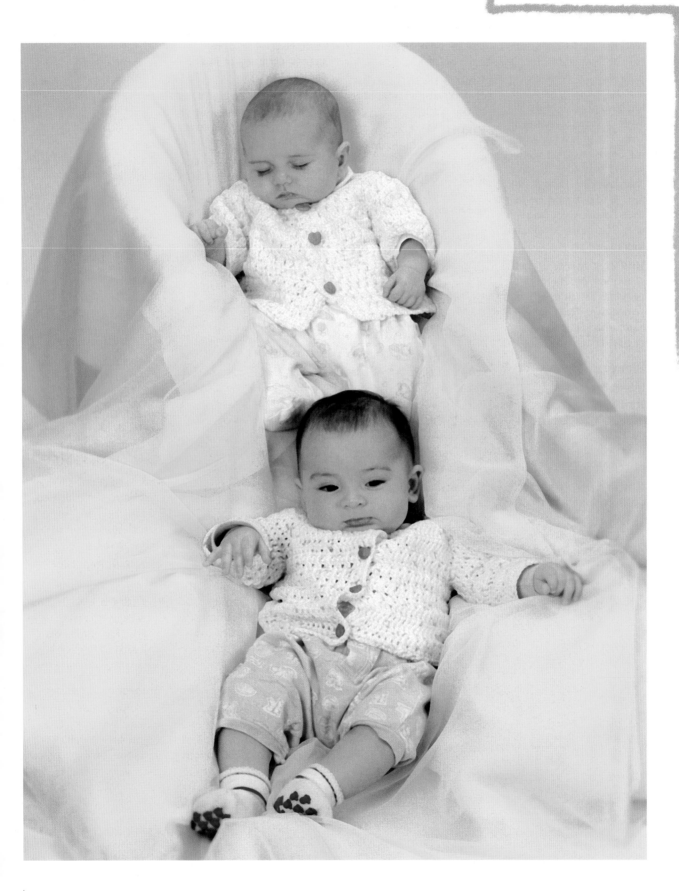

Hugs & Kisses for Baby • 99

working across opposite side of foundation ch, 3 sc in first ch, sc in each ch across, skipping the ch at the base of each of the 4 V-sts of Row 1, ending with 3 sc in last ch; working down left front work 2 sc over side edge of each row; working across bottom, 3 sc in first st, sc in each dc across, ending with 3 sc in last st, sl st to join in beg sc.

Rnd 22: Ch 1, sc in each sc around, except around neckline, [sc in next 5 sc, sc dec over next 2 sc] across neckline, join in beg sc, fasten off.

Sleeve

(Make 2)

Rnd 1: Attach MC at underarm, ch 3, work 31 dc evenly sp around armhole opening, join in top of beg ch-3. (32 dc)

Rnd 2: Ch 3, dc in each dc around, join in top of beg ch-3.

Rnds 3–6: Ch 3, dc in dc before beg ch-3, [cross-st over next 2 sts] 15 times,

join in top of beg ch-3. (16 cross-sts)

Rnds 7–10: Ch 3, dc in each dc around, join in top of beg ch-3.

Rnd 11: Ch 2, hdc in each dc around, join in top of beg ch-2.

Rnd 12: Ch 1, sc in each hdc around, join in beg sc, fasten off.

Finishing

Sew 4 blue buttons evenly sp down right front of jacket. Use natural sps on left front for buttonholes.

Girl's Jacket

Row 1: With MC, ch 70, sc in 2nd ch from hook, sc in each rem ch across, turn. (69 sc)

Row 2: Ch 2, [hdc in each of next 3 sts, 2 hdc in next st] 16 times, hdc in each of next 4 sts, turn. (85 sts)

Row 3: Beg 3-dc cl in first st, [ch 1, sk next st, 3-dc cl in next st] rep across, turn. (43 cls)

Row 4: Ch 3, [3 dc in each of next 2 ch-1 sps, 2

dc in next ch-1 sp] rep across, dc in top of last cl, turn. (114 dc)

Row 5: Beg 3-dc cl in first st, [ch 1, sk next st, 3-dc cl in next st] rep across, turn. (57 cls)

Row 6: Ch 3, [3 dc in next ch-1 sp] rep across, dc in last cl, turn. (170 dc)

Row 7: Ch 3, dc in each of next 27 sts, ch 4, sk next 29 sts (armhole opening), dc in next 56 sts, ch 4, sk next 29 sts (armhole opening), dc in each of next 28 sts, turn. (112 dc; 2 ch-4 sps)

Row 8: Ch 3, dc in each st across, turn. (120 dc)

Row 9: Beg 3-dc cl in first st, [ch 1, sk next st, 3-dc cl in next st] rep across, dc in last st, turn. (60 cls)

Row 10: Ch 3, 2 dc in each ch-1 sp across, dc in last cl, turn. (120 dc)

Rows 11–20: Rep Rows 9 and 10.

At the end of Row 20, do not turn.

Rnd 21: Working up right edge, ch 1, sc in side edge of row, ch 3, [sc in end of next row, ch 3] rep up front to beg foundation ch, sc in first ch, [sc dec over next 2 chs, sc in each of next 3 chs] rep across neckline; working down left front, [ch 3, sc in end of next row] rep down left front; working across bottom, [sc in next dc, ch 3, sk next dc] rep across, join

in beg sc, fasten off.

Sleeve

(Make 2)

Rnd 1: Attach MC at underarm, ch 3, work 35 dc evenly sp around armhole opening, join in top of beg ch-3. (36 dc)

Rnd 2: Beg 3-dc cl in same st, ch 1, [sk next dc, 3-dc cl in next dc, ch 1] rep around, join in top of beg cl. (18 ch-1 sps)

Rnd 3: Sl st into ch-1 sp, ch 3, dc in same ch-1 sp, 2 dc in each ch-1 sp around, join in top of beg ch-3. (36 dc)

Rnds 4–9: Rep Rnds 2 and 3.

Rnd 10: Ch 1, sc in same dc as beg ch-1, ch 3, sk next dc, [sc in next dc, ch 3, sk next dc] rep around, join in beg sc, fasten off.

Finishing

Sew 3 pink buttons evenly sp down left front. Use natural sps on right front for buttonholes. ♥

Keepsake Bag & Gift Box

By Mary Betz

Skill Level: Beginner

Size: Bag: 2¼ x 2½ inches

Materials

✓ Crochet cotton size 10: 20 yds yellow

✓ Size 5 steel crochet hook or size needed to obtain gauge

✓ 10 inches ¼-inch-wide white ribbon

✓ Small box with cover

✓ Decorative self-adhesive paper

Tuck special mementos from your little one's early years, such as a lock of hair or first pair of shoes, into this sweet keepsake set!

Gauge

10 sc and 10 sc rnds = 1 inch

Check gauge to save time.

Pattern Notes

Weave in loose ends as work progresses.

Sl st to join each rnd in top of beg st unless otherwise stated.

Box

Cover inside of box lid and lid with patterned plastic-coated, self-adhesive paper, then cover outside of both.

Bag

Rnd 1: Ch 22, sc in 2nd ch from hook, sc in each rem ch across to last ch, 3 sc in last ch, working on opposite side of foundation ch, sc in each ch across, 2 sc in same ch as beg sc, join. (44 sc)

Rnd 2: Ch 1, sc in each st around, join in beg sc.

Rnds 3–8: Rep Rnd 2.

Rnd 9: Ch 3, [sk next sc, dc in next sc, dc in sk sc] rep around, ending with dc over ch-3 into first sk sc, join in top of beg ch-3.

Rnd 10: Rep Rnd 2.

Rnd 11: Rep Rnd 9.

Rnds 12–16: Rep Rnd 2.

Rnd 17: Ch 4 (counts as first dc, ch 1), [sk next sc, dc in next sc, ch 1] rep around, join in 3rd ch of beg ch-4. (22 ch-1 sps)

Rnd 18: Rep Rnd 2.

Rnd 19: Ch 1, sc in same st as beg ch-1, [ch 3, sl st in top of last sc, sc in each of next 2 sc] rep around, join in beg sc, fasten off.

Starting at side edge of bag, weave ribbon through ch-1 sps of Rnd 17. Tie ends in a bow. ♥

Delight the new mother with this sweet, adorable layette set. Appliquéd leaves reflect the joy of new life!

In Leaf Baby Layette

By Sandy Abbate

Skill Level: Intermediate

Size:

Layette: 3–6 months

Blanket: 33 inches square

Materials

✓ Bernat Coordinates sport-weight yarn (6 oz skeins): 3 skeins soft turquoise #1013

✓ Size G/6 crochet hook or size needed to obtain gauge

✓ Size F/5 crochet hook

✓ 13 (⅜-inch) white pearlized buttons

✓ 5 yds ¼-inch-wide turquoise picot ribbon

✓ Yarn needle

Gauge

6 rows and 3 pattern groups = 3 inches

Check gauge to save time.

Pattern Notes

Weave in loose ends as work progresses.

Join rnds with a sl st unless otherwise stated.

Large Appliquéd Leaf

(Make 2)

Note: *Each large appliqué requires 2 leaves.*

Row 1: With G hook, ch 5, sc in 2nd ch from hook, sc in each of next 3 chs, ch 2, working on opposite side of foundation ch, sc in next 4 chs, ch 2, join in beg sc. (8 sc)

Rnd 2: Ch 1, [sc in each of next 4 sc, {2 sc, ch 2, 2 sc} in ch-2 sp] twice, join in beg sc. (16 sc)

Rnd 3: Ch 1, sc in each of next 6 sc, [2 sc, ch 2, 2 sc]

in ch-2 sp, sc in each of next 8 sc, [2 sc, ch 2, 2 sc] in ch-2 sp, sc in each of next 2 sc, join in beg sc, fasten off.

Finishing

With yarn needle and length of yarn, sew leaves tog at top for approximately ½-inch. Sew a button to center top.

Small Appliquéd Leaf

(Make 2)

Note: *Each small appliqué requires 2 leaves.*

Rnds 1 & 2: Rep Rnds 1 and 2 of large appliqué leaf.

Rep finishing the same as large appliqué.

Blanket

Row 1 (RS): With crochet hook size G, ch 123, 2 dc in 3rd ch from hook, sk 3 chs, [{1 sc, ch 3, 2 dc} in next ch, sk next 3 chs] rep across to last ch, sc in last ch, turn.

Row 2: Ch 2, 2 dc in first sc, [{sc, ch 3, 2 dc} in next ch-3 sp] rep across, ending with 1 sc in turning ch-2, turn.

Rows 3–60: Rep Row 2.

Row 61: Ch 5 (counts as first hdc, ch 3 throughout), [sc in next ch-3 sp, ch 3] rep across, turn.

Border

Rnd 1: Ch 1, 3 sc in first hdc (for corner), work 119 sc evenly sp across to 2nd ch of beg ch-5, 3 sc in 2nd ch of beg ch-5 (for corner), *working in ends of rows, work 119 sc evenly sp across side *, working across opposite side of foundation ch, 3 sc in first ch (for corner), 119 sc evenly sp across, ending with 3 sc in last ch (for corner, rep from * to *, join in beg sc. (488 sc)

Rnd 2: Sl st into center corner sc, ch 5, hdc in same st, *ch 1, sk next sc, [hdc in next sc, ch 1, sk next sc] rep to next center corner sc **, [hdc, ch 3, hdc] in center corner sc, rep from * around, ending last rep at **, join in 2nd ch of beg ch-5.

Rnd 3: Working in ch-1 and ch-3 sps, sl st in next ch sp, ch 1, [sc, ch 3, 2 dc] in same ch sp, sk next ch sp, [{sc, ch 3, 2 dc} in next ch sp, sk next ch sp] rep around, join in beg sc, fasten off.

Finishing

Make 4 sets of large appliquéd leaves. Sew 1 group of leaves to each corner. Cut 4 pieces of ribbon each 14 inches in length, tie each length of ribbon in a bow around button.

Sweater

Body

Row 1: Ch 99, rep Row 1 of blanket.

Rows 2–12: Rep Row 2 of blanket.

Row 13: Ch 1, [sc, ch 2, 2 dc] in first sc, [{sc, ch 2, 2 dc} in next ch-3 sp] rep across, ending with sc in turning ch-2, fasten off.

Row 14: With RS facing, working across opposite side of foundation ch, attach yarn in first ch, ch 1, sc in same ch, work 3 sc in each ch-3 sp across, ending with sc in last ch, turn. (74 sc)

Left front

Row 1 (WS): Ch 2 (counts as first dc throughout), dc in each of next 16 sc, turn. (17 dc)

Rows 2–6: Ch 2, dc in each dc across, turn. (17 dc)

Row 7: Sl st in next 6 sts (neck edge), ch 1, dc in next st (beg dec), dc in each of next 10 dc, turn. (11 dc)

Row 8: Ch 2, dc in each of next 8 dc, dc dec over next 2 dc, turn. (10 dc)

Row 9: Ch 2, dc in each of next 9 dc, fasten off. (10 dc)

Back

Row 1: With WS facing, attach yarn with sl st in next unworked sc of Row 14 of body, ch 2, dc in each of next 39 sc, turn. (40 dc)

Rows 2–8: Ch 2, dc in each dc across, turn. (40 dc)

Left shoulder

Row 9: Ch 2, dc in each of next 8 sts, dc dec over next 2 sts, fasten off. (10 dc)

Right shoulder

Row 9: Sk next 18 sts on Row 8 of back, attach yarn

in next st, ch 1, dc in next st (beg dec), dc in each of next 9 dc, fasten off. (10 dc)

Right front

Row 1: With WS facing, attach yarn in next st of Row 14 of body, ch 2, dc in each st across, turn. (17 dc)

Rows 2–6: Ch 2, dc in each dc across, turn.

Row 7: Ch 2, dc in next 9 dc, dc dec over next 2 dc, turn. (11 dc)

Row 8: Ch 1, dc in next st (beg dec), dc in next 9 dc, turn. (10 dc)

Row 9: Ch 2, dc in each of next 9 dc, fasten off.

With length of yarn and needle, sew shoulder seams.

Sleeve
(Make 2)

Row 1: Ch 47, rep Row 1 of blanket.

Rows 2–10: Rep Row 2 of blanket.

Row 11: Ch 1, [sc, ch 2, 2 dc] in first sc, [{sc, ch 2, 2 dc} in next ch-3 sp] rep across, ending with sc in turning ch-2, fasten off.

Sew sleeve seam.

Cuff

Rnd 1: With RS facing, working in Row 11, with hook size F, attach yarn in first ch-2 sp, ch 1, sc in same ch-2 sp, ch 1, [sc in next ch-2 sp, ch 1] rep around, join in beg sc. (11 sc; 11 ch-1 sps)

Rnd 2: Ch 2, dc in each sc and each ch-1 sp around, join in top of beg ch-2.

Rnd 3: Ch 1, sc in same st as beg ch, loosely ch 1, sk

1 st, [sc in next st, loosely ch 1, sk 1 st] rep around, join in beg sc, fasten off.

Sew sleeve into armhole opening.

Neckline trim

Row 1 (RS): With hook size F, attach yarn at neck edge, ch 1, sc in same st as beg sc, work 42 sc evenly sp around neckline, turn. (43 sc)

Row 2: Ch 2, dc in each sc across, turn.

Row 3: Ch 1, sc in first dc, [ch 1, sk next dc, sc in next dc] rep across, fasten off.

Right front placket

Row 1 (RS): With hook size F, attach yarn, ch 1, work 41 sc evenly sp up right front, turn. (41 sc)

Row 2: Ch 1, sc in first sc, [ch 2, sk 1 sc, sc in next 6 sc] 3 times, sc in each of next 19 sc, turn. (3 buttonholes)

Row 3: Ch 1, sc in each of next 19 sc, [sc in next 6 sc, 1 sc in next ch-2 sp] 3 times, sc in next sc, fasten off. (41 sc)

Left front placket

Row 1 (RS): With hook size F, attach yarn at neckline edge, ch 1, work 41 sc evenly sp down left front,

turn. (41 sc)

Rows 2 & 3: Ch 1, sc in each sc across, turn.

At the end of Row 3, fasten off.

Sew buttons opposite buttonholes.

Make 3 sets of large appliqués. Attach 1 to each left and right sweater yoke, sewing upper and lower edges of leaves to sweater. Attach 3rd set of leaves to back yoke in same manner. Cut a 14-inch length of ribbon for each set, attach ribbon around button, tie ends in a bow.

Bonnet

Row 1: Ch 55, rep Row 1 of blanket.

Rows 2–12: Rep Row 2 of blanket.

Row 13: Ch 5 (counts as first hdc, ch 3), [sc in next ch-3 sp, ch 3] rep across, ending with hdc in top of ch-2 turning ch, turn.

Row 14: Ch 3, [3 dc in next ch-3 sp, dc in next sc] rep across to beg ch-5, 3 dc in ch-5 sp, dc in 2nd ch of beg ch-5, turn.

Rows 15 & 16: Ch 3, dc in each dc across, turn.

Row 17: Ch 1, [sc, ch 3, 2 dc] in same st, sk next 3 dc, [{sc, ch 3, 2 dc} in next dc, sk next 3 dc] rep across, ending with sc in last dc, fasten off.

Sew back seam. Fold front up along Row 13.

Neckband

Row 1: With RS facing, with hook size F and working through both thicknesses at each front edge of hat, attach yarn,

ch 1, sc in same sp as beg ch-1, work 38 sc across edge, turn. (39 sc)

Row 2: Ch 3 (counts as first hdc, ch 1), sk 1 sc, hdc in next sc, [ch 1, sk 1 sc, hdc in next sc] rep across edge, turn.

Row 3: Ch 1, 2 sc in each ch-1 sp across, sl st in 2nd ch of beg ch-3, fasten off.

Make large leaf appliqué and tack to hat on left side of hat. Tie a 14-inch length of ribbon around base of button, tie ends in a bow. Cut a 36-inch length of ribbon, weave through ch-1 sps of Row 2 of neckband.

Booties

(Make 2)

Instep

Row 1: With crochet hook size F, ch 8, dc in 4th ch from hook, dc in each rem ch across, turn. (6 dc)

Rows 2 & 3: Ch 3 (counts as first dc throughout), dc in each dc across, turn.

Sides

Rnd 1: Ch 22, sl st in top of beg ch-3 of Row 3 of instep, ch 3, work 6 dc evenly sp across side edge of instep, work 6 dc across opposite side of foundation ch of instep, 7 dc across side edge of instep, dc in each of next 22 chs, join in top of beg ch-3. (42 dc)

Rnd 2: Ch 3, dc in each dc around, join in top of beg ch-3.

Sole

Rnd 3: Working in back lps for this rnd only, ch 1, sc in same st as beg ch-1, sc in each of next 6 sts, sc

dec over next 2 sts, sc in next 4 sts, sc dec over next 2 sts, sc in each of next 14 sts, sc dec over next 2 sts, sc in next 2 sts, sc dec over next 2 sts, sc in each of next 7 sts, do not join, use scrap of CC yarn to mark rnds. (38 sc)

Rnd 4: Ch 1, sc in each of next 7 sc, sc dec over next 2 sts, sc in next 2 sc, sc dec over next 2 sc, sc in next 14 sc, [sc dec over next 2 sc] twice, sc in next 7 sc, join in beg sc. (34 sc)

Rnd 5: Ch 1, sc in next 7 sc, [sc dec over next 2 sc] twice, sc in next 13 sc, [sc dec over next 2 sc] twice, sc in next 6 sc, join in beg sc. (30 sc)

Rnd 6: Ch 1, sc in each of next 7 sc, sc dec over next 2 sc, sc in next 13 sc, sc dec over next 2 sc, sc in next 6 sc, sl st in next st, leaving a length of yarn, fasten off.

Fold sole in half lengthwise, with rem length, sew seam across sole.

Cuff

Rnd 1: With crochet hook size F, attach yarn at center back of ankle, ch 1, work 29 sc evenly sp around, join in beg sc. (29 sc)

Row 2: Change to crochet hook size G, ch 2, 2 dc in same st, sk next 3 sc, [{1 sc, ch 3, 2 dc} in next sc, sk 3 sc] rep across, ending with sc in last st, turn.

Rows 3–5: Ch 2, 2 dc in first sc, [{1 sc, ch 3, 2 dc} in next ch-3 sp] rep across, ending with sc in top of turning ch-2 sp, turn.

At the end of Row 5, leaving a length of yarn, fasten off. Sew back seam of cuff.

Make 2 small leaf appliqués. Tack 1 to each instep. Do not attach ribbon to button. Cut a 16-inch length of ribbon, starting at center front, weave through ch sps of Row 5 of cuff, tie ends in a bow; rep ribbon weave on 2nd bootie. ♥

Baby Announcement Wreaths

By Sue Childress

It's a Girl!

Skill Level: Beginner

Size: 10 inches in diameter

Materials

- ✓ Sport weight cotton yarn: 1 ball each pink, green and white/pink print
- ✓ Size B/1 crochet hook or size needed to obtain gauge
- ✓ 10-inch foam wreath
- ✓ 4 yds 1½-inch-wide wire edged pink ribbon
- ✓ 4mm pre-strung pearls
- ✓ Baby related charms and ornaments
- ✓ 12-inch chenille stem
- ✓ Hot-glue gun

Share the joyous news of a new baby by displaying these delicate floral wreaths, and beautify your door at the same time!

Gauge

Pink flower = 3 inches in diameter; white flower = 2½ inches in diameter; leaf = 1 inch

Check gauge to save time.

Pattern Notes

Weave in loose ends as work progresses.

Join rnds with a sl st unless otherwise stated.

Each flower requires 15 yds and each leaf requires 5 yds.

Pattern indicates a certain number of flowers and leaves, make as many flowers and leaves as desired.

Pink Flower

(Make 6)

Rnd 1 (RS): With pink, ch 5, sl st to join in beg ch to from a ring, ch 4 (counts as first tr), 39 tr in ring, join in top of beg ch-4. (40 tr)

Rnd 2: Ch 1, sc in same tr as beg ch-1, ch 4, [sc in next tr, ch 4] rep around, join in beg sc, fasten off.

White/Pink Flower

(Make 8)

Rnd 1: With white/pink print, ch 4, sl st to join in beg ch to form a ring, ch 1, [sc in ring, ch 10] 6 times, join in beg sc. (6 ch lps)

Rnd 2: Ch 1, [sc in ch-10 lp, {ch 4, sc in same ch-10 lp} 6 times] rep in each ch-10 lp around, join in beg sc, fasten off.

Leaf

(Make 20)

Row 1: With green, ch 3, [hdc, 2 dc, 2 tr, 2 dc, hdc] in 3rd ch from hook, turn.

Rnd 2: [Ch 2, sc in next st] rep around entire outer

edge, ending with ch 2, sl st in beg st, fasten off.

Finishing

Wrap wreath with ribbon, forming a bow a center top. Form a hanging lp at end of chenille stem. With handing lp at back, secure chenille stem to wreath under bow. Glue leaves and flowers to wreath as desired. Cut a 6-bead strand of pearls and glue each end to center of each flower. Glue charms and baby related items to wreath.

It's a Boy!

Skill Level: Beginner

Size: 10 inches in diameter

Materials

- ✓ Sport weight cotton yarn: 1 ball each blue, green and white/blue print
- ✓ Size B/1 crochet hook or size needed to obtain gauge
- ✓ 10-inch foam wreath
- ✓ 4 yds 1½-inch-wide wire-edge blue ribbon
- ✓ 4mm pre-strung pearls
- ✓ Baby related charms and ornaments
- ✓ 12-inch chenille stem
- ✓ Hot-glue gun

Gauge

Blue flower = 1¾ inches; white flower = 2 inches; leaf 1 inch

Check gauge to save time.

Pattern Notes

Weave in loose ends as work progresses.

Join rnds with a sl st unless otherwise indicated.

Each flower requires 10 yds and each leaf requires 5 yds.

Pattern indicates a certain number of flowers and leaves, make as many flowers and leaves as desired.

Blue Flower
(Make 6)

Rnd 1: Ch 4, sl st to join to form a ring, ch 1, [sc in ring, ch 8] 12 times, join in beg sc.

Rnd 2: Ch 1, [12 sc in next ch-8 sp] rep around, join in beg sc, fasten off.

White/Blue Flower
(Make 10)

Rnd 1: With white/blue print, ch 5, sl st to join to form a ring, ch 1, [sc in ring, ch 6] 6 times, join in beg sc.

Rnd 2: Sl st into ch-5 sp, ch 3 (counts as first dc), 6 dc in same ch-5 sp, [7 dc in next ch-5 sp] rep around, join in top of beg ch-3, fasten off.

Finishing

Rep finishing the same as "It's a Girl!" wreath. ❤

Rainbow Stripes Baby Afghan

By Anne Halliday

Skill Level: Beginner

Size: 39 x 52 inches

Materials

✓ Coats & Clark Red Heart Super Saver worsted weight yarn (8 oz skeins): 10 oz white (MC) #311, 5 oz each light blue (A) #381, pale green (B) #363, pale yellow (C) #322, light coral (D) #327 and petal pink (E) #373

✓ Size I/9 crochet hook or size needed to obtain gauge

✓ Safety pin

✓ Yarn needle

Simple and sweet, this bright afghan will delight the new baby with a rainbow of colors! It's great for using up scraps of primary-colored yarns, too!

Gauge

5 sc plus 5 cls (length) = 4½ inches; 3 sc plus 4 cls (in width) = 4½ inches

Check gauge to save time.

Pattern Notes

Weave in loose ends as work progresses.

Afghan is crocheted vertically.

Leave a 6-inch length of yarn at beg and end of each row. Yarn ends will be worked into fringe.

To maintain same fringe consistency on both ends of afghan, each row is finished off, even if same color continues on next row.

Pattern Stitches

Cluster (cl): Ch 3, yo, insert hook in 3rd ch from hook, yo, draw up a lp, yo, draw through 2 lps on hook, yo, insert hook in same ch, yo, draw up a lp, yo, draw through 2 lps on hook, yo, draw through 3 lps on hook.

To join yarn with sc: Make a sl knot on hook, insert hook in indicated st, yo, draw up a lp, yo, draw through 2 lps on hook.

To join yarn with a sl st: Make a sl knot on hook, insert hook in indicated st, yo, draw up lp and draw through lp on hook.

To fasten off a yarn color: Ch 1, leaving a 6-inch length of yarn, cut yarn, draw up on last lp on hook until yarn pulls through.

Afghan

Row 1 (RS): With MC, ch 218, sc in 2nd ch from hook, [cl, sk next 3 chs, sc in next ch] rep across, fasten off. (54 cls)

Note: Attach safety pin in Row 1 to mark as RS of afghan.

Row 2 (WS): Attach MC with sl st in first sc, ch 5 (counts as first tr, ch 1), sc in ch sp of next cl, work cl, sc in next ch sp of next cl, ch 4, sc in next ch sp of next cl, *[work cl, sc in ch sp of next cl] twice, ch 4, sc in ch sp of next cl, rep from * across to last cl, work cl, sc in ch sp of next cl, ch 1, tr in last sc, fasten off. (17 ch-4 sps)

Row 3 (RS): Attach MC with sc in first tr, *work cl, sc in ch sp of next cl, ch 4, sc in next ch-4 sp, ch 4, sc in ch sp of next cl, rep from * across to turning ch-4, work cl,

Row 4 (WS): Attach MC with sl st in first sc, ch 4, sc in ch sp of next cl, *work cl, sc in first ch-4 sp, ch 4, sc in next ch-4 sp, work cl, sc in ch sp of next cl, rep from * to last sc, ch 1, tr in last sc, fasten off.

Row 5: With RS facing, attach MC with sc in first tr, work cl, sc in next cl, work cl, sc in next ch-4 sp, *[work cl, sc in next cl] twice, work cl, sc in next ch-4 sp, rep from * across to last cl, work cl, sc in next cl, work cl, sc in 3rd ch of ch-4, fasten off.

Row 6: With WS facing, attach A with sl st in first sc, ch 4, sc in next cl, [work cl, sc in next cl] rep across to last sc, ch 1, tr in last sc, fasten off.

Row 7: With RS facing, attach B with sc in first tr, [work cl, sc in next cl] 3 times, ch 4, sc in next cl, *[work cl, sc in next cl]

twice, ch 4, sc in next cl, rep from * across to last 2 lps, [work cl, sc in next cl] twice, work cl, sc in 3rd ch of beg ch-4, fasten off.

Row 8: With WS facing, attach C with sl st in first sc, ch 4, sc in next cl, [work cl, sc in next cl] twice, ch 4, sc in next ch-4 sp, ch 4, sc in next cl, *work cl, sc in next cl, ch 4, sc in next ch-4 sp, ch 4, sc in next cl, rep from * across to last 2 cls, [work cl, sc in next cl] twice, ch 1, tr in last sc, fasten off.

Row 9: With RS facing, join D with sc in first tr, [work cl, sc in next cl] twice, work cl, sc in next ch-4 sp, ch 4, sc in next ch-4 sp, *work cl, sc in next cl, work cl, sc in next ch-4 sp, ch 4, sc in next ch-4 sp, rep from * across to last 2 cls, [work cl, sc in next cl] twice, work cl, sc in 3rd ch of beg ch-4, fasten off.

Row 10: With WS facing, attach E with sl st in first sc, ch 4, sc in first cl, *[work cl, sc in next cl] twice, work cl, sc in next ch-4 sp, rep from * across to last 3 cls, [work cl, sc in next cl] 3 times, ch 1, tr in last sc, fasten off.

Row 11: With RS facing, join MC with sc in first tr, [work cl, sc in next cl] rep across to turning ch-4, sc in 3rd ch of beg ch-4, fasten off.

[Rep Rows 2–11] 5 times, then rep Rows 2–5.

Edging
Row 1: Working in last row of afghan, with WS

facing, attach MC with a sl st in first sc, ch 4, sc in next cl, [ch 3, sc in next cl] rep across to last sc, ch 1, tr in last sc, turn.

Row 2: Ch 1, [sl st, ch 2, 2 dc] in first tr, sk next 3 chs, [{sl st, ch 2, 2 dc} in next sc, sk next 3 chs] rep across to last tr, sl st in last tr, fasten off.

Foundation Edging
Row 1: With RS facing, working in opposite side of foundation ch of Row 1 of afghan, attach MC in first ch with sl st, ch 2, 2 dc in same st, sk next 3 chs, [{sl st, ch 2, 2 dc} in next ch, sk next 3 chs] rep across, ending with sl st in last st, fasten off.

Fringe
Cut 12-inch lengths of yarn. Attach fringe in a single lp at end of rows across top and bottom edges as follows; Matching color of fringe to row color, attach evenly sp fringe in each tr and sc, including corresponding rem length of yarn from working afghan. Trim ends evenly. ♥

His & Her Kewpie Outfits

By Maggie Petsch Chasalow

Skill Level: Beginner

Size: Fits 5-inch kewpie doll

Materials

✓ Crochet cotton size 10: Small amounts shaded pinks, shaded blues and white

✓ Size 7 steel crochet hook or size needed to obtain gauge

✓ 6 snap fasteners

✓ ½-inch white satin rose with leaves

✓ Sewing needle and thread

✓ Tapestry needle

Dress up your huggable kewpie dolls with these heart-warming outfits!

Gauge

9 dc = 1 inch

Check gauge to save time.

Pattern Notes

Weave in loose ends as work progresses.

Join rnds with a sl st unless otherwise stated.

Ch 3 counts as first dc throughout.

Ch 2 counts as first hdc throughout.

Pattern Stitches

Front post treble (fptr):
Yo hook twice, insert hook from front to back to front again around post of next st, yo, draw up a lp, [yo, draw through 2 lps on hook] 3 times.

Front post sc (fpsc):
Insert hook from front to back to front again around indicated st, yo, draw up a lp, yo, draw through 2 lps on hook.

Girl

Sundress

Skirt

Row 1: Beg at waist, with shaded pinks, ch 46, hdc in 3rd ch from hook, hdc in each rem ch across, turn. (45 hdc)

Row 2: Ch 3, dc in same st as beg ch, 2 dc in each of next 41 sts, leaving rem 3 sts unworked, turn. (84 dc)

Rnd 3: Ch 3, dc in each st around, join in top of beg ch-3, turn. (84 dc)

Rnd 4 (RS): Ch 3, dc in each st around, join in top of beg ch-3.

Rnd 5: Rep Rnd 4, fasten off.

Rnd 6 (RS): Attach white in same st as joining, ch 3, [sk next st, sl st in next st, ch 3] rep around, join in same st as beg sl st, fasten off.

Bib

Row 1 (RS): With shaded pinks, ch 3, 4 hdc in 3rd ch from hook, turn. (5 hdc)

Row 2: Ch 2, hdc in same st as beg ch, [hdc in next st, 2 hdc in next st] twice, turn. (8 hdc)

Row 3: Ch 2, hdc in same st as beg ch, 2 hdc in next st, hdc in each of next 2 sts, 2 hdc in next st, hdc in next st, 2 hdc in last st, turn. (12 hdc)

Row 4: *Ch 3, holding back on hook last lp of each st, dc in each of next 4 sts, yo, draw through all 5 lps on hook, ch 3 *, sl st in each of next 2 sts, rep from * to *, sl st in last st, do not turn.

Rnd 5: Ch 1, sc in same st as last sl st, work 5 sc evenly sp over ends of rows to bottom of bib, 3 sc in opposite side of foundation ch (bottom point of heart), 6 sc evenly sp over end of next 3 rows, 8 sc evenly sp across first lobe of bib, sl st in next 2 sl sts, 8 sc evenly sp across 2nd lobe of bib, join in beg sc, fasten off. (31 sc; 2 sl sts)

Rnd 6 (RS): Attach white in joining with sl st, [ch 3, sk next st, sl st in next st] 3 times, [ch 3, sl st in next st] twice, [ch 3, sk next st, sl st in next st] 7 times, sl st in next sl st, sl st in next sc, ch 3, [sk next st, sl st in next st, ch 3] rep around, join in same st as beg ch-3, fasten off.

Strap

(Make 2)

Row 1: With shaded pinks, ch 30, working in single vertical strands across back of ch, dc in 4th ch from hook, dc in each rem ch across, leaving a 6-inch length, fasten off.

Headband

Row 1: With shaded pinks, ch 4, sc in 2nd ch from hook, sc in each of next 2 chs, turn. (3 sc)

Rows 2–49: Working in back lps only, ch 1, sc in each of next 3 sts, turn. (3 sc)

Row 50: Working through both thicknesses of rem lp on opposite side of foundation ch and back lps only of previous row, sl st in each st across, fasten off. Turn headband inside out.

Edging

Rnd 51: Attach white with sl st over side edge of any row of headband, ch 3, [sk next row, sl st over end of next row, ch 3] rep around, join in sl st at base of beg ch-3, fasten off.

Rep edging on opposite edge of headband.

Finishing

With tapestry needle and shaded pinks, tack bottom tip of bib to center front of skirt waistband. With sewing needle and thread, sew snap fastener to back waist opening. With tapestry needle and rem length, sew a strap to each side at top of bib on WS. Cross straps at back of sundress, sew snap fasteners to ends of straps and corresponding points on back waistband.

Boy

Sunsuit

Pants

Row 1: With shaded blues, ch 46, hdc in 3rd ch from hook, hdc in each rem ch across, turn. (45 hdc)

Row 2: Ch 3, dc in same st as beg ch, [dc in each of next 5 sts, 2 dc in next st] 6 times, dc in each of next 4 sts, 2 dc in next st, leaving rem 3 sts unworked, turn. (50 dc)

Row 3: Ch 3, dc in each st across, turn.

Rnds 4–6: Ch 3, dc in each st around, join in top of beg ch. (50 dc)

First leg

Rnd 7: Ch 3, dc in each of next 24 sts, join in top of beg ch, fasten off. (25 dc)

Rnd 8: Attach white, ch 1, reverse sc in each st around, join in beg sc, fasten off.

Second leg

Rnd 7: Attach shaded

blues in next unworked st of Rnd 6, ch 3, dc in each of next 24 sts, join in top of beg ch, fasten off. (25 dc)

Rnd 8: Rep Rnd 8 of first leg.

Bib

Rows 1–3: With shaded blues, rep Rows 1–3 of bib for girl. (12 hdc)

Row 4: Ch 2, hdc in same st as beg ch, hdc in each st across to last 2 sts, 2 hdc in last st, turn. (14 hdc)

Row 5: Ch 2, hdc in each st across, turn.

Row 6: *Ch 2, holding back last lp of each st, dc in each of next 5 sts, yo, draw through all 6 lps on hook, ch 2 *, sl st in each of next 2 sts, rep from * to *, sl st in last st, do not turn.

Rnd 7: Ch 1, working over ends of rows, sc in same st as sl st, work 8 sc evenly sp to bottom of bib, 3 sc in opposite side of foundation ch (bottom point of heart), 9 sc evenly sp over ends of next 5 rows, 9 sc evenly sp across first lobe of heart, sl st between 2 sl sts, 9 sc evenly sp across 2nd lobe of heart, join in beg sc, fasten off. (39 sc)

Rnd 8 (RS): Attach white in same st as joining, ch 1, reverse sc in each st around, join in beg sc, fasten off.

Strap

(Make 2)

With shaded blues, rep strap for girl.

Cap

Rnd 1: With shaded blues,

Continued on page 113

Dainty Shells Baby Afghan

By Melissa Leapman

Skill Level: Beginner

Size: 36 x 41 inches

Materials

✓ Coats & Clark Red Heart Baby Soft yarn (6-oz skeins): 2 skeins each light rose twinkle #8722 (A), light mint twinkle #8660 (B) and light yellow twinkle #8225 (C)

✓ Size F/5 crochet hook or size needed to obtain gauge

✓ Yarn needle

This lovely textured blanket is the perfect gift for the new baby or the mom-to-be. Stitch it with love for a warm and cozy "bundle of joy!"

Gauge

In pattern, each shell = ¾ inch

Check gauge to save time.

Pattern Notes

Weave in loose ends as work progresses.

Join rnds with a sl st unless otherwise stated.

Pattern Stitches

Shell: [Dc, ch 1] twice and dc in indicated st.

3-hdc dec: [Yo hook, insert hook in next st, yo, draw up a lp] 3 times, yo, draw through all 7 lps on hook.

Afghan

Note: Color sequence through afghan is as follows, 1 row A, [2 rows each of B, C and A] rep for color pattern.

Foundation row (WS): With A, ch 218, sc in 2nd ch from hook, [sk 2 chs, shell in next ch, sk 2 chs, sc in next ch] rep across, turn.

Row 1: Change color, ch 4 (counts as first dc, ch 1), dc in first dc, [sc in center dc of next shell, shell in next sc] rep across, ending with sc in center dc of last shell, [dc, ch 1, dc] in last sc, turn.

Row 2: Ch 1, sc in first dc, [shell in next sc, sc in center dc of next shell] rep across, ending with shell in last sc, sc in 3rd ch of turning ch-4.

Rep Rows 1 and 2 in pattern

until afghan measures 40 inches, ending after 1 row worked with A, turn.

Last row: Ch 1, sc in first dc, [ch 1, sk next ch-1 sp, 3-hdc dec over next 3 sts, ch 1, sc in next dc] rep across, ending with ch 1, sk next ch-1 sp, 3-hdc dec over next 3 sts, ch 1, sc in 3rd ch of turning ch-4, fasten off.

Border

Rnd 1 (RS): Attach C with a sl st to upper right corner of afghan, ch 1, work 155 sc along top edge of afghan, 3 sc in corner, 181 sc along left edge of afghan, 3 sc in corner, 155 sc across opposite side of foundation ch, 3 sc in corner, 181 sc across rem side edge of afghan and 3 sc in corner st, join in beg sc.

Rnd 2: Ch 1, sc in same st as beg ch-1, [ch 2, sk next sc, sc in next sc] rep around entire outer edge, working [sc, ch 2] twice in each center corner sc, join in beg sc.

Rnd 3: Sl st into ch-2 sp, ch 1, [sc, ch 2, sc] in each ch-2 sp around, working [sc, ch 2, sc] twice in each corner ch-2 sp, join in beg sc, fasten off. ♥

His & Her Kewpie Outfits

Continued from page 111

ch 4, 11 dc in 4th ch from hook, join in top of beg ch. (12 dc)

Rnd 2: Ch 3, dc in same st as beg ch, *dc in next st, fptr over same st **, 2 dc in next st, rep from * around, ending last rep at **, join in top of beg ch. (24 sts)

Rnd 3: Ch 3, *2 dc in next st, dc in each of next 2 sts, fptr over same st as last dc **, dc in next st, rep from * around, ending last rep at **, join in top of beg ch. (36 sts)

Rnd 4: Ch 3, dc in next st, *2 dc in next st, dc in each of next 2 sts, fptr over next st **, dc in each of next 2 sts, rep from * around, ending last rep at **, join in top of beg ch. (42 sts)

Rnd 5: Ch 3, dc in each of next 6 sts, *fptr over same st as last dc **, dc in each of next 7 dc, rep from * around, ending last rep at **, join in top of beg ch. (48 sts)

Rnd 6: Ch 3, dc in each of next 2 sts, *2 dc in next st, dc in each of next 3 sts, fptr over next st, dc in each of next 7 dc, fptr over next st **, dc in each of next 3 sts, rep from * around, ending last rep at **, join in top of beg ch. (51 sts)

Rnds 7 & 8: Ch 3, dc in each dc and fptr over fptr around, join in top of beg ch. (51 sts)

Brim

Row 1 (RS): Working in front lps for this row only, ch 2, hdc in each of next 7 sts, 2 hdc in next st, hdc in each of next 7 sts, turn. (17 hdc)

Row 2: Ch 2, dec 1 hdc over next 2 sts, hdc in each of next 5 sts, 2 hdc in next st, hdc in each rem st to last 3 sts, dec 1 hdc over next 2 sts, hdc in last st, turn. (16 sts)

Row 3: Ch 2, hdc in each of next 7 sts, 2 hdc in next st, hdc in each rem st across, turn. (17 hdc)

Row 4: Rep Row 2. (16 hdc)

Rnd 5: Ch 1, dec 1 sc over next 2 sts, sc in each of next 12 sts, dec 1 sc over next 2 sts, work 6 sc evenly sp over side edge of 4 rows of brim, sc in each rem st of Rnd 8 of cap to opposite side of brim, work 6 sc evenly sp over ends of next 4 rows of brim, join in beg sc, fasten off.

Rnd 6: Attach white with sl st in any sc at back of cap in previous rnd, ch 1, work reverse sc around entire outer edge of cap, sk 1 st at base of brim on each side of brim, join in beg st, fasten off.

Button

Rnd 1: With white, leaving a 6-inch length at beg, ch 2, 8 sc in 2nd ch from hook, do not join. (8 sc)

Rnd 2: Working in back lps only, sl st in each of next 8 sts, join in beg sl st, fasten off.

Finishing

With rem beg 6-inch length of button; sew button to center top of cap.

With sewing needle and thread, sew 1 snap fastener to back waistline.

With tapestry needle and shaded blues, tack bottom of bib to center front waistband. Sew 1 end of each strap to each inside edge of top of bib. Cross straps at back, sew a snap fastener to free end of strap and to corresponding points at back waistband. ♥

Mix-and-Match Outfits

By Carol Carlile

Skill Level: Beginner

Size:

Boy's shirt: 6–12 months

Girl's blouse: 6–12 months

Shorts: 6–12 months

Materials

✓ Bernat Softee Baby sport weight yarn:

Boy's shirt: 2 oz pale blue, 1 oz white

Girl's blouse: 2 oz pink, 1 oz white

Shorts: 2 oz white

✓ Size G/6 crochet hook or size needed to obtain gauge

✓ ½-inch heart-shaped white button

✓ Iron-on appliqué

✓ Yarn needle

Soft and simple, these tiny garments will dress baby up in style! The mix-and-match pieces coordinate for a truly versatile gift.

Gauge

4 dc = 1 inch; 5 dc rows = 2 inches

Check gauge to save time.

Pattern Notes

Weave in loose ends as work progresses.

Join rnds with a sl st unless otherwise stated.

Ch 3 counts as first dc throughout.

Boy's Shirt

Front

Row 1: With blue, ch 42, dc in 4th ch from hook, dc in each rem ch across, turn. (40 dc)

Row 2 (RS): Ch 3, dc in each of next 9 dc, fpdc around next 4 dc, dc in each of next 12 dc, fpdc around next 4 dc, dc in each of next 10 dc, turn.

Row 3 (WS): Ch 3, dc in each of next 9 dc, bpdc around next 4 sts, dc in each of next 12 dc, bpdc around next 4 sts, dc in each of next 10 dc, turn.

Row 4 (RS): Ch 3, dc in each of next 9 dc, *sk next 2 sts, fpdc around next 2 sts, fpdc around 2 sk sts (cable twist) *, dc in each of next 12 dc, rep from * to *, dc in each of next 10 dc, turn.

Row 5 (WS): Rep Row 3.

Row 6 (RS): Rep Row 2.

Row 7 (WS): Ch 3, dc in each of next 9 dc, *sk next 2 sts, bpdc around next 2 sts, bpdc around 2 sk sts (cable twist) *, dc in each of next 12 dc, rep from * to *, dc in each of next 10 dc, turn.

Row 8: Rep Row 2.

Row 9: Rep Row 3.

Row 10: Rep Row 4.

Row 11: Rep Row 3.

Row 12: Rep Row 2.

Row 13: Rep Row 7.

Row 14: Rep Row 2.

Row 15: Rep Row 3.

Row 16: Rep Row 4.

Row 17: Rep Row 3.

Row 18: Rep Row 2.

Right neck shaping

Row 19 (WS): Ch 3, dc in next 10 dc, sk 2 sts, bpdc around next 2 sts, bpdc around 2 sk sts (cable twist), dc in each of next 6 dc, turn.

Row 20: Ch 2, dc in each of next 5 dc, fpdc around next 4 sts, dc in next 10 sts, turn.

Row 21: Ch 3, dc in next 9 dc, bpdc around next 4 sts, dc in each of next 4 sts, turn.

Row 22: Ch 2, dc in each of next 3 dc, sk next 2 sts, fpdc around next 2 sts, fpdc around 2 sk sts, dc in each of next 10 dc, turn.

Row 23: Ch 3, dc in each of next 9 dc, bpdc around next 4 sts, dc dec over next 2 sts, turn.

Row 24: Ch 2, sk 2 sts, fpdc around next 4 sts, dc in next 10 dc, turn.

Row 25: Ch 3, dc in next 11 dc, fasten off.

Left neck shaping

Row 19 (WS): Attach blue in next unworked st of Row 18, ch 3, dc in each of next 5 dc, sk 2 sts, bpdc around next 2 sts, bpdc around 2 sk sts, dc in each of next 10 dc, turn.

Row 20: Ch 3, dc in each of next 9 dc, fpdc around next 4 sts, dc in each of next 4 sts, dc dec over next 2 dc, turn.

Row 21: Ch 2, dc in next 4 dc, bpdc around next 4 sts, dc in each of next 10 dc, turn.

Row 22: Ch 3, dc in each of next 9 dc, sk next 2 sts, fpdc around next 2 sts, fpdc around 2 sk sts, dc in next 2 dc, dc dec over next 2 sts, turn.

Row 23: Ch 2, dc in next dc, bpdc around next 4 sts, dc in each of next 10 dc, turn.

Row 24: Ch 3, dc in each of next 9 dc, fpdc around next 4 sts, dc in next st, turn.

Row 25: Sl st in next 3 sts, ch 3, dc in next 11 sts, fasten off.

Back
Row 1 (WS): With blue, ch 42, dc in 4th ch from hook, dc in each rem ch across, turn. (40 dc)

Rows 2–24: Ch 3, dc in each dc across, turn.

First shoulder shaping
Row 25: Ch 3, dc in next 11 dc, fasten off.

Second shoulder shaping
Row 25: Sk next 16 sts of Row 24, attach blue in next st, ch 3, dc in each of

next 11 dc, fasten off. Holding front and back tog, sew shoulder seams. Sew side seams, Rows 1–17.

Neckline Trim
Row 1 (RS): Attach white at center front, ch 1, sc evenly sp around neckline opening, turn.

Rows 2 & 3: Ch 1, sc in each sc across, turn.

At the end of Row 3, leaving a length of yarn, fasten off.

Overlap ends at center front, sew ends tog at front center of V.

Sleeve
(Make 2)

Rnd 1 (RS): Attach blue at underarm, ch 3, work 35 dc evenly sp around armhole opening, join in top of beg ch-3, turn. (36 dc)

Rnds 2–5: Ch 3, dc in each dc around, join in top of beg ch-3, turn.

At the end of Rnd 5, fasten off.

Rnd 7 (WS): Attach white at underarm, ch 1, sc in each dc around, join in beg sc.

Rnds 8–10: Ch 1, sc in each sc around, join in beg sc, turn.

At the end of Rnd 10, fasten off.

Girl's Blouse

Front
Rows 1 (RS): With pink, ch 42, dc in 4th ch from hook, dc in each rem ch across, turn. (40 dc)

Rnds 2–17: Ch 3, dc in each dc across, turn.

Row 18 (WS): Sl st in each of next 5 sts, ch 3, dc in each of next 31 dc, leaving rem 4 sts unworked, turn. (32 dc)

Rows 19–23: Ch 3, dc in each of next 31 dc, turn. (32 dc)

First neck shaping
Row 24 (WS): Ch 3, dc in each of next 9 dc, turn. (10 dc)

Row 25: Ch 3, dc dec over next 2 sts, dc in each of next 7 dc, fasten off. (9 dc)

Second neck shaping
Row 24 (WS): Sk next 12 dc, attach pink in next dc, ch 3, dc in each of next 9 dc, turn. (10 dc)

Row 25: Ch 3, dc in next 6 dc, dc dec over next 2 dc, dc in next dc, fasten off. (9 dc)

Back
Rows 1–18: Rep Rows

1–17 of front. (32 dc)

First back opening
Row 19 (WS): Ch 3, dc in each of next 15 dc, turn. (16 dc)

Rows 20–24: Ch 3, dc in each of next 15 dc, turn.

Row 25 (WS): Ch 3, dc in each of next 6 dc, dc dec over next 2 sts, dc in next st, fasten off. (9 dc)

Second back opening
Row 19 (WS): Attach pink in next unworked dc of Row 18, ch 3, dc in each of next 15 dc, turn. (16 dc)

Rows 20–24: Ch 3, dc in each of next 15 dc, turn. (16 dc)

Row 25 (WS): Sl st in each of next 7 sts, ch 3, dc dec over next 2 sts, dc in each of next 7 dc, fasten off. (9 dc)

Sew shoulder seams. Matching rows, sew side seams Rows 1–17.

Collar
Note: Each collar section is crocheted from back opening to center to st.

First half
Row 1: Attach white at left back opening, ch 3, work 33 dc evenly sp to center front, turn. (34 dc)

Row 2: Ch 3, dc in each dc across, turn.

Row 3: [Ch 5, sl st in next st] rep across sts of Row 2 and down side edge of rows at center front, ending with last sl st in same st as last dc of Row 1 of collar, fasten off.

Second half
Row 1: Attach white in

next unworked st at front, ch 3, work 33 dc evenly sp around rem of neckline, ending at right back opening, turn. (34 dc)

Row 2: Ch 3, dc in each dc across, fasten off.

Row 3: Attach white with sl st in same st as beg ch-3 of Row 1, [ch 5, sl st in next st] rep across side edge of Rows 1 and 2 and in each st of Row 2, fasten off.

Trim

Row 1: Working through both thicknesses of collar and neckline of blouse, attach white at left back, ch 1, sc evenly sp around neckline, fasten off.

Sew button to right back neckline, using natural sps on left edge for buttonhole.

Sleeve

(Make 2)

Rnd 1 (RS): Attach pink at center underarm, ch 3, work 53 dc evenly sp around armhole opening, join in top of beg ch-3, turn. (54 dc)

Rnds 2–5: Ch 3, dc in each dc around, join in top of beg ch-3, turn.

At the end of Rnd 5, fasten off.

Rnd 6 (RS): Attach white in same st as joining, ch 1, sc in same st, sk next st, [sc in next st, sk next st] rep around, join in beg sc. (27 sc)

Rnds 7–9: Ch 1, sc in each sc around, join in beg sc, turn.

Rnd 10: [Ch 5, sl st in next st] rep around, fasten off.

Shorts

Front

Waistband

Row 1: With white, ch 10, sc in 2nd ch from hook, sc in each rem ch across, turn. (9 sc)

Rows 2–36: Ch 1, working in back lps only, sc in each st across, turn. (9 sc)

Body

Row 1: Working across side edge of rows, ch 1, [2 sc in next row, sc in each of next 5 row] 6 times, turn. (42 sc)

Rows 2–12: Ch 3, dc in each st across, turn. (42 dc)

Row 13: Ch 3, [dc dec over next 2 sts] twice, dc in each of next 32 dc, [dc dec over next 2 dc] twice, dc in next dc, fasten off. (38 dc)

Back

Waistband

Rows 1–36: Rep Rows 1–36 of front waistband.

Body

Rows 1–13: Rep Rows 1–12 of front body. (42 dc)

Rows 14 & 15: Ch 2, dc in next dc (beg dec), dc dec over next 2 sts, dc in each dc across to last 4 dc, [dc dec over next 2 dc] twice, turn. (34 dc)

At the end of Row 15, fasten off.

Crotch

Row 16: Sk next 12 dc of previous row, attach white in next dc, ch 3, dc in next 9 dc, leaving rem 12 dc unworked, turn. (10 dc)

Rows 17 & 18: Ch 3, dc in each dc across, turn. (10 dc)

Row 19: Ch 3, dc in same st as beg ch-3, 2 dc in next dc, dc in each of next 6 dc, [2 dc in next dc] twice, leaving a length of yarn, fasten off. (14 dc)

With rem length of yarn, sew Row 19 to center 14 dc sts of Row 13 of front.

Matching rows, sew side seams.

Leg trim

Rnd 1 (RS): Attach white at center crotch, ch 1, sc evenly sp around leg opening, join in beg sc.

Rnd 2: Ch 1, sc in each sc around, join in beg sc, fasten off.

Attach iron-on appliqué to right front of shorts. ♥

Ten Helpful Hints!

By Betsy Ann Day

If your foundation row tends to be too tight, use a hook one size larger just for that chain.

Add a gift tag: Include fiber content, care instructions and a personal note.

Keep a creative diary. Include pictures of your work, patterns, personal notes, yarn samples, labels, etc.

Display your hooks in a small vase.

Make a gauge swatch of ample size for each project. Launder it and evaluate your yarn's quality and drape.

To keep a pull-from-the-center skein of yarn tidy, insert it into a nylon knee-hi.

Use an old teapot as a thread holder. Thread the string through the spout.

Save all swatches. Create a one-of-a-kind mismatched vest, scarf, afghan or tote bag.

Cut all scraps of yarn into 3-inch pieces. Hang in mesh bags, or scatter them on evergreen branches. Your neighborhood birds will appreciate the nest-building material!

Join a crochet guild. Start your own chapter. Creating with others brings great joy!

Victorian Hearts Baby Coverlet

By Carol Alexander for
Crochet Trends and Traditions

Skill Level: Intermediate

Size: 31 x 41 inches

Materials

✓ Lion Brand Jamie pompadour baby yarn (1.75 oz skeins): 9 skeins fisherman #299

✓ Size C/2 crochet hook or size needed to obtain gauge

✓ 4⅔ yds ⅛-inch-wide ecru satin ribbon

✓ 12 (12mm) ecru ribbon roses with leaves

✓ Tapestry needle

This exquisite baby blanket is perfect for a spring stroll through the park. Lightweight and lacy, it will keep off the chill while making baby and carriage look beautiful!

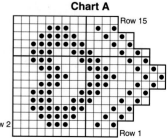

Gauge

One pattern rep Rows 6–13 = 2½ inches; 6 dc = 1 inch

Check gauge to save time.

Pattern Note

Weave in loose ends as work progresses.

Pattern Stitch

Cl: [Yo hook, draw up a lp] 5 times in indicated st, yo, draw through all 11 lps on hook, ch 1 tightly to lock.

Heart Filet Border for Short Ends of Coverlet

(Make 2)

Row 1: Ch 44, dc in 8th ch from hook (beg sp), [ch 2, sk 2 sts, dc in next st (sp)] 12 times, turn. (13 sps)

Row 2: Ch 5, dc in next dc (beg sp), [ch 2, dc in next dc] 4 times, dc in each of next 9 sts (3 bls), [ch 2, dc in next dc] twice, dc in each of next 3 sts (1 bl), ch 2, dc in each of next 3 dc sts (1 bl), turn.

Row 3: Ch 10, dc in 8th ch from hook, dc in each of next 2 chs, dc in next dc, ch 2, sk next 2 sts, dc in next dc, dc in each of next 3 sts, [ch 2, sk next 2 sts, dc in next dc] twice, dc in each of next 15 sts, [ch 2, sk next 2 sts, dc in next st] 4 times, turn.

Rows 4–15: Follow Chart A, working bls and sps as indicated.

[Rep Rows 2–15] 5 times. At the end of last rep, fasten off. (6 hearts)

Coverlet

Row 1 (RS): Ch 203, dc in 4th ch from hook, dc in each rem ch across, turn. (210 dc)

Rows 2–5: Ch 3 (counts as first dc throughout), dc in each dc across, turn. (201 dc)

Row 6: Ch 1, sc in same st as beg ch-1, [sc in next st, ch 3, sk next 2 sts, cl in next st, ch 3, sk next 2 sts] rep across, ending with sc in each of last 2 sts, turn.

Row 7: Ch 5, sc in top of first cl, [ch 3, 3 sc in top of next cl] rep across, ending with ch 2, dc in last st, turn.

Row 8: Ch 1, 3 sc in first ch sp, [sc in each of next 3 sc, 3 sc in next ch-3 sp] rep across, ending with 2 sc in last sp, sc in 3rd ch of turning ch, turn.

Row 9: Ch 3, dc in each st across, turn. (201 dc)

Rows 10–13: Ch 3, dc in each dc across, turn.

Rows 14–69: [Rep Rows 6–13] 7 times. At the end of Row 69, fasten off.

With RS facing, sl st filet

STITCH KEY
- ⊙ Block
- ☐ Space

Chart A

Row 15

Row 2

Row 1

borders to short ends of coverlet.

Edging

Attach yarn at right end of long side of coverlet in the 3rd ch of turning ch of first sp on straight edge of filet border, ch 3, 2 dc in same ch, *dc in each of next 2 ch of first sp, [dc in next dc, dc in each of next 2 chs of next sp] 12 times, dc evenly sp across edge of coverlet to next filet border, dc in each of next 2 chs of first sp of border, rep between [ ] 12 times, 3 dc in 3rd ch of turning ch of last sp, ch 2, work cl between next 2 dc groups, **{ch 2, 4 dc in next sp, ch 2, cl between next 2 dc groups} twice, ch 2, 4 dc in next sp, ch 4, work cl in lp of dc on end, ch 4, 4 dc in next sp, ch 2, cl between next 2 dc groups, rep between { } twice †, dc in next sp, cl between next 2 dc groups **, rep between ** 5 times, ending last rep at †, ch 2, 3 dc in 3rd ch of turning ch of first sp on other straight edge of border *, rep from * once, omitting 3 dc at end of rep, join with sl st in 3rd ch of beg ch-3, fasten off.

Finishing

Block coverlet. Weave ribbon through the ch sps of each border where joined to body of coverlet. Secure ribbon ends on back side. Divide rem ribbon into 12 equal lengths (approximately 8 inches each) and tie into bows. Tack bow and ribbon rose to center of each heart motif on coverlet ends as illustrated in photo. ♥

Clowning-Around Bear

By Beverly Mewhorter

Skill Level: Beginner

Size: 17 inches square

Materials

- ✓ Coats & Clark Red Heart Classic worsted weight yarn: 2 oz Mexicana #950, 1 oz light clay #275, 1 oz cherry red #912 and scrap of black #12
- ✓ Size G/6 crochet hook or size needed to obtain gauge
- ✓ 12mm black cabochons for eyes
- ✓ 6 white ¾-inch pompoms
- ✓ ¼-inch red pompom
- ✓ Fiberfill
- ✓ Hot-glue gun
- ✓ Tapestry needle

This friendly clown bear will win the hearts of boys and girls alike. Rainbows, ruffles and pompoms make him festive and fun!

Gauge

4 sc = 1 inch

Check gauge to save time.

Pattern Notes

Weave in loose ends as work progresses.

Join rnds with a sl st unless otherwise stated.

Head

Rnd 1: With light clay, ch 2, 10 sc in 2nd ch from hook, join in beg sc. (10 sc)

Rnd 2: Ch 1, 2 sc in each sc around, join in beg sc. (20 sc)

Rnd 3: Ch 1, 2 sc in first sc, sc in next sc, [2 sc in next sc, sc in next sc] rep around, join in beg sc. (30 sc)

Rnd 4: Ch 1, sc in each sc around, join in beg sc.

Rnds 5–11: Rep Rnd 4.

Rnd 12: Ch 1, sc in first sc, sc dec over next 2 sc, [sc in next sc, sc dec over next 2 sc] rep around, join in beg sc. (20 sc)

Rnd 13: Ch 1, [sc dec over next 2 sc] rep around, join in beg sc. (10 sc)

Stuff head with fiberfill.

Rnd 14: Rep Rnd 4, fasten off.

Body

Rnd 15: Attach Mexicana in first sc of previous rnd, ch 1, 2 sc in same sc as beg ch, 2 sc in each rem sc around, join in beg sc. (20 sc)

Rnd 16: Ch 1, sc in same sc as beg ch, 2 sc in next sc, [sc in next sc, 2 sc in next sc] rep around, join in beg sc. (30 sc)

Rnds 17–32: Rep Rnd 4.

Rnd 33: Ch 1, sc in same sc as beg ch, sc dec over next 2 sc, [sc in next sc, sc dec over next 2 sc] rep around, join in beg sc. (20 sc)

Stuff body with fiberfill; continue stuffing as work progresses.

Rnd 34: Ch 1, [sc dec over next 2 sc] rep around, join in beg sc. (10 sc)

Rnd 35: Rep Rnd 34, leaving a length of yarn, fasten off. (5 sc)

Weave rem length through sts to close opening and secure.

Muzzle

Rnd 1: With light clay, ch 2, 4 sc in 2nd ch from hook, join in beg sc. (4 sc)

Rnd 2: Ch 1, 2 sc in each sc around, join in beg sc. (8 sc)

Rnd 3: Ch 1, [sc in next sc, 2 sc in next sc] rep around, join in beg sc, leaving a length of yarn, fasten off. (12 sc)

Sew to face over Rnds 8–12, stuffing with fiberfill before closing.

Ear

(Make 2)

Row 1: With light clay, ch 2, 5 sc in 2nd ch from hook, turn. (5 sc)

Rnd 2: Ch 3 (counts as first dc), dc in same sc as beg ch, 2 dc in each sc across, ch 1, sl st in opposite side of foundation ch of Row 1, ch 1, sl st in top of beg ch-3 of Row 2, fasten off.

Sew ears between Rnds 3–6 at each side of head.

Leg

(Make 2)

Rnd 1: With light clay, ch 2, 8 sc in 2nd ch from hook, join in beg sc. (8 sc)

Rnd 2: Ch 1, 2 sc in each sc around, join in beg sc. (16 sc)

Rnd 3: Ch 1, sc in each st around, join in beg sc.

Rnds 4–6: Rep Rnd 3.

At the end of Rnd 6, fasten off.

Rnd 7: Attach Mexicana, ch 1, sc in each sc around, join in beg sc.

Rnd 8: Ch 1, [sc in each of next 3 sc, 2 sc in next sc] 4 times, join in beg sc. (20 sc)

Rnds 9–18: Rep Rnd 3.

At the end of Rnd 18, leaving a length of yarn, fasten off.

Stuff legs with fiberfill and sew to bottom of body.

Arm
(Make 2)

Rnd 1: With light clay, ch 2, 8 sc in 2nd ch from hook, join in beg sc. (8 sc)

Rnd 2: Ch 1, 2 sc in each sc around, join in beg sc. (16 sc)

Rnd 3: Ch 1, sc in each sc around, join in beg sc.

Rnds 4 & 5: Rep Rnd 3.

At the end of Rnd 5, fasten off.

Rnd 6: Attach Mexicana, ch 1, sc in each sc around, join in beg sc.

Rnds 7–15: Rep Rnd 3.

At the end of Rnd 15, leaving a length of yarn, fasten off.

Stuff arms with fiberfill and sew between Rnds 19–25 at each side of body.

Hat

Rnd 1: With Mexicana, ch 30, sl st to join to form a ring, ch 1, sc in each ch around, join in beg sc. (30 sc)

Rnd 2: Ch 1, sc in each sc around, join in beg sc.

Rnds 3 & 4: Rep Rnd 2.

Rnd 5: Ch 1, [sc in each of next 3 sc, sc dec over next 2 sc] rep around, join in beg sc. (24 sc)

Rnds 6 & 7: Rep Rnd 2.

Rnd 8: Ch 1, [sc in each of next 2 sc, sc dec over next 2 sc] rep around, join in beg sc. (18 sc)

Rnds 9 & 10: Rep Rnd 2.

Rnd 11: Ch 1, [sc in next sc, sc dec over next 2 sc] rep around, join in beg sc. (12 sc)

Rnds 12 & 13: Rep Rnd 2.

Rnd 14: Ch 1, [sc dec over next 2 sc] rep around, join in beg sc. (6 sc)

Rnds 15 & 16: Rep Rnd 2.

Rnd 17: Ch 1, [sc dec over next 2 sc] 3 times, join in beg sc, fasten off. (3 sc)

Stuff hat with fiberfill and sew to top of head.

Ruffles

Hat ruffle

With cherry red, ch 31, 3 sc in 2nd ch from hook, 3 sc in each rem ch across, fasten off.

Sew ruffle to bottom of hat.

Neck ruffle

Row 1: With cherry red, ch 21, 3 sc in 2nd ch from hook, 3 sc in each rem ch across, turn.

Row 2: Ch 3, dc in each sc across, fasten off.

With seam at center back, sew ruffle around neckline.

Arm ruffle
(Make 2)

With cherry red, ch 17, 3 sc in 2nd ch from hook, 3 sc in each rem ch across, fasten off.

Sew ruffle to each arm over Rnd 6.

Leg ruffle
(Make 2)

With cherry red, ch 19, 3 sc in 2nd ch from hook, 3 sc in each rem ch across, fasten off.

Sew ruffle to each leg over Rnd 7.

Finishing

With black, embroider mouth over muzzle.

Secure eyes in place above muzzle. For children under 3, with black, ch 2, 4 sc in 2nd ch from hook, join, fasten off and sew in place or with black embroider eyes above muzzle.

Glue white pompom to each leg ruffle, glue 3 white pompoms down center front of chest and glue last white pompom to top of hat. For nose, glue red pompom to center of muzzle. ♥

Pretty in Pink Baby Doll & Pillow

By Beverly Mewhorter

Skill Level: Beginner

Size:

Dress: Fits 10-inch baby doll

Pillow: 18 inches in diameter

Materials

- ✓ Coats & Clark Red Heart baby pompadour yarn: 2¼ oz light pink #722
- ✓ Coats & Clark Red Heart Classic worsted weight yarn: 4½ oz white #1
- ✓ Sizes F/5 and H/8 crochet hooks or size needed to obtain gauge
- ✓ 10-inch baby doll
- ✓ 77 inches ⅜-inch-wide light pink satin ribbon
- ✓ 6 white ribbon carnations with green leaves
- ✓ Fiberfill
- ✓ Hot-glue gun
- ✓ Tapestry needle

Gauge

With H hook, 5 sc = 2 inches; With F hook, 9 dc = 2 inches

Check gauge to save time.

Pattern Notes

Weave in loose ends as work progresses.

Sl st to join each rnd in top of beg ch-3 unless otherwise stated.

Ch 3 counts as first dc throughout.

Pillow

Sides

(Make 2)

Rnd 1: With hook size H and white, ch 4, 11 dc in 4th ch from hook, join. (12 dc)

Rnd 2: Ch 3, dc in same st, 2 dc in each dc around, join. (24 dc)

Rnd 3: Ch 3, dc in same st as beg ch, dc in next dc, [2 dc in next dc, dc in next dc] rep around, join. (36 dc)

Rnd 4: Ch 3, dc in same st, dc in each of next 2 dc, [2 dc in next dc, dc in each of next 2 dc] rep around, join. (48 dc)

Rnd 5: Ch 3, dc in same st as beg ch, dc in each of next 3 dc, [2 dc in next dc, dc in each of next 3 dc]

rep around, join. (60 dc)

Rnd 6: Ch 3, dc in same st as beg ch, dc in each of next 4 dc, [2 dc in next dc, dc in each of next 4 dc] rep around, join. (72 dc)

Rnd 7: Ch 3, dc in same st as beg ch, dc in each of next 5 dc, [2 dc in next dc, dc in each of next 5 dc] rep around, join. (84 dc)

Rnd 8: Ch 3, dc in same st as beg ch, dc in each of next 6 dc, [2 dc in next dc, dc in each of next 6 dc] rep around, join. (96 dc)

Rnd 9: Ch 3, dc in same st as beg ch, dc in each of next 7 dc, [2 dc in next dc, dc in each of next 7 dc] rep around, join. (108 dc)

Rnd 10: Ch 3, dc in same st, dc in each of next 8 dc, [2 dc in next dc, dc in each of next 8 dc] rep around, join. (120 dc)

Rnd 11: Ch 3, dc in same st as beg ch, dc in each of next 9 dc, [2 dc in next dc, dc in each of next 9 dc] rep around, join. (132 dc)

Rnd 12: Ch 3, dc in same st as beg ch, dc in each of next 10 dc, [2 dc in next dc, dc in each of next 10 dc] rep around, join, fasten

off. (144 dc)

Joining

Rnd 13: Holding both sides tog, matching sts and working through both thicknesses, attach white, ch 1, 2 sc in same st, sc in each of next 11 sts, [2 sc in next st, sc in each of next 11 sts] rep around, stuffing with fiberfill before closing, join in beg sc, fasten off.

Ruffle

Rnd 14: With hook size F, attach light pink in any sc of Rnd 13, ch 3, 2 dc in same st as beg ch, 3 dc in each sc around, join, fasten off. (468 dc)

Doll Dress

Bodice

Row 1: Beg at waist, with hook size F and light pink, ch 37, sc in 2nd ch from hook, sc in each rem ch across, turn. (36 sc)

Row 2: Ch 1, sc in each st across, turn.

Row 3: Rep Row 2.

Row 4: Ch 1, sc in each of next 7 sc, ch 12, sk next 5 sts, sc in each of next 12 sc, ch 12, sk next 5 sts, sc in each of next 7 sc, turn. (26 sc; 2 ch-12 sps)

Rows 5–7: Ch 1, sc in each st across, turn. (50 sc)

Row 8: Ch 1, sc in first sc, sc dec over next 2 sc, [sc in next sc, sc dec over next 2 sc] 15 times, sc dec over last 2 sc, turn. (33 sc)

Row 9: Ch 1, [sc dec over next 2 sc] 16 times, sc in last sc, turn. (17 sc)

Row 10: Rep Row 2.

Row 11: Working in back lps for this row only, ch 3, 4 dc in same st as beg ch, 5 dc in each st across, turn. (85 dc)

Row 12: Ch 3, dc in each dc across, fasten off.

Sleeve

(Make 2)

Rnd 1: With hook size F and light pink, ch 19, sl st to join to form a ring, ch 1, sc in each ch around, join in beg sc. (19 sc)

Rnds 2–10: Ch 1, sc in each sc around, join in beg sc.

Rnd 11: Ch 3, 4 dc in same st as beg ch, 5 dc in each st around, join in top of beg ch-3, fasten off.

Sew sleeve into armhole opening.

Skirt

Row 1: Working in opposite side of foundation ch of bodice, with hook size F, attach light pink, ch 1, sc in each ch across, turn. (36 sc)

Row 2: Ch 3, 3 dc in same st as beg ch, 4 dc in each rem st across, turn. (144 dc)

Row 3: Ch 3, dc in each dc across, turn.

Rows 4–16: Rep Row 3.

Row 17: Rep Row 2. (720 dc)

Row 18: Rep Row 3, leaving a length of yarn, fasten off.

Matching ends of rows, sew Rows 1–18 of back opening of skirt closed.

Bonnet

Rnd 1: With hook size F and light pink, ch 2, 8 sc in 2nd ch from hook, join in beg sc. (8 sc)

Rnd 2: Ch 1, 3 sc in each sc around, join in beg sc. (24 sc)

Rnd 3: Ch 1, sc in each sc around, join in beg sc.

Rnd 4: Rep Rnd 3.

Rnd 5: Ch 1, sc in first sc, 2 sc in next sc, [sc in next sc, 2 sc in next sc] 11 times, join in beg sc. (36 sc)

Rnds 6–12: Rep Rnd 3.

Rnd 13: Ch 3, 4 dc in same st as beg ch, [5 dc in next sc] 19 times, ch 12, sl st in 3rd ch of beg ch-3, fasten off.

With ruffle facing forward, slip bonnet onto doll.

Finishing

Weave a 16-inch length of ribbon through Row 9 of bodice. Place dress on doll, tie ribbon ends in a bow at back neckline.

Cut a 36-inch length of ribbon; attach at center to center front of pillow with a double knot. Place waistline of doll centered over ribbon attached to pillow center, bring strands around waist and tie ends in a bow. This holds doll in place on pillow when not being played with.

Cut rem length of ribbon into 5 equal lengths of 5 inches each. *Glue 5-inch length of ribbon at center to Rnd 11; fold ends to center and glue in place. Glue a carnation to center of ribbon bow. Rep from * 4 more times evenly sp around Rnd 11 of pillow.

Glue rem carnation to bodice just below ruffle. ♥

Tooth-Saver Pillow

By Debi Yorston

Skill Level: Beginner

Size: 10 x 11 inches

Materials

✓ Worsted weight yarn: 2½ oz variegated (MC) and 1 oz matching solid (CC)

✓ Size I/9 crochet hook or size needed to obtain gauge

✓ ⅜-inch heart-shaped button

✓ 1 yd 1-inch-wide matching pregathered lace

✓ Small safety pin or other marker

✓ Hot-glue gun

✓ 8-inch square pillow form

✓ Tapestry needle

Eagerly awaiting a reward from the tooth fairy has never been more exciting. This fun-loving project will help your child go from anxiety to anticipation over losing a tooth.

Gauge

14 sc and 16 sc rows = 4 inches

Check gauge to save time.

Pattern Notes

Weave in loose ends as work progresses.

Join rnds with a sl st unless otherwise stated.

Front & Back

(Make 2)

Row 1: With MC, ch 27, sc in 2nd ch from hook, sc in each rem ch across, turn. (26 sc)

Rows 2–32: Ch 1, sc in each sc across, turn.

Rnd 33: Ch 1, sc evenly sp around entire outer edge, working 3 sc in each corner st, join in beg sc, fasten off.

Pocket

Note: Do not join rnds; mark first st of each rnd with safety pin or other marker.

Rnd 1: With CC, ch 2, 6 sc in 2nd ch from hook. (6 sc)

Rnd 2: Work 2 sc in each sc around. (12 sc)

Rnd 3: [Sc in next sc, 2 sc in next sc] rep around. (18 sc)

Rnd 4: [Sc in each of next 2 sc, 2 sc in next sc] rep around. (24 sc)

Rnd 5: [Sc in each of next 3 sc, 2 sc in next sc] rep around, join in beg sc, fasten off. (30 sc)

Fold edge over as shown in photo. Using tapestry needle and CC, tack center of folded edge down; sew pocket in center of RS

pillow front.

Glue button to Rnd 1 of pocket.

Joining

Rnd 1: Holding front and back WS tog, working through both thicknesses and matching sts, attach CC with a sl st in any corner st, ch 1, 3 sc in same st, sc evenly sp around, working 3 sc in each corner st, inserting pillow form before closing, join in beg sc.

Rnd 2: Ch 1, sc in same st as beg ch, ch 3, [sk next sc, sc in next sc, ch 3] rep around, join in beg sc, fasten off.

Glue lace to back of Rnd 2. ♥

Heartwarming

House Warmers

Add a special touch to home-sweet-home with this collection of pretty and practical accents! Whether dressing up your own home, or giving a special gift to friends who are moving into a new home or apartment, you're sure to find many delightful items to crochet and share in this chapter!

How Does Your Garden Grow?

Skill Level: Beginner

Size: 48½ x 57 inches

Materials
- ✓ Coats & Clark TLC worsted weight yarn (5 oz per skein): 15 oz butterscotch #5263, 15 oz medium blue #5823, 5 oz emerald #5687, 3 oz each medium pink #5745 and cognac #5288
- ✓ Size I/9 crochet hook or size needed to obtain gauge
- ✓ Tapestry needle

Simple and unpretentious, this cheerful 1937 afghan is full of primitive charm! With yellow trellises and sweet appliquéd flowers, you'll find plenty of reasons to "grow" this beautiful garden.

Gauge
Motifs = 6½ inches square

Check gauge to save time.

Pattern Notes
Weave in loose ends as work progresses.

Join rnds with a sl st unless otherwise stated.

Ch 3 counts as first dc throughout.

Blue Block
(Make 31)

Row 1: Starting at lower edge, with medium blue, ch 25, dc in 4th ch from hook, dc in each rem ch across, turn. (23 dc)

Row 2: Working in front lps for this row only, ch 3, dc in each of next 2 sts, [ch 1, sk 1 st, dc in next st] twice, dc in each of next 10 sts, [ch 1, sk 1 st, dc in next st] twice, dc in each of next 2 sts, turn.

Row 3: Working in back lps for this row only, ch 3, dc in each of next 2 sts, [ch 1, sk ch-1 sp, dc in next st] twice, dc in each of next 10 sts, [ch 1, sk ch-1 sp, dc in next st] twice, dc in each of next 2 sts, turn.

Row 4: Working in front lps for this row only, ch 3, dc in each of next 2 sts, [dc in next ch-1 sp, dc in next dc] twice, dc in each of next 10 sts, [dc in next ch-1 sp, dc in next dc] twice, dc in each of next 2 sts, turn. (23 dc)

Row 5: Working in back lps for this row only, ch 3, dc in each st across, turn.

Row 6: Working in front lps for this row only, ch 3, dc in each st across, turn.

Row 7: Rep Row 5.

Rows 8 & 9: Rep Rows 2 and 3.

Row 10: Rep Row 4, fasten off.

Rnd 11: Attach emerald in any st, ch 1, sc evenly sp around entire outer edge of block, working 3 sc in each corner st, join in beg sc, fasten off.

Butterscotch Block
(Make 32)

Row 1: Starting at lower edge with butterscotch, ch 25, dc in 4th ch from hook, dc in each rem ch across, turn. (23 dc)

Row 2: Ch 3, dc in each of next 2 dc, [ch 1, sk next dc, dc in next dc] 9 times, dc in each of next 2 dc, turn.

Rows 3–9: Ch 3, dc in each of next 2 dc, [ch 1, sk ch-1 sp, dc in next dc] 9 times, dc in each of next 2 dc, turn.

Row 10: Ch 3, dc in each of next 2 dc, [dc in next ch-1 sp, dc in next dc] 9 times, dc in each of next 2 dc, turn. (23 dc)

Rnd 11: Ch 1, sc evenly sp around entire outer edge, working 3 sc in each corner st, join in beg sc, fasten off.

Joining
Using diagram as a guide, with WS facing place blocks in position alternately. Working in top lp only of sc sts, sew blocks tog.

Edging
Rnd 1: Attach butterscotch in any center corner sc, ch 1, *[sc, ch 3, sc] in center corner sc, ch 3, sk next 3

Afghan Assembly

sc, [sc in next sc, ch 3, sk next 3 sc] rep across edge to next corner sc, rep from * around entire outer edge, join in beg sc, fasten off.

Rnd 2: Attach medium blue in corner ch-3 sp, ch 3, 4 dc in same corner ch-3 sp, ch 1, [3 dc in next ch sp, ch 1] rep across to next corner ch sp, *5 dc in next corner ch-3 sp, ch 1, [3 dc in next ch sp, ch 1] rep across to next corner ch sp, rep from * around, join in top of beg ch-3.

Rnd 3: Ch 1, sc in each dc and each ch-1 sp around, working 3 sc in each center corner dc, join in beg sc, fasten off.

Plant

Flowerpot
(Make 31)

Row 1: With cognac, ch 6, sc in 2nd ch from hook, sc in each rem ch across, turn. (5 sc)

Row 2: Ch 1, sc in each sc across, turn.

Row 3: Ch 1, 2 sc in first sc, sc in each sc across to last sc, 2 sc in last sc, turn. (9 sc)

Row 5: Rep Row 2, fasten off.

Sew flowerpot at center on medium blue block just above dc row.

Leaf
(Make 31)

Row 1: With emerald, ch 14, sl st in 2nd ch from hook, sc in each of next 2 chs, dc in each of next 2 chs, tr in each of next 3 chs, dc in each of next 3 chs, sc in next ch, sl st in next ch, ch 7 (for stem), fasten off.

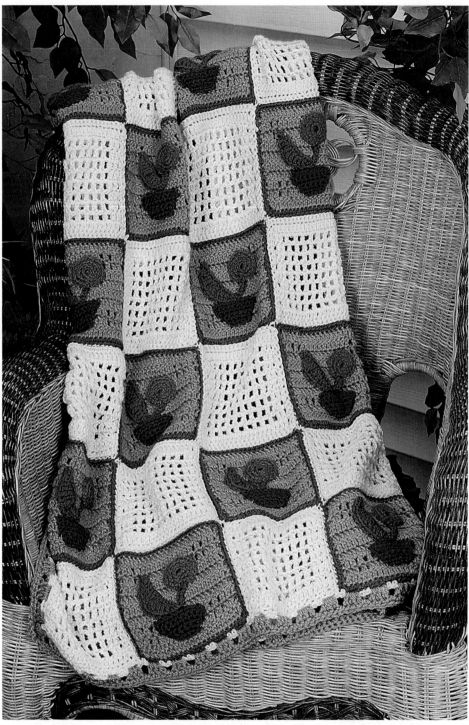

Sew leaf in place, turning stem upwards.

Flower
(Make 31)

Rnd 1: With medium pink, ch 2, 8 sc in 2nd ch from hook, join in beg sc. (8 sc)

Rnd 2: Working in back lps only, ch 1, sc in first st, 2 sc in each of next 7 sts, join in beg sc. (15 sc)

Rnd 3: Working in back lps only, ch 1, [sc in each of next 2 sts, 2 sc in next st] 5 times, sl st in next st, fasten off.

Sew flower to top of stem. ❖

Floral Candle Centerpiece

By Sue Childress

Skill Level: Beginner

Size: 6 inches tall

Materials

- ✓ Sport weight cotton yarn: 1 ball each lilac and pink
- ✓ Size C/2 crochet hook or size needed to obtain gauge
- ✓ 6-inch in diameter x 2-inch deep foam disk
- ✓ 3 x 6-inch candle
- ✓ 3 yds 3-inch-wide wired matching floral ribbon
- ✓ Small filler flowers
- ✓ Craft glue
- ✓ 18-gauge floral wire
- ✓ Floral tape
- ✓ Stamens
- ✓ Tapestry needle

Gauge

Lilac flower = 2½ inches; pink flower = 2 inches
Check gauge to save time.

Pattern Notes

Weave in loose ends as work progresses.

Join rnds with a sl st unless otherwise stated.

Pattern Stitch

Fptr: Yo hook twice, insert hook front to back to front again around vertical post of indicated st, yo, draw up a lp, [yo, draw through 2 lps on hook] 3 times.

Lilac Flower

(Make 5)

Rnd 1: Leaving a length of lilac at beg, ch 3, 7 dc in 3rd ch from hook, join in top of beg ch-3. (8 dc)

Row 2: Ch 3, 2 dc in same st as beg ch-3, 3 dc in each rem dc around, join in top of beg ch-3. (24 dc)

Rnd 3: Ch 3, 2 dc in back lps of same st as joining, 3 dc in front lp of same st as joining, [working in back lps only, 3 dc in next st, working in front lps only, 3 dc in same st] rep around, join in top of beg ch-3, fasten off.

Pink Flower

(Make 8)

Rnd 1: With pink, ch 5, 9 tr in 5th ch from hook, join in top of beg ch-5. (10 tr)

Rnd 2: Ch 5, fptr around next tr, [3 tr in next tr, fptr around next tr] rep around, ending with 2 tr in same st as beg ch-5, join in top of beg ch-5.

Rnd 3: Ch 1, sc in same tr, ch 3, [sc in next tr, ch 3] rep around, join in beg sc, fasten off.

Finishing

Cover foam disk with ribbon, gluing in place as work progresses. Glue candle in center of disk. Make a bow from ribbon and secure to disk with wire and glue.

Using wire and stamens, wrap flowers with floral tape. Push flowers into place around candle.

Wrap filler flowers with tape and stamens for accent.

Arrange filler flowers at random to give a pretty accent. Secure with glue as work progresses. ❖

This pretty centerpiece makes a perfect Mother's Day gift! Stitch its delicate flowers, then enjoy arranging them into a beautiful decorative accent.

Irish Linen Edging

Skill Level: Beginner

Size: Edging: ¾-inch-wide

Materials

✓ Crochet cotton size 10: 1 ball pink

✓ Size 7 steel crochet hook or size needed to obtain gauge

✓ 14-inch in diameter hemstitched linen doily

Dress up a simple piece of round linen with this enchanting edging. The finished piece will look exquisite under a vase of fresh flowers!

Gauge

Rnds 1–3 of edging = ¾ inch; 7 sc = 1 inch

Check gauge to save time.

Pattern Notes

Weave in loose ends as work progresses.

Join rnds with a sl st unless otherwise stated.

Edging

Rnd 1 (RS): Attach pink in any sp of edging of linen doily, ch 1, sc evenly sp around entire outer edge, ending with multiples of 13 sts, join in beg sc.

Rnd 2: Ch 1, beg in same st as beg ch, [sc in next st, hdc in next st, dc in each of next 3 sts, hdc in next st, sc in next 9 sts] rep around, join in beg sc.

Rnd 3: Sl st in next hdc, ch 8, dc in 5th ch from hook, *[dc in next dc, ch 5, dc in last dc] 3 times, dc in next hdc, sk 3 sc, dc in next sc, ch 5, dc in last dc, dc in next sc **, dc in next hdc, ch 5, dc in last dc, rep from * around, join in 3rd ch of beg ch-8, fasten off. ❖

Summertime Kitchen Set

By Sue Childress

Skill Level: Beginner

Size:

Towel: 16 x 24 inches

Hot Pad: 8½ inches square

Dishcloth: 7¼ x 9 inches

Materials

✓ Reynolds Saucy worsted weight cotton yarn (100 grams per ball) 1 ball MC

✓ Size G/6 crochet hook or size needed to obtain gauge

✓ 16 x 24-inch terry kitchen towel

✓ ¾-inch button

✓ Loop braid (optional)

✓ Batting

✓ Sewing needle and thread

✓ Yarn needle

The whole family will enjoy the vibrant beauty of this cheerful kitchen ensemble. A shiny cotton yarn makes it extra special!

Gauge

4 dc = 1 inch

Check gauge to save time.

Pattern Notes

Weave in loose ends as work progresses.

Join rnds with a sl st unless otherwise stated.

Towel preparation: Cut 7½ inches from end of towel and set aside. With larger piece, turn raw edge under ½-inch and st lp braid in place at top of towel. If you prefer not to use lp braid, st top of towel and use small crochet hook or stiletto to punch holes in top edge of towel.

Cut the 7½-inch piece in half to form 2 squares. St lp braid around outer edge of 1 piece; then layer batting and the 2 towel squares tog. Pin toweling tog and st, leaving an opening for turning. Turn RS out, st opening closed.

Pattern Stitch

3-dc cl: [Yo hook, insert hook in indicated st, yo, draw up a lp, yo, draw through 2 lps on hook] 3 times in same st, yo, draw through all 4 lps on hook.

Towel

Row 1: Working across edge of towel, attach MC, ch 1, work 59 sc evenly sp across, turn. (59 sc)

Row 2: Ch 2 (counts as first hdc throughout), hdc in each st across, turn.

Row 3: Ch 3 (counts as first dc throughout), dc in each of next 3 sts, [sk next 3 sts, 7 dc in next st, sk next 3 sts, dc in each of next 4 sts] 5 times, turn.

Row 4: Ch 3, dc in each of next 3 sts, *[sk next dc, ch 1, 3-dc cl in next dc] 3 times, sk next dc, ch 1, dc in each of next 4 dc, rep from * across, turn.

Row 5: Ch 3, dc in each dc, dc in each ch-1 sp, dc in top of each cl across, turn. (59 dc)

Row 6: Ch 2, hdc in each st across, turn. (59 hdc)

Rows 7 & 8: Rep Rows 3 and 4.

Row 9: Ch 3, [dc dec over next 2 dc, dc in next dc, sk next ch-1 sp, 2 dc in each of next 3 ch-1 sps, dc in next dc] 4 times, dc dec over next 2 dc, dc in next dc, sk next ch-1 sp, [2 dc in next ch-1 sp] twice, sk next ch-1 sp, dc in next dc, dc dec over next 2 dc, dc in next dc, turn.

Row 10: Ch 3, [dc dec over next 2 dc, dc in next dc] 15 times, turn. (31 dc)

Row 11: Ch 3, dc dec over next 2 dc, dc in each dc across to last 3 dc, dc dec over next 2 dc, dc in next dc, turn. (29 dc)

Row 12: Ch 3, [dc dec over next 2 dc, dc in next dc] 9 times, dc in last dc, turn. (20 dc)

Rows 13–15: Rep Row 11. (14 dc)

Row 16: Ch 3, dc in each of next 5 dc, dc dec over next 2 dc, dc in each of next 6 dc, turn. (13 dc)

Row 17: Ch 3, dc in each of next 2 dc, sk next 3 dc, 7 dc in next dc, sk next 3 dc, dc in each of next 3 dc, turn.

Row 18: Ch 3, dc in each of next 2 dc, [ch 1, sk next dc, 3-dc cl in next dc] 3 times, sk next dc, ch 1, dc in each of next 3 dc, turn.

Row 19: Ch 3, dc in each of next 2 dc, dc in next ch-1 sp, 2 dc in each of next 2 ch-1 sps, dc in next ch-1 sp, dc in each of next 3 dc, turn. (12 dc)

Row 20: Ch 2, hdc in each dc across, turn.

Row 21: Ch 2, hdc in each of next 4 hdc, ch 2, sk next 2 hdc (buttonhole opening), hdc in each of next 5 hdc, turn.

Row 22: Ch 2, hdc in each of next 3 hdc, sk next hdc, 2 hdc in next ch-2 sp, sk next hdc, hdc in each of next 4 hdc, turn. (10 hdc)

Rows 23 & 24: Ch 1, sc

dec over next 2 sts, sc in each st across to last 2 sts, sc dec over next 2 sts, turn. (6 sc)

At the end of Row 24, fasten off.

Sew button to center of Row 10.

Hot Pad

Rnd 1: Attach yarn in any corner, ch 1, [3 sc in corner, work 21 sc evenly sp across edge] 4 times, join in beg sc. (96 sc)

Rnd 2: Sl st into center sc of corner 3-sc group, ch 3, 6 dc in same corner sc as beg ch-3, *[ch 1, sk next sc, cl in next sc] rep across to corner, ch 1 **, 7 dc in 2nd sc of corner 3-sc group, rep from * around, ending last rep at **, join in top of beg ch-3, sl st into center dc of 7-dc group, ch 10 (for hanging lp), sl st in same dc, fasten off.

Dishcloth

Row 1: Ch 38, sc in 2nd ch from hook, sc in each rem ch across, turn. (37 sc)

Row 2: Ch 2, hdc in each st across, turn.

Row 3: Ch 3, dc in each of next 3 sts, [sk next 3 sts, 7 dc in next st, sk next 3 sts, dc in each of next 4 sts] rep across, turn.

Row 4: Ch 3, dc in each of next 3 dc, *[sk next dc, ch 1, 3-dc cl in next dc] 3 times, ch 1, sk next dc, dc in each of next 4 dc, rep from * across, turn.

Row 5: Ch 3, dc in each dc, dc in each ch-1 sp and dc in top of each cl across, turn. (37 dc)

Row 6: Ch 3, dc in each of next 3 dc, [sk next 3 dc, 7 dc in next dc, sk next 3 dc, dc in each of next 4 dc] rep across, turn.

Rows 7–12: Rep Rows 4–6.

Row 13: Rep Row 4.

Row 14: Ch 2, hdc in each dc, hdc in each ch-1 sp and hdc in each cl across, turn. (37 hdc)

Row 15: Ch 1, sc in each hdc across, fasten off. ❖

Silk Roses Bouquet

By Nazanin Fard

Skill Level: Intermediate

Size: Flowers approximately 2½ inches in diameter

Materials

- ✓ YLI 100 percent silk 4mm ribbon (5 yds per spool): 10 yds each medium pink #24 and light pink #83
- ✓ Size E/4 crochet hook or size needed to obtain gauge
- ✓ 4 pieces 18-gauge floral wire for stems
- ✓ ½-inch-wide green floral tape
- ✓ Dried baby's breath
- ✓ Silk ivy leaves

Gauge

5 dc = 1 inch

Check gauge to save time.

Pattern Notes

Weave in loose ends as work progresses.

Join rnds with a sl st unless otherwise stated.

Roses

(Make 4)

Rnd 1: With silk ribbon, make a sl knot, ch 4

A gift of lovely flowers means more when you create the flowers yourself! Crochet these little beauties in any floral color for someone you love.

(counts as first dc, ch 1), [dc, ch 1] 9 times in sl knot, join in 3rd ch of beg ch-4. Pull the end of the sl knot to make it tight. (10 ch-1 sps)

Rnd 2: Ch 1, *[sc, hdc, dc] in next ch-1 sp, [dc, hdc, sc] in next ch-1 sp, rep from * around, join in beg sc. (5 petals)

Rnd 3: Holding petals forward, [sl st around next dc of Rnd 1, ch 3, sk next dc] rep around.

Rnd 4: Ch 1, [{sc, hdc, dc, tr, dc, hdc, sc} in next ch-3 sp] rep around, join in beg sc. (5 petals)

Rnd 5: Hold petals forward, ch 1, [sl st around next sk dc on Rnd 1, ch 4] rep around, join.

Rnd 6: Ch 1, [{sc, hdc, dc, 2 tr, dc, hdc, sc} in next ch sp] rep around, join in beg sc, fasten off.

Finishing

Pass a length of wire through ch-1 sp of Rnd 1 and push it through the ch sp across from it. Fold the wire in half. Starting at the edge of the rose, wrap floral tape around the wire, cut floral tape at base of wire. Rep with rem flowers.

Place flowers tog, add baby's breath and ivy leaves. When satisfied with the shape, secure flowers by wrapping floral tape around the bouquet. ❖

Butterfly Magnets

By Stacey Graham

Skill Level: Beginner

Size: 2 x 2¼ inches

Materials

- ✓ Embroidery floss: 1 skein each MC and CC
- ✓ Size 7 steel crochet hook or size needed to obtain gauge
- ✓ Flower stamen
- ✓ 2 inches tan chenille stem
- ✓ ½-inch round magnet
- ✓ Craft glue
- ✓ Hot-glue gun

Gauge

4 sc = ½ inch

Check gauge to save time.

Pattern Notes

Weave in loose ends as work progresses.

Join rnds with a sl st unless otherwise stated.

Work with 6 plies of embroidery floss held tog throughout.

Pattern Stitches

Shell: [2 dc, ch 2, 2 dc] in indicated st.

Ch-2 p: Ch 2, sl st in top of last sc.

Ch-3 p: Ch 3, sl st in top of last sc.

Butterfly

Rnd 1: With MC. Ch 8, sl st to join to form a ring, ch 1, 12 sc in ring, join in beg sc. (12 sc)

Rnd 2: Ch 3 (counts as first dc throughout), dc in same st, ch 2, [2 dc in next st, ch 2] rep around, join in

Brighten up a refrigerator or filing cabinet with these life-size butterflies! Use varied stitches and a sport-weight cotton yarn to give them lively detail.

top of beg ch-3. (12 ch-2 sps)

Rnd 3: Sl st into ch-2 sp, ch 3, [dc, ch 2, 2 dc] in same ch-2 sp, * ch 3, dc in next ch-2 sp, ch 3, shell in next ch-2 sp, [2 dc, 2 tr, 2 dtr, ch 2, 2 dtr, 2 tr, 2 dc] in next ch-2 sp, sl st in next ch-2 sp, [2 dc, 2 tr, 2 dtr, ch 2, 2 dtr, 2 tr, 2 dc] in next ch-2 sp **, shell in next ch-2 sp, rep from *, ending last rep at **, join in top of beg ch-3, fasten off.

Rnd 4: Attach CC in ch-2 sp of first shell of previous rnd, ch 1, *[sc, ch-2 p, sc] in ch-2 sp of shell, 2 sc in next ch-3 sp, [sc, ch-2 p, sc] in next dc, 2 sc over next ch-3 sp, [sc, ch-2 p, sc] in next ch-2 sp of shell, sc in each of next 8 sts, [2 dc, ch-3 p, 2 dc] in next ch sp, sc in each of next 6 sts, sl st in next sl st, sc in each of next 6 sts, [2 dc, ch-3 p, 2 dc] in next ch sp, sc in each of next 8 sts, rep from *, join in beg sc, fasten off.

Finishing

Fold butterfly motif in half, with all dtr sts at top. Fold stamen in half; attach to butter-

fly by wrapping chenille piece over folded butterfly with stamen in place, overlapping ends of chenille stem at back. With glue, secure chenille stem at back.

Glue magnet to center back of butterfly. ❖

Dainty Dishcloths

By Stacey Graham

Fan Dishcloth

Skill Level: Beginner

Size: 7½ x 11½ inches

Materials

✓ Worsted weight cotton: 52 yds MC, 12 yds CC

✓ Embroidery floss: 1 skein each 3 flower colors and 1 green

✓ Size E/4 crochet hook or size needed to obtain gauge

✓ Size B/1 crochet hook

✓ Yarn needle

You'll be happy to do the dishes when accompanied by these bright and cheerful helpers! Lace and flower details make them truly pretty projects.

Gauge
4 dc = 1 inch; 2 dc rows = 1 inch

Check gauge to save time.

Pattern Notes
Weave in loose ends as work progresses.

Join rnds with a sl st unless otherwise stated.

Ch 3 counts as first dc throughout.

Use crochet hook size B for flowers and leaves only.

Dishcloth
Row 1 (RS): With MC and hook size E, ch 8, sl st to join to form a ring, ch 3, 10 dc in ring, turn. (11 dc)

Row 2 (WS): Ch 3, dc in same st as beg ch-3, [bpdc around next st, 2 dc in next st] 5 times, turn. (17 sts)

Row 3 (RS): Ch 3, dc in next st, [fpdc around next post st, dc in each of next 2 sts] rep across, turn.

Row 4 (WS): Ch 3, dc in next st, [bpdc around next post st, dc in next st, 2 dc in next st] 4 times, bpdc around next post st, dc in each of next 2 sts, turn. (21 sts)

Row 5: Ch 3, dc in next st, [fpdc around post st, dc in each of next 3 sts] 4 times, fpdc around next post st, dc in next 2 sts, turn.

Row 6: Ch 3, dc in next st, [bpdc around next post st, dc in next st, 2 dc in next st, dc in next st] 4 times, bpdc around next post st, dc in next 2 sts, turn. (25 sts)

Row 7: Ch 3, dc in next st, [fpdc around next post st, dc in next 3 sts, 2 dc in next st] 4 times, fpdc around next post st, dc in each of next 2 sts, turn. (29 sts)

Row 8: Ch 3, dc in next st, [bpdc around next post st, dc in each of next 5 sts] 4 times, bpdc around next st, dc in each of next 2 sts, turn.

Row 9: Ch 3, dc in next st, [fpdc around next post st, dc in next 2 sts, 2 dc in next st, dc in each of next 2 sts] 4 times, fpdc around next post st, dc in each of next 2 sts, turn. (33 sts)

Row 10: Ch 3, dc in next st, [bpdc around next post st, dc in next 5 sts, 2 dc in next st] 4 times, bpdc around next st, dc in next 2 sts, turn. (37 sts)

Row 11: Ch 3, dc in next st, [fpdc around next post st, dc in next 3 sts, 2 dc in next st, dc in each of next 3 sts] 4 times, fpdc around next st, dc in each of next 2 sts, turn. (41 sts)

Row 12: Ch 3, dc in next st, [bpdc around next post st, dc in each of next 7 sts, 2 dc in next st] 4 times, bpdc around next post st, dc in each of next 2 sts, turn. (45 sts)

Row 13: Ch 3, dc in next st, [fpdc around next post st, dc in each of next 9 sts] 4 times, fpdc around next post st, dc in next 2 sts, turn.

Row 14: Ch 3, dc in next st, [bpdc around next post st, dc in next 4 sts, 2 dc in next st, dc in each of next

4 sts] 4 times, bpdc around next post st, dc in each of next 2 sts, turn. (49 sts)

Row 15: Ch 3, dc in next st, [fpdc around post st, dc in each of next 10 sts] 4 times, fpdc around next st, dc in next 2 sts, turn.

Row 16: Ch 1, sc in each st across, fasten off. (49 sc)

Edging
Rnd 1: With RS facing, attach CC in side edge of Row 15, ch 1, working over ends of rows, work 2 sc over side edge of end st down to foundation ring of Row 1, 5 sc over foundation ch, 2 sc over side edge of end st of each row to Row 16, sk next st, [5 dc in next st, sk next st, sc in next st] rep across, join in beg sc, fasten off.

Flowers
(Make 4 each color)

Rnd 1: With 6-plies embroidery floss flower color and hook size B, leaving a length at beg, ch 2, [sc, hdc, dc, tr, dc, hdc] 5 times in 2nd ch from hook, join in beg sc, fasten off.

Leaf
(Make 6)

Rnd 1: With 6-plies green embroidery floss and hook

size B, ch 9, sc in 2nd ch from hook, sc in next ch, hdc in each of next 2 chs, dc in each of next 2 chs, tr in next ch, [tr, ch 4, sc, ch 4, tr] in last ch, working on opposite side of foundation ch, tr in next ch, dc in each of next 2 chs, hdc in each of next 2 chs, sc in each of next 2 chs, join in beg sc, fasten off. Sew flowers and leaves to lower portion of fan as desired.

Heart Dishcloth

Skill Level: Beginner

Size: 8½ x 9½ inches

Materials
✓ Worsted weight cotton: 46 yds MC, 10 yds CC

✓ Size E/4 crochet hook or size needed to obtain gauge

✓ Yarn needle

Gauge
2 shell rows = 1 inch

Check gauge to save time.

Pattern Notes
Weave in loose ends as work progresses.

Join rnds with a sl st unless otherwise stated.

Pattern Stitch
Shell: [2 dc, ch 2, 2 dc] in indicated st.

Double shell: [2 dc, ch 2] twice and 2 dc in indicated st.

V-st: [Dc, ch 2, dc] in indicated st.

Dishcloth
Row 1: With MC, ch 4, dc, ch 2, 2 dc in 4th ch from hook, turn.

Row 2: Ch 4 (counts as first dc, ch 1 throughout), shell in ch-2 sp of shell, ch 1, sk 1 dc, dc in end dc, turn.

Row 3: Ch 3 (counts as first dc throughout), V-st in next ch-1 sp, shell in ch-2 sp of shell, V-st in next ch-1 sp, dc in end dc, turn.

Row 4: V-st in ch sp of V-st, shell in ch-2 sp of shell, V-st in ch sp of V-st, dc in end dc, turn.

Row 5: Ch 3, shell in V-st, shell in shell, shell in V-st, dc in end dc, turn.

Row 6: Ch 3, shell over shell, double shell in next shell, shell in next shell, dc in end dc, turn.

Row 7: Ch 3, [shell over

Continued on page 139

Bouquet of Lilies

By Stacey Graham

Skill Level: Intermediate

Size: Lily: 7 inches in diameter

Materials

- ✓ DMC Cebelia crochet cotton size 10: 190 yds white #5200, 122 yds light rose #3326, 130 yds lavender #210
- ✓ DMC Cebelia crochet cotton size 20: 164 yds lavender #210
- ✓ Size 7 steel crochet hook or size needed to obtain gauge
- ✓ 3 large floral stamen centers
- ✓ Floral tape
- ✓ 26 (22-gauge) floral wires
- ✓ 6 (18-gauge) floral wires
- ✓ Large fern leaf spray
- ✓ Spray off-white/forest green filler spray
- ✓ Wire cutters
- ✓ Vase
- ✓ Floral foam brick to fit vase

Delight a special someone with the multicolored lilies that grace this elegant bouquet. Crocheted around stem wire, these lovely flowers look real and alive!

Gauge

2 shell rows = 1 inch; 2 shells = 1¼ inches

Check gauge to save time.

Pattern Notes

Weave in loose ends as work progresses.

Join rnds with a sl st unless otherwise stated.

Ch 3 counts as first dc on petal pattern only.

Pattern Stitches

V-st: [Dc, ch 2, dc] in indicated st.

Shell: [2 dc, ch 2, 2 dc] in indicated st.

Petals

(Make 26)

Row 1: With white, ch 12, dc in 4th ch from hook, dc in each rem ch across, turn. (10 dc)

Row 2: Ch 3, [sk 2 sts, shell in next st] twice, dc in last st, turn.

Row 3: Ch 3, [shell over shell] twice, dc in last dc, turn.

Row 4: Ch 3, shell over

shell, ch 1, shell over shell, dc in last dc, turn.

Row 5: Ch 3, shell over shell, V-st in ch-1 sp, shell over shell, dc in last dc, turn.

Row 6: Ch 3, shell over shell, shell over V-st, shell over shell, dc in last dc, turn.

Row 7: Ch 3, [shell over shell, ch 1] twice, shell over shell, dc in last dc, turn.

Row 8: Rep Row 7.

Row 9: Continuing with white, attach size 30 lavender cotton and working with both strands, ch 3, [shell over shell, ch 1] twice, shell in shell, dc in last dc, turn.

Row 10: Rep Row 7, fasten off white only.

Row 11: Continuing with lavender, attach light rose, working with both strands, ch 3, [shell over shell, ch

1] twice, shell over shell, dc in last dc, turn.

Row 12: Ch 3, [shell over shell] 3 times, dc in last dc, turn.

Row 13: Ch 3, shell over shell, ch 1, V-st over next shell, ch 1, shell over shell, dc in last dc, turn.

Row 14: Ch 3, shell over shell, ch 1, dc in ch sp of V-st, ch 1, shell over shell, dc in end dc, turn.

Row 15: Ch 3, 2 dc in ch sp of shell, ch 1, dc in single dc, ch 2, 2 dc in ch sp of next shell, dc in end dc, turn. (9 dc)

Row 16: Ch 3, dc in next 2 dc, sk next dc, dc in each of next 3 dc, turn. (6 dc)

Row 17: Ch 3, sk next dc, dc dec over next 2 dc, sk next dc, dc in last dc, turn. (3 dc)

Row 18: Ch 2, [yo, insert hook in next dc, yo, draw

through 2 lps on hook] twice, yo, draw through all 3 lps on hook, fasten off.

Edging

With size 10 lavender cotton, work a row of sc evenly sp around edge of petal encasing folded 22-gauge wire with 3 sc in side edge of each row and 3 sc at tip of petal.

Finishing

Flowers

(Make 3)

With stamen and 18-gauge wire in center, tightly wrap 3 petals tog with floral tape; add last 3 petals spaced evenly among first group; wrap tightly.

Flower bud

(Make 2 sets)

Fold 2 petals slightly from top to bottom.

With 18-gauge wire in center, wrap with floral tape. Attach a 2nd bud 3 inches below first bud; cut wire and tape to main stem.

Insert foam brick into vase. Arrange flowers, buds, fern spray and filler spray in vase. ❖

Dainty Dishcloths

Continued from page 137

shell] twice, ch 1, [shell over shell] twice, dc in end dc, turn.

Row 8: Ch 3, [shell over shell] twice, V-st in ch-1 sp, [shell over shell] twice, dc in end dc, turn.

Row 9: Ch 3, [shell over shell] twice, shell in ch-2 sp of V-st, [shell over shell] twice, dc in end dc, turn.

Row 10: Ch 3, [shell over shell, ch 1] 4 times, shell over shell, dc in end dc, turn.

Row 11: Ch 3, [shell over

shell, ch 1] twice, double shell in next shell, [ch 1, shell over shell] twice, dc in end dc, turn.

Row 12: Ch 3, shell over shell, [ch 1, shell over shell] 5 times, dc in end dc, turn.

Row 13: Ch 3, [shell over shell, ch 1] twice, shell over shell, V-st in next ch-1 sp, [shell over shell, ch 1] twice, shell over shell, dc in end dc, turn.

Row 14: Ch 3, [shell over shell, ch 1] twice, shell

over shell, dc in ch-2 sp of V-st, [shell over shell, ch 1] twice, shell over shell, dc in end dc, turn.

First lobe

Row 15: Ch 3, shell over shell, ch 1] twice, shell over shell, dc in next dc, turn.

Row 16: Rep Row 15.

Row 17: Ch 3, 2 dc in ch-2 sp of shell, ch 1, shell over shell, ch 1, 2 dc in next ch-2 sp of shell, dc in end dc, turn.

Row 18: Ch 3, dc in next 2 dc, 3 dc in next ch-2 sp of shell, dc in each of next 3 dc, fasten off.

Second lobe

Rep Rows 15–18 for 2nd lobe, beg at outer edge. At the end of Row 18, do not fasten off.

Edging

Rnd 1: Ch 1, working around entire outer edge, work 2 sc over side edge of each row, sc in each dc and 3 sc at bottom point and 1 sc at center top between lobes, join in beg sc, fasten off.

Rnd 2: Beg at center top between lobes, attach CC, ch 1, sc in each of next 2 sts, [ch 3, sc in each of next 2 sts] rep around, join in beg sc, fasten off. ❖

Country Checks Breakfast Set

By Charlene Finiello

Skill Level: Intermediate

Size:

Tea Cozy: Fits 5–6 inch teapot

Hot Pad: 6½ inches in diameter

Egg Cozy: 2½ inches tall

Materials

✓ Coats & Clark Red Heart Super Saver worsted weight yarn: 3 oz cornmeal #320, small amounts medium sage #632 and light celery #615

✓ Size H/8 crochet hook or size needed to obtain gauge

✓ Yarn needle

Gauge

7 dc and 3 dc rows = 2 inches

Check gauge to save time.

Pattern Notes

Weave in loose ends as work progresses.

Join rnds with a sl st unless otherwise stated.

Ch 3 counts as first dc throughout.

Roll a small ball of cornmeal; set aside.

Pattern Stitch

4-dc cl: Leaving MC on hook, [yo with CC, insert hook in next st, yo, draw up a lp, yo, draw through 2 lps on hook] 4 times in same st, drop CC to back of work, pick up MC, yo, draw through all 5 lps on hook. Continue working with MC; carry CC loosely on WS until next cl.

Tea Cozy

Rnd 1 (RS): With cornmeal, ch 12, sl st to join to form a ring, ch 1, [2 sc in next ch, sc in next ch] 6 times, join in beg sc. (18 sc)

Rnd 2: Working in back lps for this rnd only, ch 3, [2 dc in next st] rep around, ending with dc in same st as beg ch-3, join in top of beg ch-3. (36 dc)

Rnd 3: Working in back lps only, ch 3, dc in next st, *drop cornmeal to back of work, pick up celery, 4-dc cl in next st, drop celery before final yo, with cornmeal, yo, draw through all 5 lps on hook **, dc in each of next 2 sts, rep from * around, join in top of beg ch-3, turn. (24 dc; 12 cls; 48 sts total)

Note: While working Rnd 3, you have only worked 36 st; however, above each cl are 2 sts for a total of 48 sts.

Handle opening

Row 4 (WS): Working in front lps for this row only, ch 3, dc in each st across, turn. (48 dc)

Row 5 (RS): Working in back lps only, ch 3, dc in next st, *make 4-dc cl with medium sage, drop medium sage before final yo, with cornmeal, yo, draw through all 5 lps on hook **, dc in each of next 3 sts, rep from * across, ending last rep at **, dc in each of next 2 sts, turn.

First side spout opening

Row 6 (WS): Working in front lps only, dc in each of next 30 sts, turn.

Row 7 (RS): Working in back lps only, ch 3, dc in next st, *with celery make 4-dc cl, drop celery, with cornmeal, dc in next 4 sts, rep from * across, ending with dc in last 2 sts, turn. (6 cls; 4 dc between each, 2 dc at beg and end)

Row 8 (WS): Working in front lps only, ch 3, dc in next 4 sts, [dc dec over next 2 sts, dc in next 4 sts] 4 times, dc dec over next 2 sts, dc in each of next 2 sts, dc dec over next 2 sts, dc in next dc, draw up a lp, remove hook, do not fasten off.

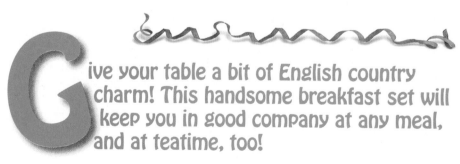

G ive your table a bit of English country charm! This handsome breakfast set will keep you in good company at any meal, and at teatime, too!

Second side spout opening

Row 6 (WS): Attach small ball of cornmeal at right-hand side of 2nd section, working in front lps only, ch 3, dc in each of next 27 sts, dc dec over next 2 sts, dc in next dc, turn. (30 sts)

Row 7 (RS): Working in back lps only, ch 3, dc in next st, *with celery make 4-dc cl in next st, with cornmeal **, dc in next 4 sts, rep from * across, ending last rep at **, dc in next 2 sts, turn.

Row 8 (WS): Rep Row 8 of first side of spout, fasten off.

Row 9 (RS): Pick up dropped lp from first side, working in back lps only, dc in next dc, *with medium sage 4-dc cl in next st, with cornmeal **, dc in next 4 dc, rep from * across first side, ending last rep at **, dc in next 2 dc, working across 2nd side, dc in each of next 2 sts, rep from * across 2nd side, ending last rep at **, dc in next 2 sts, turn.

Rnd 10 (WS): Working in front lps, ch 3, dc dec over next 2 sts, dc in next 2 sts, [dc dec over next 2 sts, dc in next 4 sts] rep around, ending with dc in 5 dc, sl st to join in top of beg ch-3, turn.

Rnd 11 (RS): Working in back lps only, ch 1, sc in each st around, join in beg sc, fasten off.

Finishing

Attach cornmeal in handle opening, ch 1, sc evenly sp around opening, join in beg sc, fasten off.

Attach cornmeal in spout opening, ch 1, sc evenly sp around opening, join in beg sc, fasten off.

Hot Pad

Front

Rnd 1 (RS): With cornmeal, ch 2, 6 sc in 2nd ch from hook, join in beg sc. (6 sc)

Rnd 2: Working in back lps only, ch 3, 3 dc in each of next 5 sts, 2 dc in same st as beg ch-3, join in top of beg ch-3. (18 dc)

Rnd 3: Working in back lps only, ch 3, dc in next st, *with celery work 4-dc cl **, dc in next st, 2 dc in next st, rep from * around, ending last rep at **, dc in same st as beg ch-3. (6 cls; 3 dc between each)

Rnd 4: Working in back lps only, ch 3, dc around, inc 18 dc evenly sp around, join in top of beg

Continued on page 143

Scrap Thread Pot Holders

By Angela Tate

Skill Level: Beginner

Size:

Hexagon Pot Holder: 8 inches in diameter

Rectangular Pot Holder: 6½ x 8 inches

Materials

✓ Crochet cotton size 10: 100 yds various colors for motifs, 100 yds each of white and cream

✓ Size 6 steel crochet hook or size needed to obtain gauge

✓ Tapestry needle

Gauge

8 dc = 1 inch; 5 dc rows or rnds = 1½ inches
Check gauge to save time.

Pattern Notes

Weave in loose ends as work progresses.

Join rnds with a sl st unless otherwise stated.

Ch 3 counts as first dc throughout.

Rnds 1 and 2 of each motif requires approximately 2½ yards each.

Hexagon Pot Holder

Front

First motif

Rnd 1 (RS): With motif colored cotton, ch 4, sl st to join to form a ring, ch 3, 11 dc in ring, join in top of beg ch-3. (12 dc)

Rnd 2: Ch 3, dc in same dc as beg ch-3, 2 dc in each rem dc around, join in top of beg ch-3, fasten off. (24 dc)

Rnd 3: Attach cream in any dc, ch 1, [sc in each of next 2 dc, ch 4] rep around, join in beg sc, fasten off.

Second motif

Rnds 1 & 2: Rep Rnds 1 and 2 of first motif.

Rnd 3 (joining): Attach cream in any dc of Rnd 2, ch 1, *[sc in each of next 2 dc, ch 2, sl st in corresponding lp of adjacent motif, ch 2, rep from * across 1, 2, 3

or 4 adjacent motifs, then finish rem of motif as for Rnd 3 of first motif.

Rep 2nd motif until a total of 19 motifs are completed and joined. Joining in rows of 3, 4, 5, 4 and 3 to complete hexagon pot holder.

Back

Rnd 1 (RS): With cream, ch 6, sl st to join to form a ring, ch 3, 11 dc in ring, join in top of beg ch-3. (12 dc)

Rnd 2: Ch 3, dc in same st as beg ch-3, 2 dc in each rem dc around, join in top of beg ch-3. (24 dc)

Rnd 3: Ch 3, dc in each of next 2 dc, 5 dc in next dc, [dc in each of next 3 dc, 5 dc in next dc] 5 times, join in top of beg ch-3.

Rnd 4: Ch 3, dc in each dc around, working 3 dc in each center dc of each 5-dc group, join in top of beg ch-3.

Rnd 5: Ch 3, dc in each dc around, working 5 dc in each center dc of each 3-dc group, join in top of beg ch-3.

Rnds 6–12: Rep Rnds 4 and 5. At the end of Rnd 12, fasten off. (31 dc across each side; 3 dc in each corner; total 204 dc around)

Assembly

Rnd 1: With WS of front and back tog, with front facing, attach cream, ch 1, working in dc sts of Rnd 12, sc in each st around, catching ch lps of front motifs in the first, 3rd, 14th, 16th, 28th and 30th dc between inc of each corner, 2 lps on each side edge of motifs and 4 lps at each of 6 corners are attached to back. (36 ch-4

ade with scraps of leftover thread in rainbow of colors, these pretty trivets are fun to crochet!

lps are attached to back.

Rnd 2: Ch 1, [sc in sc, ch 1, sk 1 sc] rep around, join in beg sc, ch 12, sl st in same sc (hanging lp), ch 1, 24 sc over ch-12 hanging lp, fasten off.

Press lightly with steam iron.

Rectangular Pot Holder

Front

First motif

Rnds 1 & 2: Rep Rnds 1 and 2 of first motif of hexagon pot holder.

Rnd 3: With white, rep Rnd 3 of first hexagon motif.

Second motif

Rnds 1 & 2: Rep Rnds 1 and 2 of first motif.

Rnd 3: Attach white in any dc, ch 1, *[sc in each of next 2 dc, ch 2, sl st in corresponding lp of adjacent motif, ch 2] 3 times, rep from * across 1, 2 or 3 adjacent motifs, then finish as for first motif Rnd 3. Rep 2nd motif until a total of 20 are completed and joined. Motifs are joined in 4 rows of 5 motifs each.

Back

Row 1: With white, ch 52, dc in 4th ch from hook, dc in each rem ch across, turn. (50 dc)

Rows 2–20: Ch 3, dc in each dc across, turn. At the end of Row 20, fasten off.

Assembly

Rnd 1: Place WS of front and back tog, with front facing, attach white in first dc at any corner, ch 1, sc in each st around, catching 3 free lps of each front motif around outer edge and 6 lp of motifs at each corner, sl st to join in beg sc.

Rnd 2: Ch 1, [sc in next sc, ch 4, sk 1 sc] rep around, sl st to join in beg sc, ch 12, sl st in same st (hanging lp), ch 1, 24 sc over hanging lp, sl st in base of lp, fasten off. Press lightly with steam iron. ❖

Country Checks Breakfast Set

Continued from page 141

ch-3. (48 dc)

Rnd 5: Working in back lps only, ch 3, 2 dc in next st, dc in next st, *with medium sage, 4-dc cl in next st **, with cornmeal, dc in next st, 2 dc in next st, dc in next st, rep from * around, ending at **, join in top of beg ch-3, fasten off medium sage. (72 sts)

Back

Rnds 1 & 2: With cornmeal, rep Rnds 1 and 2 of front. (18 dc)

Rnd 3: Working in back lps only, ch 3, dc around, inc 12 dc evenly sp

around, join in top of beg ch-3. (30 dc)

Rnd 4: Working in back lps only, ch 3, dc around, inc 18 dc evenly sp around, join in top of beg ch-3. (48 dc)

Rnd 5: Working in back lps only, ch 3, dc around, inc 24 dc around, join in top of beg ch-3, fasten off. (72 dc)

Joining

Rnd 6: Holding both mat sections tog, with front facing, attach cornmeal, ch 1, working in back lps only, sc in each st around, join, fasten off.

Egg Cozy

Note: Make 4 egg cozies in various colors as shown. Alternating color combinations.

Rnd 1: With MC, ch 4, 15 dc in 4th ch from hook, join in top of beg ch-4. (16 dc)

Rnd 2: Working in back lps only, ch 3, dc in next 2 sts, *with CC, 4-dc cl in next st **, with MC, dc in each of next 3 sts, rep from * around, ending last rep at **, join in top of beg ch-3. (20 sts)

Rnd 3: Working in back lps only, ch 3, dc in each st around, join in top of beg ch-3.

Rnd 4: Working in back

lps only, ch 3, dc in each of next 3 sts, *with CC, 4-dc cl in next st **, with MC, dc in each of next 4 sts, rep from * around, ending last rep at **, join in top of beg ch-3.

Rnd 5: Working in back lps only, with MC, ch 1, sc in each st around, join in beg sc, fasten off.

Top loop

With MC, leaving a length at beg, ch 10, leaving a length of yarn, fasten off.

Pull beg and ending lengths through top, secure around a st at center top, fasten off. ❖

Heart's Fancy Trivets

By Diane Poellot

Skill Level: Intermediate

Size:

Large Trivet: 10½ inches in diameter

Small Trivet: 6½ inches in diameter

Materials

✓ Worsted weight yarn: 3 oz white, 2 oz red

✓ Size I/9 crochet hook or size needed to obtain gauge

✓ Small safety pins or other markers

✓ Yarn needle

Crochet this set of large and small trivets to protect your table from hot dishes.

Gauge

Rnds 1–3 of back = 3½ inches in diameter

Check gauge to save time.

Pattern Notes

Weave in loose ends as work progresses.

Join rnds with a sl st unless otherwise stated.

Ch 3 counts as first dc throughout.

Pattern Stitches

V-st: [Dc, ch 2, dc] in indicated st.

Split 4-dc cl: [Ch 3, holding back on hook last lp of each dc, dc in same st, dc in each of next 4 sts, yo,

draw through all 5 lps on hook, ch 3, sl st in same st as last dc] twice.

Joining st (jst): Holding back on hook last lp of each st, tr in sl st in center of heart on front, dc in same st as last dc on back, yo, draw through all 3 lps on hook.

Large Trivet

Front

Rnd 1: With red, ch 6, sl st to join to form a ring, ch 1, 18 sc in ring, join in beg sc.

Rnd 2: Ch 3, 4 dc in same st as beg ch, [ch 2, sk next 2 sc, sc in next sc, ch 2 *, sk next 2 sc, 5 dc in next sc] 3 times, ending last rep

at *, join in 3rd ch of beg ch-3.

Rnd 3: Ch 3, dc in same st, [dc in each of next 3 dc, 2 dc in next dc, ch 2, dc in next sc, ch 2 *, 2 dc in next dc] 3 times, ending last rep at *, join in 3rd ch of beg ch-3.

Rnd 4: [Split 4-dc cl, ch 2, V-st in next dc *, ch 2, sl st in next dc] 3 times, ending last rep at *, dc in sl st closing Rnd 3, turn.

Rnd 5: Sl st back into ch-2 sp of V-st, turn, ch 3, 4 dc in same sp, [ch 3, sc in top of next cl, ch 6, sc in top of next cl, ch 3 *, 5 dc in ch-2 sp of next V-st] 3 times, ending last rep at *, join in 3rd ch of beg ch-3.

Rnd 6: Ch 3, dc in same st as joining, [dc in each of next 3 dc, 2 dc in next dc, ch 3, sc in next ch-3 sp, ch 4, V-st in next ch-6 sp, ch 4, sc in next ch-3 sp, ch 3 *, 2 dc in next dc] 3 times, ending last rep at *, join in 3rd ch of beg ch-3.

Rnd 7: *Split 4-dc cl, ch 3, V-st in next ch-4 sp, [V-st, ch 2, dc] in next V-st (Mark center dc with small safety pin), V-st in next ch-4 sp, ch 3, rep from * around, join in sl st closing Rnd 6, fasten off.

Back

Rnd 1: With white, ch 4, sl st to join to form a ring, ch 3, 11 dc in ring, join in 3rd ch of beg ch-3. (12 dc)

Rnd 2: Ch 3, dc in same st as joining, 2 dc in each dc around, join in top of beg ch-3. (24 dc)

Rnd 3: Rep Rnd 2. (48 dc)

Rnd 4: Ch 3, dc in same st as joining, dc in each of

next 3 dc, [2 dc in next dc, dc in each of next 3 dc] rep around, join in 3rd ch of beg ch-3. (60 dc)

Rnd 5: Ch 3, dc in same st as joining, dc in each of next 4 dc, [2 dc in next dc, dc in each of next 4 dc] rep around, join in 3rd ch of beg ch-3. (72 dc)

Rnd 6: Ch 3, dc in same st as joining, dc in each of next 5 dc, [2 dc in next dc, dc in each of next 5 dc] rep around, join in 3rd ch of beg ch-3. (84 dc)

Rnd 7: Ch 3, dc in same st as joining, dc in each of next 6 dc, [2 dc in next dc, dc in each of next 6 dc] rep around, join in 3rd ch of beg ch-3. (96 dc)

Joining

Rnd 8: Holding front and back with WS tog and front facing, ch 6, dc in same st as joining, ch 2, dc in center (Marked) dc on front and same st on back, ch 2, [dc, ch 2, tr] in same st as last dc on back, *sk next 3 sts, sl st in next st, sk next 3 sts, [tr, ch 2, {dc, ch 2} 3 times, tr] in next st, sk next 3 sts, sl st in next st, sk next 3 sts, [tr, ch 2, dc, ch 2, jst, ch 2, dc, ch 2, tr] in next st, sk next 3 sts, sl st in next st, sk next 3 sts, [tr, ch 2, {dc, ch 2} 3 times, tr] in next st, sk next 3 sts, sl st in next st, sk next 3 sts **, [tr, ch 2, dc, ch 2] in next st, dc in center (Marked) dc of front and same st on back, ch 2,

[dc, ch 2, tr] in same st on back, rep from * around, ending last rep at **, join in 4th ch of beg ch-6, fasten off.

Small Trivet

Front

Rnds 1–4: Rep Rnds 1–4 of front for large trivet. At end of Rnd 4, fasten off.

Back

Rnds 1–4: Rep Rnds 1–4 of back for large trivet. At the end of Rnd 4, fasten off.

Joining

Rnd 5: Holding front and back with WS tog and front facing, ch 6, dc in same st as joining, ch 2, *dc through both thicknesses in ch-2 sp of V-st on front and same st as last dc on back, ch 2, [dc, ch 2, tr] in same st on back only, sk next 4 sts, sl st in next st, sk next 4 sts, [tr, ch 2, dc, ch 2] in next st, dc through both thicknesses in sl st at center of heart on front and same st as last dc on back, ch 2, [dc, ch 2, tr] in same st on back only, sk next 4 sts **, [tr, ch 2, dc] in next st, rep from * around, ending last rep at **, join in 4th ch of beg ch-6, fasten off. ❖

Peach Blossom Doily

By Ruth Shepherd

Skill Level: Intermediate

Size: 10½ inches square

Materials

✓ Sport weight acrylic fiber yarn (1¾ oz balls) 1 ball each white and peach

✓ Size E/4 crochet hook or size needed to obtain gauge

✓ Yarn needle

Gauge

Rnds 1–4 = 2½ inches square

Check gauge to save time.

Pattern Notes

Weave in loose ends as work progresses.

Join rnds with a sl st unless otherwise stated.

Doily

Rnd 1 (RS): With peach, ch 6, sl st to join to form a ring, ch 3 (counts as first hdc, ch 1), [hdc in ring, ch 1] 7 times, join in 2nd ch of beg ch-3. (9 hdc; 8 ch-1 sps)

Rnd 2: Ch 1, sc in same st as beg ch-1, [ch 5, sc in

next hdc] 7 times, ch 2, dc in beg sc to form last ch-5 lp. (8 ch-5 lps)

Rnd 3: Ch 1, sc in same sp as beg ch-1, *[ch 5, sc in same ch-5 lp] twice, ch 3, sc in next ch-5 lp, ch 3 **, sc in next ch-5 lp, rep from * around, ending last rep at **, join in beg sc. (8 ch-5 lps; 8 ch-3 lps)

Rnd 4: Sl st into 3rd ch of next ch-5 lp, ch 1, sc in same ch-5 lp, *ch 5, sc in next ch-5 lp, [ch 3, sc in next ch-3 sp] twice, ch 3 **, sc in next ch-5 lp, rep from * 3 times, ending last rep at **, join in beg sc. (4 ch-5 sps; 12 ch-3 sps)

Rnd 5: Ch 4 (counts as first dc, ch 1), dc in ch-5 sp, [ch 1, dc in same ch-5 sp] 6 times, ch 5, sk next ch-3 sp, sc in next ch-3 sp, ch 5, dc in next ch-5 sp, *[ch 1, dc in same ch-5 sp] 7 times, ch 5, sk next ch-3 sp, sc in next ch-3 sp, ch 5 **, dc in next ch-5 sp, rep from * twice, ending last rep at **, join in

3rd ch of beg ch-5.

Rnd 6: Ch 4 (counts as first hdc, ch 2), *hdc in next dc, [ch 2, hdc in next dc] 6 times, ch 8 **, hdc in next dc, ch 2, rep from * around, ending last rep at **, join in 2nd ch of beg ch-4.

Rnd 7: Ch 5 (counts as first hdc, ch 3), *hdc in next hdc, [ch 3, hdc in next hdc] 6 times, [ch 3, work 1 sc over ch sps of Rnds 5 and 6 directly below] twice, ch 3 **, hdc in next hdc, ch 2, rep from * 3 times, ending last rep at **, join in 2nd ch of beg ch-5.

Rnd 8: Ch 1, sc in same hdc as beg ch-1, ch 3, *hdc in next hdc, [ch 3, hdc in next hdc] twice, ch 8, hdc in next hdc, [ch 3, hdc in next hdc] twice, ch 3, sc in next hdc, ch 5 **, sc in next hdc, ch 3, rep from * 3 times, ending last rep at **, join in beg sc.

Rnd 9: Sl st into ch-3 sp, ch 1, 3 sc in same ch-3 sp, *[ch 1, 3 sc in next ch-3 sp] twice, [4 sc, ch 3, 4 sc] in next corner ch-8 sp, [ch 1, 3 sc in next ch-3 sp] 3 times, ch 1, 5 sc over next

ch-5 sp, ch 1 **, 3 sc over next ch-3 sp, rep from * around, ending last rep at **, join in beg sc, fasten off. (32 ch-1 sps; 4 ch-3 corner sps)

Rnd 10 (RS): Attach white in any corner ch-3 sp, ch 1, [sc, ch 3, sc] in corner ch-3 sp, [ch 3, sc in next ch-1 sp] 8 times, ch 3, *[sc, ch 3, sc] in next corner ch-3 sp, ch 3, [sc in next ch-1 sp, ch 3] 8 times, rep from * twice, join in beg sc. (36 ch-3 sps; 4 corner ch-3 sps)

Rnd 11: Ch 6, hdc in 3rd ch from hook, *hdc in ch-3 sp, ch 3, hdc in 3rd ch from hook, hdc in ch-3 sp, ch 3, hdc in 3rd ch from hook, [hdc in next sc, ch 3, hdc in 3rd ch from hook] 10 times, rep from * 3 times, ending last rep with [hdc in next sc, ch 3, hdc in 3rd ch from hook] 9 times, join in 3rd ch of beg ch-6.

Rnd 12: Ch 6, *hdc in 3rd ch from hook, hdc in next hdc, ch 3, hdc in 3rd ch from hook, hdc in same hdc, ch 3, hdc in 3rd ch from hook, hdc in next hdc, ch 3, hdc in 3rd ch

from hook, hdc in same hdc, ch 3, hdc in 3rd ch from hook, [hdc in next hdc, ch 3, hdc in 3rd ch from hook] 10 times, ch 3, rep from * 3 times, ending with last rep, [hdc in next hdc, ch 3, hdc in 3rd ch from hook] 9 times, join in 3rd ch of beg ch-6.

Rnd 13: Ch 6, hdc in 3rd ch from hook, hdc in next hdc, [ch 3, hdc in 3rd ch

from hook, hdc in next hdc] twice, ch 3, hdc in 3rd ch from hook, hdc in same hdc, ch 3, hdc in 3rd ch from hook, hdc in next hdc, ch 3, hdc in 3rd ch from hook, hdc in same hdc, ch 3, hdc in 3rd ch from hook, [hdc in next hdc, ch 3, hdc in 3rd ch from hook] 12 times, rep from * 3 times, ending last rep with [hdc in next hdc,

ch 3, hdc in 3rd ch from hook] 10 times, join in 3rd ch of beg ch-6, fasten off.

Rnd 14: Attach peach in any hdc, ch 6, hdc in 3rd ch from hook, hdc in same hdc, *hdc in next hdc, ch 3, hdc in 3rd ch from hook, hdc in same hdc, rep from * around, join in 3rd ch of beg ch-6.

Rnd 15: Ch 1, sc in same

st as beg ch-1, *ch 5, sl st in 3rd ch from hook, ch 2 **, sc in each of next 2 hdc, rep from * around, ending last rep at **, sc in next st, join in beg sc, fasten off. ❖

Goldfish Bath Set

By Beverly Mewhorter

Skill Level: Beginner

Size:

Large Fish: 7 inches long

Medium Fish: 6½ inches long

Small Fish: 3 inches long

Materials

✓ Worsted weight yarn: 2 oz vibrant orange, small amount black

✓ Baby pompadour yarn: Small amount light blue

✓ Crochet cotton size 10: Small amount black

✓ Size G/6 crochet hook or size needed to obtain gauge

✓ Crochet hook size E/4

✓ Bath towel, hand towel and washcloth

✓ Sewing needle and thread

✓ Tapestry needle

Add some fishy fun to your bath with these whimsical shower accessories.

Gauge

4 sc = 1 inch

Check gauge to save time.

Pattern Notes

Weave in loose ends as work progresses.

Join rnds with a sl st unless otherwise stated.

Large Fish

(Make 1)

Row 1: With hook size G and vibrant orange, ch 7, sc in 2nd ch from hook, sc in each rem ch across, turn. (6 sc)

Row 2: Ch 1, 2 sc in first sc, sc in each sc across to last sc, 2 sc in last sc, turn. (8 sc)

Row 3: Rep Row 2. (10 sc)

Row 4: Ch 1, sc in each sc across, turn.

Row 5: Rep Row 4.

Row 6: Rep Row 2. (12 sc)

Rows 7–14: Rep Row 4.

Rows 15–17: Ch 1, sc dec over next 2 sc, sc in each sc across to last 2 sc, sc dec over next 2 sc, turn. (6 sc)

Rows 18–22: Rep Row 2. (16 sc)

Row 23: Ch 3, dc in same st as beg ch-3, dc in each of next 2 sc, hdc in each of next 2 sc, sc in next sc, sl st in each of next 2 sc, sc in next sc, hdc in each of next 2 sc, dc in each of next 3 sts, 2 dc in next st, fasten off.

Mouth

Row 1: Working in opposite side of foundation ch, attach vibrant orange, ch 1, sc in each ch across, turn. (6 sc)

Row 2: Ch 2, hdc in same st as beg ch-2, hdc in next st, sl st in each of next 2 sts, hdc in next st, 2 hdc in last st, fasten off.

Medium Fish

(Make 1)

Row 1: With hook size G and vibrant orange, ch 5, sc in 2nd ch from hook, sc in each rem ch across, turn. (4 sc)

Rows 2–22: Rep Rows 2–22 of large fish. (14 sc)

Row 23: Ch 3, dc in same st as beg ch-3, dc in each of next 3 sc, hdc in next sc, sc in next sc, sl st in each of next 2 sts, sc in next st, hdc in next st, dc in each of next 3 sts, 2 dc in last st, fasten off.

Mouth

Row 1: Attach vibrant orange in opposite side of foundation ch, ch 1, sc in each ch across, turn.

Row 2: Ch 1, 2 sc in first sc, sl st in each of next 2 sc, 2 sc in next sc, fasten off.

Small Fish

(Make 4)

Row 1: Ch 3, sc in 2nd ch from hook, sc in next ch, turn. (2 sc)

Row 2: Ch 1, sc in each sc across, turn.

Row 3: Ch 1, 2 sc in each sc across, turn. (4 sc)

Row 4: Ch 1, 2 sc in first sc, sc in each of next 2 sc, 2 sc in last sc, turn. (6 sc)

Rows 5 & 6: Rep Row 2.

Row 7: Ch 1, sc dec over next 2 sc, sc in each of next 2 sc, sc dec over next 2 sc, turn. (4 sc)

Row 8: Ch 1, [sc dec over next 2 sc] twice, turn. (2 sc)

Row 9: Rep Row 3. (4 sc)

Row 10: Rep Row 4. (6 sc)

Row 11: Ch 2, hdc in same st as beg ch-2, sc in next sc, sl st in each of next 2 sc, sc in next sc, 2 hdc in last sc, fasten off.

Features

With tapestry needle and black yarn, using photo as a guide, embroider eyes on fish. With black crochet cotton, embroider 2 V-sts as indicated in photo.

Bubbles

(Make 14)

With hook size E and light blue, ch 3, 6 hdc in 3rd ch from hook, join in top of beg ch-3, fasten off. (7 hdc)

Finishing

On bath towel, arrange and sew large fish, 2 small fish and 6 bubbles.

On hand towel, arrange and sew medium fish, 1 small fish and 5 bubbles.

On washcloth, arrange and sew 1 small fish and 3 bubbles. ❖

Dapper Duckling

By Laura Gebhardt

Skill Level: Beginner

Size: 3 x 5 inches

Materials

- ✓ Cotton worsted weight yarn: 1 oz yellow
- ✓ Size G/6 crochet hook or size needed to obtain gauge
- ✓ 1½-inch in diameter yellow pompom
- ✓ 2 x 3¼ bar soap
- ✓ 2mm animal eyes
- ✓ Scrap orange felt
- ✓ Craft glue
- ✓ Yarn needle

Gauge

3 cls = 2 inches; 3 cl rnds = 2 inches
Check gauge to save time.

Pattern Notes

Weave in loose ends as work progresses.

Join rnds with a sl st unless otherwise stated.

Pattern Stitches

3-dc cl: [Yo hook, insert hook in indicated st, yo, draw up a lp, yo, draw through 2 lps on hook] 3 times, yo, draw through all 4 lps on hook.

Beg 3-dc cl: Ch 2 (counts as first dc), [yo hook, insert hook in indicated st, yo, draw up a lp, yo, draw through 2 lps on hook] twice, yo, draw through all 3 lps on hook.

Body

Rnd 1 (RS): With yellow, ch 5, sl st to join to form a ring, ch 1, 10 sc in ring, join in beg sc. (10 sc)

Rnd 2: Ch 4 (counts as first dc, ch 1), dc in same sc, [dc, ch 1, dc] in each sc around, join in 3rd ch of beg ch-4. (10 ch-1 sps)

Rnd 3: Sl st into next ch sp, beg 3-dc cl in same ch-1 sp, ch 2, [3-dc cl in next ch-1 sp, ch 2] rep around, join in top of beg cl. (10 3-dc cl; 10 ch-2 sps)

Rnds 4–8: Rep Rnd 3.

Rnd 9: Sl st into ch sp, beg 3-dc cl in same ch sp, ch 1, [3-dc cl in next ch-2 sp, ch 1] rep around, join in top of beg cl, fasten off.

Tail Tie

With yellow, ch 50, sl st in 2nd ch from hook, sl st in each rem ch across, fasten off.

Finishing

Weave tail tie through ch-1 sps of Rnd 9 of body; insert soap, pull tail ends to close opening, tie ends in a bow. With bow facing upward for tail, place on flat surface. From orange felt, cut beak. Glue beak to center front on pompom. Glue eyes evenly sp above beak. Glue head to Rnd 3 at center top of body. ❖

Soft & Simple Face Cloth

By Aline Suplinskas

Skill Level: Beginner

Size: 7¼ x 8 inches

Materials

✓ Crochet cotton size 10: 80 yds pink, 70 yds white

✓ Size 6 steel crochet hook or size needed to obtain gauge

✓ Tapestry needle

Delicate and pretty, this dainty cloth is designed to be gentle! Make a set in several colors for your own bath or kitchen, as well as some to give friends!

Gauge

1 long sc and 3 sc = ½ inch; 10 rows = 1 inch

Check gauge to save time.

Pattern Notes

Weave in loose ends as work progresses.

Join rnds with a sl st unless otherwise stated.

Cloth

Row 1: With white, ch 49, sc in 2nd ch from hook, sc in each rem ch across, turn. (48 sc)

Row 2: Ch 1, sc in each st across to last step of last st, drop white, draw lp of pink through last 2 sts on hook, turn.

Row 3: With pink, ch 1, [sc in each of next 3 sc, long sc in 2 rows below] rep across, turn.

Row 4: Ch 1, sc in each st across to last step of last st, drop pink, draw lp of white through last 2 sts on hook, turn.

Row 5: With white, ch 1, sc in first st, [long sc in 2 rows below, sc in each of next 3 sts] rep across, ending with sc in each of last 2 sts, turn.

Rows 6–58: Rep Rows 2–5; ending last rep with Row 2, fasten off white, do not turn.

Edging

Rnd 1: With pink, ch 1, sc in same st as last st (corner), working across side, [ch 1, sk 1 row, sc in next row] rep across each side, working across top and bottom, [ch 1, sk 1 st, sc in next st] rep across and work [sc, ch 1, sc] in each corner, join in beg sc, fasten off. ❖

Row 5: Sl st into ch sp, ch 4 (counts as first dc, ch 1), [dc, ch 1] 4 times in same ch sp, *[dc, ch 1] 5 times in next ch sp, rep from * across, fasten off.

Row 6: Working on opposite edge of edging in ch sps, attach cotton, ch 1, [sc, ch 3, sl st in 3rd ch from hook, sc] in same ch sp, *[sc, ch 3, sl st in 3rd ch from hook, sc] in next ch sp, rep from * across, fasten off.

Steam-press edging. Sew edging to desired position across width of towel.

Shell Edging

Row 1: Ch 9, 2 dc in 4th ch from hook, ch 3, 3 dc in next ch (shell), dc in last ch, turn.

Row 2: Ch 3, [shell of 3 dc, ch 3, 3 dc] in ch-3 sp, dc in top of turning ch, turn.

Rep Row 2 until a total of 51 shells are completed.

Row 3: Working across side edge of strip, sl st over side edge of last row, [ch 3, 3 dc, ch 5, sl st in 5th ch from hook, 3 dc] over side edge of row, [sl st over side edge of next row, {3 dc, ch 5, sl st in 5th ch from hook, 3 dc} over side edge of next row] rep across, fasten off.

Steam-press edging. Sew edging to desired position across width of towel. ❖

Guest Towel Edgings

By Nazanin Fard

Skill Level: Beginner

Size:

Scallop Edging: 1⅜ x 16 inches

Shell Edging: 1 x 16 inches

Materials

✓ Crochet cotton size 10: 125 yds white

✓ Size 7 steel crochet hook or size needed to obtain gauge

✓ 2 burgundy 16 x 25-inch hand towels

✓ Sewing needle and thread

Make your guests feel pampered with this pair of delicate edgings tacked onto hand towels.

Gauge

9 dc = 1 inch

Check gauge to save time.

Pattern Notes

Weave in loose ends as work progresses.

Materials listed will make both edgings.

Ch 3 counts as first dc throughout.

Scallop Edging

Row 1: Ch 8, dc in 6th ch from hook, ch 1, sk 1 ch, dc in next ch, turn. (3 dc; 2 ch-1 sps)

Row 2: Ch 4 (counts as first dc, ch 1 throughout), dc in next dc, ch 1, sk next ch, dc in next ch, turn.

[Rep Row 2] 57 times. (59 mesh rows total)

Row 3: Working over side edge of rows, ch 3, 2 dc in same sp, [ch 3, sc in next sp, ch 3, 3 dc in next sp] 29 times, turn.

Row 4: Ch 1, sc in first dc, ch 3, [sc in next ch sp, ch 3] rep across, ending with sc in last dc, turn.

Patriotic Coasters

By Beverly Mewhorter

Skill Level: Beginner

Size: 4 inches

Materials

✓ Worsted weight yarn: Small amounts cherry red, white and royal blue

✓ Size F/5 crochet hook or size needed to obtain gauge

✓ Tapestry needle

Protect your table by serving up summer beverages on these bright and colorful coasters.

Gauge

4 dc = 1 inch

Check gauge to save time.

Pattern Notes

Weave in loose ends as work progresses.

Join rnds with a sl st unless otherwise stated.

Ch 3 counts as first dc throughout.

Pattern Stitch

Shell: [2 dc, ch 2, 2 dc] in indicated st.

First Coaster

Rnd 1: With cherry red, ch 4, 15 dc in 4th ch from hook, join in top of beg ch-4, fasten off. (16 dc)

Rnd 2: Attach white in any dc, ch 3, [dc, ch 2, 2 dc] in same st as beg ch, sk 1 dc, [shell in next dc, sk next dc] rep around, join in top of beg ch-3, fasten off. (8 shells)

Rnd 3: Attach royal blue in any ch-2 sp of shell, ch 3, [dc, ch 2, 2 dc] in same ch-2 sp, sc in sp between shells, [shell in next ch-2 sp of shell, sc in sp between shells] rep around, join in top of beg ch-3, fasten off. (8 shells; 8 sc)

Second Coaster

Rnd 1: With royal blue, rep Rnd 1 of first coaster.

Rnd 2: With white, rep Rnd 2 of first coaster.

Rnd 3: With cherry red, rep Rnd 3 of first coaster. ❖

Regency Floral Afghan

By Carol Alexander for
Crochet Trends & Traditions

Skill Level: Advanced

Size: 48 x 63 inches

Materials

✓ Patons Canadiana worsted weight yarn (3.5 oz balls): 5 balls loden #162, 4 balls each hot pink #430 and bisque #6, 1 ball willow #58

✓ Size H/8 crochet hook or size needed to obtain gauge

✓ Yarn needle

Gauge

Motif measures 9¾ x 14 inches

Check gauge to save time.

Pattern Notes

Weave in loose ends as work progresses.

Join rnds with a sl st unless otherwise stated.

Pattern Stitches

Dtr cl: *Yo hook 3 times, insert hook in indicated st, yo, draw up a lp, [yo, draw through 2 lps on hook] 3 times, rep from * 3 times in indicated st, yo, draw through all 5 lps on hook.

Beg dtr cl: Ch 4 (counts as first dtr), *yo hook 3 times, insert hook in indicated st, yo, draw up a lp, [yo, draw through 2 lps on hook] 3 times, rep from * twice, yo, draw through all 4 lps on hook.

Dc cl: [Yo hook, insert hook in indicated st, yo, draw up a lp, yo, draw through 2 lps on hook] 5 times, yo, draw through all 6 lps on hook.

Beg dc cl: Ch 2 (counts as first dc), [yo hook, insert hook in indicated st, yo, draw up a lp, yo, draw through 2 lps on hook] 4 times, yo, draw through all 5 lps on hook.

Shell: [Dc, ch 1] 4 times in same sp.

Beg shell: Ch 4 (counts as first dc, ch 1), [dc, ch 1] 3 times in same sp.

First Motif

Rnd 1: With hot pink, ch 16, 2 dc in 4th ch from hook, dc in each of next 11 chs, 5 dc in last ch, working on opposite side of foundation ch, dc in each of next 11 chs, 2 dc in last ch, join in 4th ch of beg ch, draw loden through; drop hot pink. (32 dc)

Rnd 2: Working in back lps for this rnd only, beg dtr cl in same st, [ch 3, dtr cl in next st] twice, {ch 2, sk next 2 sts, dtr cl in next st} 4 times, rep between [ ] 3 times, rep between { } 4 times, rep between [ ] twice, ch 3, join in top of beg dtr cl, fasten off.

Add inner leaves

Working in rem free lps of Rnd 1, attach willow in any dc, [ch 1, hdc in same st, ch 2, sc around post of hdc just made, dc in same st, sk next st of Rnd 1, sl st in next st] rep around, ending with sl st in base of beg ch, fasten off. (16 leaves)

First flower

With RS facing, attach hot pink around post of 3rd dc of 5-dc group at either end of Rnd 1, [ch 1, {sc, dc, ch 1, dc} around post of same dc, sl st around post of next dc] 3 times, ch 1, [sc, dc, ch 1, dc] around post of same dc, turn piece so that dc is on other side of Rnd 1 are on top, sl st around post of 4th free dc from first petal, rep between [ ] 4 times, ending with sl st in sc of first petal, fasten off.

First flower center

Attach hot pink to center of flower at bottom of any petal, [ch 2, sl st to center at base of next petal] 8 times, fasten off.

Second flower

Sk next 2 dc sts on Rnd 1 from 4th petal of first flower, attach hot pink around post of next dc, rep between [ ] of first flower 3 times, ch 1, [sc, dc, ch 1, dc] around post of same dc, turn piece to work on other side of Rnd 1, sl st around post of 6th free dc from 5th petal of first flower, rep between [ ] of first flower 4 times, ending with sl st in sc of first petal, fasten off.

Second flower center

With hot pink, rep first flower center.

Third flower

Attach hot pink around post of 3rd dc of 5-dc group at opposite end of Rnd 1, rep first flower and first flower center.

Rnd 3: Attach bisque in the first ch-3 sp of Rnd 2 at either end, beg dc cl in same sp, *ch 3, dc cl in same sp, [ch 3, {dc, cl, ch 3, dc cl} in next sp] 3 times *, [ch 3, dc cl in next sp] 5 times, rep from * to *, [ch 3, dc cl in next sp] 4 times, sl st in top of *Continued on page 157*

Continued on page 157

Deluxe Lap Robe

By Irene Stock

Skill Level: Beginner

Size: 30 inches across top; 40 inches long

Materials

✓ Red Heart Classic worsted weight yarn (3 oz per skein): 4 skeins each white #1 and pale rose #755

✓ Size I/9 crochet hook or size needed to obtain gauge

✓ Yarn needle

Delight an older friend with this thoughtful gift—a lap afghan with pockets for the hands and feet. It's just right for keeping warm!

Gauge

5 pattern reps = 4 inches; 10 pattern rows = 4 inches

Check gauge to save time.

Pattern Notes

Weave in loose ends as work progresses.

Join rnds with a sl st unless otherwise stated.

Carry yarn not in use loosely along side.

Change color in last sc of indicated row; pull next color through 2 lps of end sc.

Body

Row 1: With pale rose, ch 112, dc in 4th ch from hook, sk next 2 chs, sc in next ch, [ch 2, dc in same ch as sc, sk next 2 chs, sc in next ch] rep across, turn.

Row 2: Ch 2, dc in same st as beg ch-2, sc in ch-2 sp, [ch 2, dc in same sp, sc in next ch-2 sp] rep across, change to white in last sc, drop pale rose, turn.

Rows 3 & 4: Rep Row 2, at the end of Row 4, change to pale rose, drop white, turn.

Rows 5 & 6: Rep Row 2. Rep Rows 3–6 until 23 pale rose and 22 white stripes have been worked, fasten off.

Bottom Insert

With pale rose, ch 28, rep instructions for body until 8 pale rose and 7 white

stripes have been worked, fasten off.

Center first row of insert to first row of bottom; pin in place. Bring remainder of first row around sides of insert; pin in place and sew.

Edging

Rnd 1 (WS): Attach

white, work around in pattern, around entire piece, join in beg sc, turn.

Rnd 2 (RS): Work in pattern around, join in beg sc, fasten off.

Pockets

(Make 2)
Rep instructions for bottom insert until 5 pale rose

stripes and 4 white stripes have been completed, fasten off.

Edging

Rnds 1 & 2: Rep Rnds 1 and 2 of edging for body.

Ties

(Make 2)
With white, ch 101, sl st in

2nd ch from hook, sl st in each rem ch across, fasten off.

Tie knot in each end.

Fold tie in half; pull fold through lp 5 patterns from side and 2nd row from top; pull ends through lp and pull tight. ❖

Regency Floral Afghan

Continued from page 155

beg cl, fasten off.

Rnd 4: Attach hot pink in 2nd ch-3 sp from beg dc cl of Rnd 3, [beg dc cl, ch 3, dc cl] in same sp, [ch 3, dc cl in next ch-3 sp, ch 3, {dc cl, ch 3, dc cl} in next ch-3 sp] twice, {ch 3, dc cl in next sp} 6 times, rep between [ ] 3 times, rep between { } 7 times, ch 3, join in top of beg cl, fasten off.

Rnd 5: Attach bisque in first ch-3 sp of Rnd 4, [beg dc cl, ch 3, dc cl] in same sp, [[{ch 3, dc cl in next ch-3 sp} twice, ch 3, {dc cl, ch 3, dc cl} in next ch-3 sp] twice, †ch 3, dc cl in next sp †, rep between † 5 times, rep between [ ] 3 times, rep between † 8 times, ch 3, join in top of beg dc cl, fasten off.

Rnd 6: Attach loden in first ch-3 sp of Rnd 5, ch 1, {2 sc, ch 2, 2 sc} in same sp, [4 sc in each of next 3 ch-3 sps, {2 sc, ch 2, 2 sc} in next ch-3 sp] twice, {4 sc in next ch-3 sp} 6 times, rep between [ ] 3 times, {4

sc in next ch-3 sp} 9 times, join in beg sc.

Rnd 7: Sl st to first corner ch-2 sp, beg shell in same sp, †*sk 4 sts, **[sc, ch 1] twice in next st, sk 3 sts, shell in next st, sk 3 sts **, [sc, ch 1] twice in next st, sk 3 sts, shell in next corner ch-2 sp *, rep from * to *, sk 4 sts, rep from ** to ** 4 times, [sc, ch 1] twice in next st, sk 3 sts †, shell in next corner ch-2 sp, rep from † to †, join in 3rd ch of beg ch-4, fasten off.

Second Motif

Rnds 1–6: Rep Rnds 1–6 of first motif.

Rnd 7 (Joining): Work same as Rnd 7 of first motif except join shells on joining side as follows:

First corner shell: Work [{dc, ch 1} twice, dc, drop lp from hook, with WS of first motif facing, insert hook from right side of first motif through corresponding corner dc on first motif, draw dropped lp through, ch 1, dc in same corner sp on 2nd motif, ch 1];

Each shell across side: Work [dc, ch 1, {dc, drop lp from hook, insert hook from right side through corresponding dc of first motif, draw dropped lp through, ch 1} twice, dc, ch 1];

Last corner shell: Work dc, ch 1, dc, drop lp from hook and join to corresponding corner dc on first motif in same manner as before, complete rem of rnd same as for first motif.

Referring to diagram for placement, make and join 21 more motifs, working all joining sides same as for 2nd motif.

Tassels

(Make 10)

Cut 25 strands of loden, 12 inches long each. Holding all strands tog, tie separate length of yarn tightly around strands at center. Fold strands in half at tied point and tie a 14-inch length of yarn tightly around folded strands 1¼-inch below top. Using tying lengths at top of tassel, sew tassels securely to points on motifs across top and bottom ends of afghan. ❖

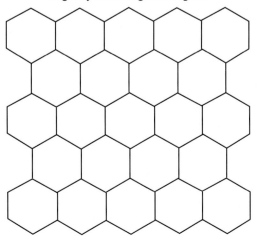

Regency Floral Afghan Diagram

Checks 'n' Cherries

By Daria McGuire for Women of Design

Skill Level: Beginner

Size: Fits boutique-style tissue box

Materials

✓ Bernat Berella "4" worsted weight yarn: 2 oz black #8994, 1½ oz white #8942, 1 oz scarlet #8933 and ½ oz deep sea green #8876

✓ Size H/8 crochet hook or size needed to obtain gauge

✓ Size G/6 crochet hook

✓ Safety pin or marker

✓ Yarn needle

Add to the delight of cherry cobblers and pies this cherry boutique tissue topper. The bright, three-dimensional cherries on each side of the design are a striking contrast to the black-and-white check pattern.

Gauge

9 sc and 9 sc rows = 2 inches

Check gauge to save time.

Pattern Notes

Weave in loose ends as work progresses.

Join rnds with a sl st unless otherwise stated.

To change color in dc, work dc with working color until 2 lps rem on hook, yo, with next color draw through rem 2 lps on hook to complete dc.

Work over yarn not in use with working color.

Ch 3 counts as first dc throughout.

Side

(Make 4)

Row 1: With hook size H and white, ch 22, dc in 4th ch from hook, dc in next 2 chs, changing to black in last dc made, [dc in each of next 4 chs, changing to white in 4th dc, dc in each of next 4 chs, changing to black in 4th dc] twice, turn. (20 dc)

Row 2: With black, ch 3, dc in each of next 3 dc, changing to white in last dc made, [dc in each of next 4 dc, changing to black in 4th dc, dc in each of next 4 dc, changing to white in 4th dc] twice, fasten off black, turn.

Row 3: With white, ch 3, dc in each dc across, turn. (20 dc)

Rows 4–7: Rep Row 3.

Row 8: Rep Row 3, changing to black in last dc, turn.

Row 9: Rep Row 2, do not fasten off black, turn.

Row 10: With white, ch 3, dc in each of next 3 dc, changing to black in 4th dc, [dc in each of next 4 dc, changing to white in 4th dc, dc in each of next 4 dc, changing to black in 4th dc] twice, fasten off white, do not fasten off black, turn.

Edging

Rnd 1: With hook size G, ch 1, sc evenly sp around entire outer edge, working 3 sc in each corner st, join in beg sc, fasten off.

Top

Row 1 (WS): With hook size H and black, ch 21, sc in 2nd ch from hook, sc in each rem ch across, turn. (20 sc)

Rows 2–8: Ch 1, sc in each sc across, turn.

Tissue opening, first side

Row 9: Ch 1, sc in each of next 5 sc, turn.

Row 10: Ch 1, sc in each of next 5 sc, fasten off, turn.

Tissue opening, second side

Row 9: Sk next 10 sc of Row 8 for tissue opening, attach black in next sc, ch 1, sc in same sc as beg ch-1, sc in next 4 sc, turn.

Row 10: Rep Row 10 of first half. (5 sc)

Row 11: With WS facing, attach black in first sc at outer edge, ch 1, sc in same st as beg ch, sc in each of next 4 sc, ch 10, sc in each of next 5 sc, turn.

Row 12: Ch 1, sc in each of next 5 sc, sc in each of next 10 chs, sc in each of next 5 sc, turn. (20 sc)

Rows 13–19: Ch 1, sc in each sc across, turn.

Edging

Rnd 1: With hook size G, ch 1, sc evenly sp around entire outer edge, working 3 sc in each corner, join in beg sc, fasten off.

Tissue opening trim

Rnd 1: With hook size G, attach black in tissue opening, ch 1, sc evenly sp around opening, join in beg sc, fasten off.

Cherry

(Make 12)

Note: Do not join rnds; mark first st of each rnd with safety pin or other

small marker.

Rnd 1: With hook size G and scarlet, ch 4, sl st to join to form a ring, ch 1, 6 sc in ring. (6 sc)

Rnd 2: Work 2 sc in each sc around. (12 sc)

Rnd 3: [Sc dec over next 2 sc] 6 times, leaving a length of yarn, fasten off.

Stuff cherry with yarn to desired firmness. Thread rem length of yarn through

top of Rnd 3; draw up tightly; secure.

Stem

With hook size G, attach deep sea green with a sl st in center top of cherry, ch 7, leaving a length of yarn, fasten off.

Leaf
(Make 8)

Row 1: With hook size G and deep sea green, ch 9,

sc in 2nd ch from hook, sc in next ch, hdc in next ch, dc in each of next 3 chs, hdc in next ch, sc in next ch, leaving a length of yarn, fasten off.

Finishing

Tack 3 cherry stems tog at top of stem; attach 2 leaves to opposite sides of stems at joining. Attach 1 cherry cl securely to center of side between 8th and

9th rows, leaving cherries and stems hanging freely. Rep for rem 3 sides.

With black yarn and yarn needle, whipstitch all 4 sides tog; sew top to sides.

With hook size G, attach black with sl st to any corner at top edge, ch 1, sc evenly sp around top edge, join in beg sc, fasten off.

Rep around lower edge. ❖

Christmas Spirit

Make the Christmas season extra-special by filling your home with festive crochet and by creating one-of-a-kind gifts for family and friends!

Holly Jolly Apron

By Laura Gebhardt

Skill Level: Beginner

Size: One size fits all

Materials

✓ Worsted weight cotton: 7 oz white, 3½ oz red, 1¼ oz green

✓ Size G/6 crochet hook or size needed to obtain gauge

✓ Yarn needle

Gauge

11 sts = 3 inches; 11 rows = 4 inches

Check gauge to save time.

Pattern Notes

Weave in loose ends as work progresses.

Join rnds with a sl st unless otherwise stated.

Ch 3 counts as first dc throughout.

Pattern Stitch

Picot (p): Ch 3, sl st in top of last st made.

Apron

Row 1: Beg at waist, with white, ch 82, dc in 4th ch from hook, dc in each rem ch across, turn. (80 dc)

Row 2: Ch 1, sc in each st across, turn.

Row 3: Ch 3, dc in each st across, turn.

Rows 4–25: Rep Rows 2 and 3.

Row 26: Rep Row 2.

Row 27: Ch 2, dc in next st (beg dec), dc in each st across to last 2 sts, dc dec over next 2 sts, turn. (78 dc)

Row 28: Ch 1, sc dec over next 2 sts, sc in each st across to last 2 sts, sc dec over next 2 sts, turn. (76 sc)

Rows 29–32: Rep Rows 27 and 28. (68 sts)

At the end of Row 32, fasten off.

Waistband

Row 1 (RS): Attach white in opposite side of foundation ch, ch 1, sc in same ch, sc in next ch, sc dec over next 2 chs, [sc in each of next 2 chs, sc dec over next 2 chs] rep across, turn. (60 sc)

Rows 2–5: Ch 1, sc in each sc across, turn. At the end of Row 5, fasten off.

Edging

Row 1 (RS): Attach white in side edge of Row 1 of apron, ch 1, sc in same st as beg ch, sc evenly sp down side edge working 3 sc to 2 rows, sc evenly sp across Row 32 of apron, sc evenly sp up opposite side edge of apron working 3 sc to 2 rows, fasten off. (164 sc)

Row 2 (RS): Attach red in first sc of previous row, ch 3, dc in same st, 2 dc in each sc, turn. (328 dc)

Row 3: Ch 3, dc in same st, [dc in next st, 2 dc in next st] rep across previous row, fasten off.

Row 4 (RS): Attach green in first dc of previous row, ch 1, sc in same dc, [ch 3, {yo, insert hook in last sc, yo, draw up a lp, yo, draw through 2 lps on hook} twice in same sc, yo, draw through all 3 lps on hook, sk next 2 dc, sc in next dc] rep across edge, fasten off.

Pocket

Row 1: Beg at bottom of pocket, with white, ch 17, sc in 2nd ch from hook, sc in each rem ch across, turn. (16 sc)

Rows 2 & 3: Ch 1, 2 sc in first sc, sc in each sc across to last sc, 2 sc in last sc, turn. (20 sc)

Rows 4–21: Ch 1, sc in each sc across, turn.

Row 22: Ch 1, sc evenly sp down side edge of pocket, sc across opposite side of foundation ch, sc evenly sp up opposite side edge of pocket, fasten off.

Holly leaf

(Make 2)

Rnd 1 (RS): With green, ch 10, sc in 2nd ch from hook, hdc in next ch, [dc in next ch, hdc in each of next 2 chs] twice, 3 sc in last ch, working on opposite side of foundation ch, [hdc in each of next 2 chs, dc in next ch] twice, hdc in next ch, 2 sc in same ch as beg sc, join in beg sc. (20 sts)

Rnd 2: Ch 1, sc in same st as beg ch, sc in next hdc, [sc, p] in next dc, sc in each of next 2 hdc, [sc, p] in next dc, sc in next 3 sts, [sc, p] in next sc, sc in each of next 3 sts, [sc, p] in next dc, sc in each of next 2 hdc, [sc, p] in next dc, sc in next 2 sts, 3 sc in next sc, join in beg sc, leaving a length of yarn, fasten off.

Berry

(Make 3)

Rnd 1: With red, ch 2, 6 sc in 2nd ch from hook, join in beg sc, leaving a length of yarn, fasten off.

Sew leaves and berries to RS of pocket. Sew pocket to apron in desired position.

Tie

(Make 2)

Row 1 (RS): Attach white in side edge of waistband, ch 1, working in ends of rows, sc in each row across, turn. (5 sc)

Row 2: Ch 1, sc in each sc across, turn.

Continued on page 169

Christmas Candy Afghan

By Diane Poellot

Skill Level: Intermediate

Size: 49 x 66 inches

Materials

✓ Coats & Clark Red Heart Classic worsted weight yarn (3½ oz per skein): 55 oz cherry red #912 and 20 oz eggshell #111

✓ Size J/10 crochet hook or size needed to obtain gauge

✓ Yarn needle

The circular blocks of this fascinating afghan look just like Christmas peppermints!

Gauge

Motif = 8 inches in diameter; Rnd 1 = 1¼ inches in diameter

Check gauge to save time.

Pattern Notes

Weave in loose ends as work progresses.

Join rnds with a sl st unless otherwise stated.

Ch 3 counts as first dc throughout.

Pattern Stitch

Braid lp: Ch 8, sl st in top of last st made.

Motif

(Make 56)

Rnd 1 (RS): With eggshell, ch 5, sl st to join to form a ring, ch 3, dc in ring, [braid lp, 2 dc in ring] 7 times, join in top of beg ch-3, fasten off. (16 dc; 8 braid lps)

Rnd 2: Attach cherry red with sc between any 2 dc sts, ch 2, dc in same sp, braid lp, dc in same sp, [{braid lp, 2 dc, braid lp, dc} in sp between next 2 dc] rep around, join in top of beg ch-2. (16 braid lps)

Rnd 3: Sl st into next dc, ch 3, dc in same st, [braid lp, sk next dc, 2 dc in next dc] rep around, braid lp, join in top of beg ch-3. (16 braid lps)

Rnd 4: Ch 3, dc in same st as beg ch, [2 dc in next st, braid lp, 2 dc in next st] rep around, join in top of beg ch-3, fasten off. (16 braid lps)

Rnd 5: Attach eggshell in 3rd dc of any 4-dc group, ch 1, sc in same sc as beg ch, sc in next 3 sc, [braid lp, sc in next 4 dc] rep around, ending with braid lp, leaving a length of yarn for braid lp joining, fasten off.

Rnd 6: Attach cherry red with sc in any sc, sc in next sc, [ch 10, sc in each of next 2 sc] rep around, leaving a length of yarn for braid lp joining, fasten off.

Braiding Loops

Starting at center braid lps of Rnds 1–4 from center outward, [insert hook in eggshell lp, {insert hook in lp, draw lp through lp on hook} 3 times, remove hook] 8 times. Working on rem cherry red lps between, [insert hook in lp of Rnd 2, {insert hook in next lp, draw lp through lp on hook} twice, remove hook] 8 times.

Note: Leave all ch-10 lps of Rnd 6 unworked.

Continued on page 169

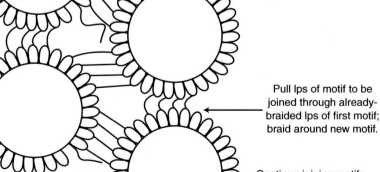

Work braid lp join at end of each motif.

Joining Diagram

Pull lps of motif to be joined through already-braided lps of first motif; braid around new motif.

Continue joining motifs until afghan is 7 x 8 motifs.

Santa Air Freshener

By Beverly Mewhorter

Skill Level: Beginner

Size: 9½ inches tall

Materials

✓ Coats & Clark Red Heart Classic worsted weight yarn: 1½ oz white #1, 1 oz cherry red #912, small amount paddy green #686

✓ Size G/6 crochet hook or size needed to obtain gauge

✓ 5½-inch air-freshener doll

✓ 12mm gold jingle bell

✓ 1⅛-inch plastic ring

✓ 12 inches ¼-inch-wide red ribbon

✓ Hot-glue gun

✓ Yarn needle

With his stocking cap and miniature holiday wreath, this jolly Santa will brighten your decor and keep the air fresh, too!

Gauge

4 sc = 1 inch

Check gauge to save time.

Pattern Notes

Weave in loose ends as work progresses.

Join rnds with a sl st unless otherwise stated.

Coat

Row 1: With cherry red, ch 19, sc in 2nd ch from hook, sc in each of next 3 chs, ch 5, sk next 2 chs, sc in each of next 6 chs, ch 5, sk next 2 chs, sc in each of next 4 chs, turn. (14 sc; 2 ch-5 sps)

Row 2: Ch 1, sc in each sc and each ch across, turn. (24 sc)

Row 3: Ch 1, [sc dec over next 2 sc] rep across, fasten off. (12 sc)

Row 4: Attach cherry red in opposite side of foundation ch, ch 1, sc in each ch across, turn. (18 sc)

Row 5: Ch 1, [sc in each of next 2 sc, 2 sc in next sc] rep across, turn. (24 sc)

Row 6: Ch 1, sc in each sc across, turn.

Rows 7 & 8: Rep Row 6.

Row 9: Ch 1, [sc in each of next 3 sc, 2 sc in next sc] rep across, turn. (30 sc)

Rows 10–23: Rep Row 6. At the end of Row 23, fasten off.

Ruffle edging

Attach white in last sc of Row 23, ch 1, 6 sc in same sc as beg ch, work 6 sc in each st across row, working up side edge of rows, work 6 sc in each row to neckline, work 6 sc in each of 12 sc across neckline, fasten off.

Sleeve

(Make 2)

Rnd 1: With cherry red, ch 10, sl st to join to form a ring, ch 1, sc in each ch around, join in beg sc. (10 sc)

Rnds 2–7: Ch 1, sc in each sc around, join in beg sc. At the end of Rnd 7, fasten off.

Rnd 8: Attach white in first sc of previous rnd, ch 1, 6 sc in same st as beg ch, work 6 sc in each rem sc around, join in beg sc, fasten off.

Sew sleeves into armhole openings of coat. Place coat on doll, sew front opening closed.

Hat

Rnd 1: With cherry red, ch 24, sl st to join to form a ring, ch 1, sc in each ch around, join in beg sc. (24 sc)

Rnd 2: Ch 1, sc in each sc around, join in beg sc.

Rnd 3: Rep Rnd 2.

Rnd 4: Ch 1, [sc in next

Happy Holidays Pin

By Gloria Graham

Skill Level: Beginner

Size: 1¾ inches in diameter

Materials

✓ Crochet cotton size 10: 7 yds green

✓ Size 9 steel crochet hook or size needed to obtain gauge

✓ 1-inch plastic ring

✓ ¾-inch pin back

✓ 2 (½-inch) gold bells

✓ 9 frosted rose E beads

✓ 6mm baby's breath bead

✓ Small red bow

✓ Craft glue

Now you can be inspired by holiday cheer all season long! Make this dainty wreath as an elegant pin, or use it as a super topper for gift-wrapped packages.

ending last rep at **, join in top of beg ch-3. (8 shells; 8 sc)

Rnd 4: Ch 1, sc in joining, sc in next dc, *[sc, ch 2, sc] in ch-2 sp of shell, sc in each of next 2 dc, ch 2 **, sc in each of next 2 dc, rep from * around, ending last rep at **, join in beg sc, fasten off.

Gauge

3 sc = ¼ inch
Check gauge to save time.

Pattern Notes

Weave in loose ends as work progresses.
Join rnds with a sl st unless otherwise stated.

Wreath

Rnd 1 (RS): Attach green cotton to plastic ring, ch 1, work 48 sc over ring, join in beg sc. (48 sc)

Rnd 2: Ch 1, sc in first sc, ch 2, sk next 2 sc, [sc in next sc, ch 2, sk next 2 sc]

15 times, join in beg sc. (16 ch-2 sps)

Rnd 3: Sl st into ch-2 sp, [ch 3, 1 dc, ch 2, 2 dc] in same ch-2 sp, *ch 2, sc in next ch-2 sp, ch 2 **, [2 dc, ch 2, 2 dc] in next ch-2 sp, rep from * around,

Finishing

Glue bells, bow and 6mm bead to center front bottom of wreath. Glue 3 frosted beads in a group evenly sp at each side and center top of wreath. Glue pin back to back top of wreath. ★

Santa Air Freshener

sc, sc dec over next 2 sc] rep around, join in beg sc. (16 sc)

Rnds 5 & 6: Rep Rnd 2.

Rnd 7: Ch 1, [sc in next sc, sc dec over next 2 sc] rep around, sc in last sc, join in beg sc. (11 sc)

Rnds 8–11: Rep Rnd 2.

Rnd 12: Ch 1, [sc dec over next 2 sc] 5 times, sc in next sc, join in beg sc. (6 sc)

Rnd 13: Ch 1, [sc dec over next 2 sc] 3 times, join in beg sc, fasten off. (3 sc)

Ruffle

Attach white in opposite side of foundation ch, ch 1, 6 sc in each ch around, join in beg sc, fasten off.

Attach jingle bell to Rnd 13 of hat; tack point of hat to side edge. Place hat on doll.

Wreath

Rnd 1: Attach paddy green to plastic ring, ch 1, work 18 sc over ring, join in beg sc.

Rnd 2: Ch 1, sc in same sc as beg ch, ch 4, [sc in next sc, ch 4] rep around, join in beg sc, fasten off.

Tie ribbon in a bow at top of wreath; place wreath in doll's hand and secure with glue. ★

String of Lights Garland

By Gloria Graham

Skill Level: Beginner

Size: 1¼ x 2½ inches

Materials

- ✓ Crochet cotton size 10: 24 yds gray, 20 yds each red, blue, green, gold, orange and white
- ✓ Size 7 steel crochet hook or size needed to obtain gauge
- ✓ 12 (8mm) jump rings
- ✓ 12 (6mm) jump rings
- ✓ 12 (1½-inch) eye pins
- ✓ Gold craft cord
- ✓ Craft glue
- ✓ Fiberfill
- ✓ Tapestry needle

Gauge

9 hdc = 1 inch
Check gauge to save time.

Pattern Notes

Weave in loose ends as work progresses.

Just like real Christmas lights, these cheerful bulbs have a glowing beauty all their own! Use them to decorate a tree, or string them across a doorway or mantel.

Join rnds with a sl st unless otherwise stated.

Beg each rnd with ch 2 to count as first hdc, pattern will simply indicate hdc.

Materials listed will make a set of 12 lights.

Each bulb requires 10 yards bulb color and 2 yards gray.

Bulb

Rnd 1 (RS): Starting at tip of bulb with bulb color, ch 3, 5 hdc in 3rd ch from hook, join in top of beg ch. (6 hdc)

Rnd 2: Work 2 hdc in each hdc around, join in top of beg ch-2. (12 hdc)

Rnd 3: Hdc in each hdc around, join in top of beg ch-2.

Rnd 4: [Hdc in each of next 3 hdc, 2 hdc in next hdc] rep around, join in top of beg ch-2. (15 hdc)

Rnd 5: [Hdc in each of next 4 hdc, 2 hdc in next hdc] rep around, join in top of beg ch-2. (18 hdc)

Rnd 6: [2 hdc in next st, hdc in each of next 2 hdc] 6 times, join in top of beg ch-2. (24 hdc)

Rnd 7: [2 hdc in next hdc,

Holly Jolly Apron

Continued from page 163

Row 3: Ch 1, sc dec over next 2 sc, sc in next sc, sc dec over next 2 sc, turn. (3 sc)

Row 4: Rep Row 2.

Row 5: Ch 1, sc dec over next 2 sc, sc in next sc, turn. (2 sc)

Row 6: Rep Row 2.

Row 7: Ch 1, sc dec over next 2 sc, ch 130, sl st in 2nd ch from hook, sl st in each rem ch across, sl st into last sc dec, fasten off. ★

Christmas Candy Afghan

Continued from page 164

Insert hook in first cherry red lp of Rnd 4 after fasten-off point of Rnd 5, [insert hook in next eggshell lp, draw eggshell lp through cherry lp of hook, insert hook in next cherry red lp, draw through eggshell lp on hook] rep around, remove hook.

With rem length of yarn, using Figs. 1 and 2 as a guide, weave last lp as indicated.

Fig. 1
Braid Lp joining
Beg Point of Braid
Lp Joining

First Sc   Last Sc

Fig. 2
To join motifs, pull lps from 2nd motif as shown; braid as usual.

First Sc   Last Sc

Joining

Using joining diagram as a guide, braid all lps around first motif of Rnd 6 (ch-10 lps). To join next motif, pull 4 unbraid lps from 2nd motif through 4 braid lps of first motif; braid rem lps around. Continue joining motifs in this manner (4 lps for each join) working braid lp joining on each motif as it is joined.

Edging

Rnd 1: Working around entire outer edge, attach eggshell in any sc, ch 1, sc in same st, sc in next 3 sc, [braid lp, sc in next 4 sc] rep around, join in beg sc, fasten off.

Rnd 2: Attach cherry red with sc in 3rd sc of previous rnd, sc in next sc, [braid lp, sc in next 4 sc] rep around (braid lps should be positioned in center between previous rnd of braid lps), ending with sc in last 2 sc, ch 8, leaving a length of yarn, fasten off.

Beg in first eggshell lp next to last cherry red ending, braid lps around entire outer edge alternating colors, work braid lp joining, fasten off. ★

---

hdc in each of next 5 hdc] 4 times, join in top of beg ch-2. (28 hdc)

Rnd 8: Rep Rnd 3.

Rnd 9: [2 hdc in next hdc, hdc in each of next 6 hdc] 4 times, join in top of beg ch-2. (32 hdc)

Rnd 10: Rep Rnd 3.

Rnd 11: [Hdc in each of next 2 hdc, hdc dec over next 2 hdc] 8 times, join in top of beg ch-2. (24 hdc)

Rnd 12: [Hdc in each of next 2 hdc, hdc dec over next 2 hdc] 6 times, join in top of beg ch-2. (18 hdc)

Rnd 13: [Hdc in next hdc, hdc dec over next 2 sts] 6 times, join in top of beg ch-2, fasten off.

Stuff firmly with fiberfill.

Rnd 14: Attach gray with sl st in any hdc of Rnd 13,

hdc in each st around, join in top of beg ch-2. (12 hdc)

Rnds 15–17: Ch 1, sc in each st around, join in beg sc.

At the end of Rnd 17, leaving a length of gray, fasten off. Stuff firmly with fiberfill. Weave rem length through sts, knot to secure, fasten off.

Finishing

Twisting sideways, open 6mm jump ring, slide on eye pin and 8mm jump ring; close 6mm jump ring. Dot glue on eye pin and insert into gray end of bulb; allow to dry completely. String bulbs on gold cord through 8mm jump ring; spacing bulbs 5 inches apart, tie knot over each jump ring to secure bulb on cord. ★

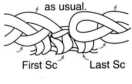

Christmas Spirit • 169

Pineapple Teardrop Ornament

By Gloria Graham

Skill Level: Intermediate

Size: 3½ x 7½ inches

Materials

- ✓ Crochet cotton size 10: 55 yds white
- ✓ Size 7 steel crochet hook or size needed to obtain gauge
- ✓ 1 yd 1½-inch-wide sheer white wire-edged ribbon
- ✓ 10mm x 20mm pearl drop bead with cap
- ✓ 4mm jump ring
- ✓ Large gold bell cap
- ✓ 8-inch length gold thread
- ✓ 2mm prestrung white pearl beads
- ✓ Assortment small flowers
- ✓ Small balloon
- ✓ Fabric stiffener
- ✓ Poster board
- ✓ Tape
- ✓ Plastic wrap
- ✓ Craft glue

Gauge

3 shell rnds = 1 inch
Check gauge to save time.

Pattern Notes

Weave in loose ends as work progresses.

Join rnds with a sl st unless otherwise stated.

Ch 3 counts as first dc throughout; ch 3 replaces first dc of a rnd.

Ch 2 counts as first hdc throughout; ch 2 replaces first hdc of a rnd.

When a rnd begs with a dc, simply ch 3, as the same when a rnd begs with a hdc, simply ch 2.

Pattern Stitches

Shell: [2 dc, ch 2, 2 dc] in indicated st.

Double shell: [2 dc, ch 3] twice and 2 dc in indicated st.

V-st: [Dc, ch 2, dc] in indicated st.

Ornament

Rnd 1 (RS): Ch 18, sl st to join to form a ring, ch 1, sc in each ch around, join in beg sc. (18 sc)

Rnd 2: Ch 1, [2 sc in next sc, sc in each of next 2 sc] 6 times, join in beg sc. (24 sc)

Rnd 3: [2 dc in next st, ch 2, sk next st] rep around, join in beg dc. (24 dc, 24 ch-2 sps)

Rnd 4: Sl st into ch-2 sp, shell in each ch-2 sp around, join in beg dc. (12 shells)

Rnd 5: [Shell in next shell, ch 1, {2 dc, ch 4, 2 dc} in next ch-2 sp of shell, ch 1] 6 times, join in beg dc.

Rnd 6: [Shell in next shell, ch 1, 6 tr in next ch-4 sp, ch 1] rep around, join in beg dc. (6 shells; 6 pineapple bases)

Rnd 7: [Shell in next shell, {tr in next tr, ch 1} 5 times,

tr in next tr] rep around, join in top of beg dc.

Rnd 8: [Shell in next shell, {sc in next tr, ch 3} 5 times, sc in next tr] rep around, join in beg dc.

Rnd 9: [Shell in next shell, {sc in next ch-3 sp, ch 3} 4 times, sc in next ch-3 sp] rep around, join in top of beg dc.

Rnd 10: [Shell in next shell, {sc in next ch-3 sp, ch 3} 3 times, sc in next ch-3 sp] rep around, join in top of beg dc.

Rnd 11: [Shell in next shell, ch 1, {sc in next ch-3 sp, ch 3} twice, sc in next ch-3 sp, ch 1] rep around, join in top of beg dc.

Rnd 12: [Double shell in next shell, ch 2, sc in next ch-3 sp, ch 3, sc in next

This year, add some Victorian elegance to your holiday decor. This delicate ornament will create a sense of perfect beauty anywhere it's displayed.

ch-3 sp, ch 2] rep around, join in top of beg dc.

Rnd 13: [{Shell in ch-2 sp of shell} twice, ch 4, sc in next ch-3 sp, ch 4] rep around, join in top of beg dc.

Rnd 14: [{Shell in next shell} twice, {tr, ch 2, tr} in next sc] rep around, join in top of beg dc.

Rnd 15: [Shell in next shell, dc in sp between shells, shell in next shell, sc in next ch-2 sp] rep around, join in top of beg dc.

Rnd 16: [Shell in next shell, V-st in single dc between shells, shell in next shell] rep around, join in top of beg dc. (12 shells; 6 V-sts)

Rnd 17: [Dc in ch-2 sp of shell, shell in V-st, dc in next ch-2 sp of shell] rep around, join in beg dc. (6 shells)

Rnd 18: Sl st into ch-2 sp of shell, [shell in ch-2 sp of shell, V-st between 2 single dc sts] rep around, join in top of beg ch-3. (6 shells; 6 V-sts)

Rnds 19 & 20: [Shell in next shell, V-st in next V-st] rep around, join in top of beg dc.

Rnd 21: [Shell in next shell, dc in ch-2 sp of V-st] rep around, join in top of beg dc.

Rnd 22: [Shell over next shell] rep around, join in beg dc.

Rnd 23: [Shell in next shell, V-st in next shell] rep around, join in top of beg dc.

Rnd 24: [Shell in next shell, dc in ch-2 sp of V-st] rep around, join in top of beg dc.

Rnd 25: [3 dc in ch-2 sp of shell, dc in single dc worked in V-st] rep around, join in top of beg dc. (12 dc)

Rnd 26: [Dc dec over next 2 dc, dc in next dc] 4 times, join in top of beg dc. (8 dc)

Rnd 27: [Dc dec over next 2 dc] 4 times, join in top of beg dc, fasten off. (4 dc)

Finishing

Form a cone with poster board that conforms to the pointed shape of ornament; cover cone with plastic wrap and insert into ornament. Insert balloon through Rnd 1 opening; inflate balloon and secure. Saturate ornament with fabric stiffener; let dry completely. Pop balloon and remove cone.

Glue gold bell cap to bottom of ornament; attach pearl drop bead to cap with jump ring.

Form a multiloop bow with ribbon. Using photo as a guide, decorate top with flowers and pearls. Secure bow at center top of ornament. For hanging lp, attach gold thread to center top. ★

Pineapple Bell Ornament

By Gloria Graham

Skill Level: Beginner

Size: 2¼ x 2½ inches

Materials

✓ Crochet cotton size 10: 22 yds white

✓ Size 7 steel crochet hook or size needed to obtain gauge

✓ 2mm prestrung white pearl beads

✓ Assorted small flowers

✓ 8-inch length gold thread

✓ 2½-inch foam bell form

✓ Plastic wrap

✓ Fabric stiffener

✓ Craft glue

Gauge

2 shell rnds = ½ inch

Check gauge to save time.

Pattern Notes

Weave in loose ends as work progresses.

Join rnds with a sl st unless otherwise stated.

Ch 3 counts as first dc throughout.

Pattern Stitches

Shell: [2 dc, ch 2, 2 dc] in indicated st.

Beg shell: [Ch 3, dc, ch 2, 2 dc] in indicated st.

Picot (p): Ch 3, sl st in 3rd ch from hook.

Bell

Rnd 1 (RS): With white, ch 8, sl st to join to form a ring, ch 1, 12 sc in ring, join in beg sc. (12 sc)

Rnd 2: Ch 3, dc in next st, ch 2, [dc in each of next 2 sts, ch 2] rep around, join in top of beg ch-3.

Rnd 3: Sl st into ch-2 sp, beg shell in ch-2 sp, [shell in next ch-2 sp] rep around, join in top of beg ch-3. (6 shells)

Rnd 4: Sl st into ch-2 sp of shell, beg shell in same ch-2 sp, 6 dc in next ch-2 sp, [shell in next ch-2 sp, 6 dc in next ch-2 sp] rep around, join in top of beg ch-3. (3 shells; 3 pineapple bases)

Rnd 5: Sl st into ch-2 sp, beg shell in same ch-2 sp, *ch 2, [dc in next dc of pineapple base, ch 1] 5 times, dc in next dc of pineapple, ch 2 **, shell in ch-2 sp of shell, rep from * around, ending last rep at **, join in top of beg ch-3.

Rnd 6: Sl st into ch-2 sp, beg shell in same ch-2 sp, *[sc in next dc of pineapple, ch 3] 5 times, sc in next dc of pineapple **, shell in next shell, rep from * around, ending last rep at **, join in top of beg ch-3.

Rnd 7: Sl st into ch-2 sp, beg shell in same ch-2 sp, *[sc in next ch-3 sp, ch 3] 4 times, sc in next ch-3 sp **, shell in next shell, rep from * around, ending last rep at **, join in top of beg ch-3.

Rnd 8: Sl st into ch-2 sp, beg shell in same ch-2 sp, *[sc in next ch-3 sp, ch 3] 3 times, sc in next ch-3 sp **, shell in next shell, rep from * around, ending last rep at **, join in top of beg ch-3.

Rnd 9: Sl st into ch-2 sp, beg shell in ch-2 sp, *ch 2, [sc in next ch-3 sp, ch 3] twice, sc in next ch-3 sp, ch 2 **, shell in next shell, rep from * around, ending last rep at **, join in top of beg ch-3.

Rnd 10: Sl st into ch-2 sp, beg shell in ch-2 sp, *ch 3, [sc in next ch-3 sp, ch 3] twice **, shell in next shell, rep from * around, ending last rep at **, join in top of beg ch-3.

Continued on page 176

This dainty little bell will look so nice on your tree you'll want to make a whole tree's worth of them!

Golden Angel Ornament

By Gloria Graham

Skill Level: Beginner

Size: 3½ inches tall

Materials

- ✓ Crochet cotton size 20: 25 yds white
- ✓ Size 9 steel crochet hook or size needed to obtain gauge
- ✓ 20mm x 25mm drop crystal with cap
- ✓ 15mm 3-ring crown (collar)
- ✓ 20mm gold filigree (halo)
- ✓ 20mm gold bead cap
- ✓ 2 (8mm) faceted crystal beads
- ✓ 2 x 2½ inches gold filigree wings
- ✓ 26 (2.5mm) gold beads
- ✓ 1¼-inch white rose with flat bow
- ✓ 8-inch length 2 plies gold embroidery floss
- ✓ Fabric stiffener
- ✓ Craft glue
- ✓ Poster board
- ✓ Tape
- ✓ Plastic wrap

With her lovely white dress and sparkling gold accents, this tiny angel harkens back to "days of yore."

Gauge

Tr shell = ⅜ inch

Check gauge to save time.

Pattern Notes

Weave in loose ends as work progresses.

Join rnds with a sl st unless otherwise stated.

Pattern Stitches

Shell: [2 tr, ch 2, 2 tr] in indicated st.

3-tr cl: *Yo hook twice, insert hook in indicated st, yo, draw up a lp, [yo, draw through 2 lps on hook] twice, rep from * twice, yo, draw through all 4 lps on hook.

Beg 3-tr cl: Ch 3 (counts as first tr, *yo hook twice, insert hook in indicated st, yo, draw up a lp, [yo, draw through 2 lps on hook] twice, rep from * once, yo, draw through all 3 lps on hook.

Picot (p): Ch 3, sl st in top of dc.

Dress

Rnd 1 (RS): With white, ch 10, sl st to join to form a ring, ch 3 (counts as first dc throughout), 15 dc in ring, join in top of beg ch-3. (16 dc)

Rnd 2: Beg 3-tr cl in first st, ch 2, sk next st, [3-tr cl in next st, ch 2, sk next st] rep around, join in top of beg cl. (8 cl; 8 ch-2 sps)

Rnd 3: Sl st into ch-2 sp, [beg 3-tr cl, ch 2, 3-tr cl] in same ch-2 sp, [3-tr cl, ch 2, 3-tr cl] in each rem

Continued on page 176

Natural Star Ornaments

By Katherine Eng

Skill Level: Beginner

Size: 3½–4 inches

Materials

- ✓ Lion Brand Kitchen cotton: ½ oz natural #098 each ornament
- ✓ Size E/4 crochet hook or size needed to obtain gauge
- ✓ 12mm rounded pearl shank button each ornament
- ✓ Sewing needle and thread
- ✓ Yarn needle

This trio of all-cotton stars will add beauty to your Christmas tree and shine with a perfect, natural light, befitting the season.

Gauge

Rnd 1 = 1¾ inches

Check gauge to save time.

Pattern Notes

Weave in loose ends as work progresses.

Join rnds with a sl st unless otherwise stated.

Ch 3 counts as first dc throughout.

Pattern Stitch

Shell: [3 dc, ch 2, 3 dc] in indicated st.

Back

Rnd 1 (RS): Ch 4, sl st to join to form a ring, ch 3, 2 dc in ring, ch 2, [3 dc in ring, ch 2] 4 times, join in top of beg ch-3, sl st in next dc.

Rnd 2: Ch 1, sc in same dc, [shell in next ch-2 sp, sc in center dc of next 3-dc group] 4 times, shell in next ch-2 sp, join in beg sc, fasten off.

Front

Rnds 1 & 2: Rep Rnds 1 and 2 of back, do not fasten off.

Joining

Rnd 3: Holding WS of front and back tog and matching sts, sl st through both thicknesses of sc, *ch 3, sk next 2 dc, sc in next dc, ch 2, [sc, ch 3, sc] in next ch-2 sp, ch 2, sc in next dc, ch 3, sk next 2 dc **, sl st in next sc, rep from * around, working [sl st, ch 30, sl st] for hanging lp in any sc between shells, ending last rep at **, fasten off.

Sew button to center front of Rnd 1. ★

Poinsettia Plaid Wreath

By Sue Childress

Skill Level: Beginner

Size: 12 inches in diameter

Materials

✓ Schachenmayr Nomotta Catania sport weight cotton (50 grams per ball): 1 ball each yellow, red and green

✓ Size D/3 crochet hook or size needed to obtain gauge

✓ 12-inch chenille stem

✓ 12-inch extruded-foam wreath form

✓ 5 yds 2½-inch-wide plaid wire-edged ribbon

✓ 6 (30mm) round acrylic crystal ornaments

✓ Gold embroidery floss

✓ Glue

✓ Yarn needle

Greet your guests in holiday style! Bright, cheerful poinsettias combine with Christmas tartan fabric for a wonderful festive accent!

Gauge

Rnds 1 and 2 of poinsettia = 2¼ inches in diameter

Check gauge to save time.

Pattern Notes

Weave in loose ends as work progresses.

Join rnds with a sl st unless otherwise stated.

Pattern Stitches

Beg pc: Ch 2, 4 dc in indicated st, remove hook, insert hook in top of beg ch-2, pick up dropped lp and draw through st on hook.

Popcorn (pc): 5 dc in indicated st, remove hook, insert hook in first dc of 5-dc group, pick up dropped lp, draw through st on hook.

Poinsettia

(Make 5)

Rnd 1 (RS): With yellow, ch 5, sl st to join to form a ring, beg pc in ring, ch 2, [pc in ring, ch 2] 4 times, join in top of beg pc. (5 pc; 5 ch-2 sps)

Rnd 2: Sl st into ch-2 sp, [beg pc, ch 2, pc, ch 2] in same ch-2 sp, [pc, ch 2] twice in each rem ch-2 sp around, join in top of beg pc, fasten off. (10 pc; 10 ch-2 sps)

Rnd 3: Attach red in any ch-2 sp, [ch 2 (counts as first hdc), hdc, dc, 2 tr, 3 dtr, 2 tr, dc, 2 hdc] in same ch-2 sp, [2 hdc, dc, 2 tr, 3 dtr, 2 tr, dc, 2 hdc] in each rem ch-2 sp around, join in top of beg ch-2. (10 petals)

Rnd 4: Ch 1, [sc, ch 3, sc] in first st of petal, *[sc in next st of petal, {sc, ch 3, sc} in next st of petal] 6 times, rep from * around, join in beg sc, fasten off.

Leaf
(Make 10)

Rnd 1 (RS): With green, ch 11, 3 tr in 5th ch from hook, tr in each of next 2 chs, dc in each of next 3 chs, 6 hdc in next ch, working on opposite side of foundation ch, dc in each of next 3 chs, tr in each of next 2 chs, 4 tr in same ch as beg tr sts, join in top of ch-4.

Rnd 2: Ch 1, [sc, ch 3, sc] in same st as beg ch, [sc in next st, {sc, ch 3, sc} in next st] rep around, join in beg sc, fasten off.

Finishing
Cover wreath with ribbon using glue to secure as work progresses. Make a bow and attach to wreath with chenille stem, leaving enough stem to form a hanging lp. Glue flowers and leaves as desired to wreath. Cut six lengths of gold embroidery floss; string one acrylic ornament on each strand and tie strands tog to make a cluster. Attach to chenille stem under bow. ★

Pineapple Bell Ornament
Continued from page 172

Rnd 11: Sl st into ch-2 sp of shell, ch 3, dc, ch 2, [2 dc, ch 3] twice in same ch-2 sp, *sk next ch-3 sp, [2 dc, ch 2] 3 times in next ch-3 sp, sk next ch-3 sp **, [2 dc, ch 2] 3 times in next ch-2 sp of shell, rep from * around, ending last rep at **, join in top of beg ch-3.

Rnd 12: Sl st into ch-2 sp, beg shell in same ch-2 sp, shell in next ch-2 sp, sk next ch sp, [{shell in next ch-2 sp} twice, sk next ch sp] rep around, join in top of beg ch-3.

Rnd 13: Ch 1, sc in each dc around, [sc, p, sc] in each ch-2 sp, join in beg sc, fasten off.

Finishing
Cover foam bell form with plastic wrap. Saturate crocheted bell with fabric stiffener and place over bell form. Allow to dry completely.

Glue flowers to center top of bell. Weave pearl beads, forming lps as desired, around upper portion of bell.

For hanging lp, attach gold thread to top of bell. ★

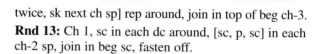

Golden Angel Ornament
Continued from page 173

ch-2 sp around, join in top of beg cl. (16 cl; 8 ch-2 sps)

Rnd 4: Ch 1, [sc in top of cl, 2 sc in ch-2 sp] rep around, join in beg sc. (32 sc)

Rnd 5: Ch 1, [sc in each of next 3 sc, ch 2, sk next sc] rep around, join in beg sc. (24 sc; 8 ch-2 sps)

Rnd 6: Sl st into ch-2 sp, [ch 4, tr, ch 2, 2 tr] in same ch-2 sp, shell in each rem ch-2 sp around, join in top of beg ch-4. (8 shells)

Rnd 7: Sl st into ch-2 sp, ch 4 (counts as first tr throughout), 5 tr in same ch-2 sp, [6 tr in next ch-2 sp] rep around, join in top of beg ch-4. (48 tr)

Rnd 8: Beg 3-tr cl over next 3 tr, ch 3, [3-tr cl over next 3 tr, ch 3] rep around, join in top of beg cl. (16 cl; 16 ch-3 sps)

Rnd 9: Ch 1, [sc in top of cl, 3 sc in next ch-3 sp] rep around, join in beg sc. (64 sc)

Rnd 10: Rep Rnd 5.

Rnd 11: Sl st into ch-2 sp, ch 1, [{sc, dc, p, sc} in ch-2 sp, ch 1, sk next sc, sc in next sc, ch 1] rep around, join in beg sc, fasten off.

Sleeve
(Make 2)

Rnd 1: With white, ch 5, 9 tr in 5th ch from hook, join in top of beg ch-5. (10 tr)

Rnd 2: Rep Rnd 2 of dress. (5 cl; 5 ch-2 sps)

Rnd 3: Sl st into next ch-2 sp, ch 4, 2 tr in same ch-2 sp, [3 tr in next ch-2 sp] rep around, join in top of beg ch-4. (15 tr)

Rnd 4: Ch 1, 2 sc in first tr, sc in each of next 14 tr, join in beg sc. (16 sc)

Rnd 5: Rep Rnd 5 of dress.

Rnd 6: Rep Rnd 11 of dress.

Finishing
Form a poster board cone shape that fits inside of dress; cover form with plastic wrap.

Sew sleeves to opposite sides of Rnd 1 of dress.

Saturate dress with fabric stiffener and place over form shaping sleeves in cone shape. Allow to dry completely; remove form.

Glue gold bead cap to top of dress; glue filigree halo over cap on drop crystal; glue drop crystal on top of gold bead cap. Attach gold embroidery floss to top for hanging lp. Glue 7 gold beads to each sleeve as shown and 12 beads around bottom of dress.

Glue wings to back of dress and rose to center front bodice. ★

Baby Angel Ornament

By Beverly Mewhorter

Skill Level: Beginner

Size: 4 inches tall

Materials

✓ Worsted weight yarn: Small amounts white and peach, scrap of black

✓ Size G/6 crochet hook or size needed to obtain gauge

✓ 2 (4mm) black cabochons

✓ Small amount yellow curly hair

✓ Red ribbon rose

✓ Hot-glue gun

✓ 5-inch gold chenille stem

✓ Tapestry needle

Gauge

4 sc = 1 inch

Check gauge to save time.

Pattern Notes

Weave in loose ends as work progresses.

Join rnds with a sl st unless otherwise stated.

Ch 3 counts as first dc throughout.

Body

Row 1: With white, ch 4, 5 dc in 4th ch from hook, turn. (6 dc)

Row 2: Ch 3, dc in same st as beg ch, 2 dc in each st across, turn. (12 dc)

Rows 3 & 4: Ch 3, dc in each st across, turn.

Row 5: [Ch 4, sl st in next st] rep across, fasten off.

Arm

(Make 2)

Row 1: Beg at top of arm, with white, ch 3, sc in 2nd ch from hook, sc in next ch, turn. (2 sc)

Row 2: Ch 1, sc in each of next 2 sc, turn.

Row 3: Ch 1, [2 sc in next sc] twice, fasten off. (4 sc)

Head

Rnd 1: With peach, ch 2, 6 sc in 2nd ch from hook, join in beg sc. (6 sc)

Rnd 2: Ch 1, 2 sc in each sc around, join in beg sc, fasten off. (12 sc)

Wing

(Make 2)

Row 1: With white, ch 4, sc in 2nd ch from hook, sc in each rem ch across, turn. (3 sc)

This fun-loving little angel can't wait to adorn your Christmas tree! Sweet and simple, she'll add whimsical charm to your Yuletide decor.

Row 2: Ch 1, sc in each sc across, turn.

Rows 3 & 4: Ch 1, 2 sc in first sc, sc in each sc across to last sc, 2 sc in last sc, turn. (7 sc)

Row 5: Ch 3, [sc in next sc, ch 3] 5 times, sl st in last sc, fasten off.

Finishing

With black, separate plies of yarn, working with 1 ply, embroider mouth on head. Glue cabochons in place above mouth for eyes. Glue curly hair to head. Form chenille stem into a halo and glue to top of head. Glue head to top of body, arms to front body over Rows 2 and 3. Glue rose between arms. Glue wings to back body over Row 2.

For hanging lp, cut a 6-inch length of white and attach to top of head. ★

Canine Christmas Stocking

By Cheryl Helbig

Skill Level: Beginner

Size: 9½ x 14 inches

Materials

✓ Caron Christmas Gold worsted weight yarn (1¾ oz per skein): 3 skeins lace #1952

✓ Size I/9 crochet hook or size needed to obtain gauge

✓ 1 yd 1¼-inch-wide plaid ribbon

✓ 3 novelty buttons

✓ Hot-glue gun

✓ Tapestry needle

Gauge

10 sc = 3 inches; 8 sc rows = 2 inches

Check gauge to save time.

Pattern Notes

Weave in loose ends as work progresses.

Join rnds with a sl st unless otherwise stated.

Front

Row 1: With lace, ch 21, sc in 2nd ch from hook, sc in each rem ch across, turn. (20 sc)

Row 2: Ch 1, 2 sc in first sc, sc in each sc across to last sc, 2 sc in last sc, turn. (22 sc)

Rows 3–7: Rep Row 2. (32 sc)

Row 8: Ch 1, sc in each sc across, turn.

Row 9: Rep Row 8.

Row 10: Ch 1, sc dec over next 2 sc, sc in each sc across to last 2 sc, sc dec over next 2 sc, turn. (30 sc)

Rows 11–15: Rep Row 10. (20 sc)

Row 16: Ch 1, sl st in first sc, sc in each sc across to last sc, sl st in last sc, turn. (18 sc; 2 sl sts)

Row 17: Ch 1, sk first sl st, sc in each sc across to last sl st, turn. (18 sc)

Rows 18–34: Rep Row 8.

Rows 35–41: Rep Row 2. (32 sc)

Rows 42 & 43: Rep Row 8.

Rows 44–49: Rep Row 10. (20 sc)

Row 50: Rep Row 8, do not turn.

Rnd 51: Ch 1, work 50 sc evenly sp down side edge of rows (place a marker in first sc), working across opposite side of foundation ch, *sc in each of first 2 sts, hdc in next st, dc in next st, tr in next st, dc in next st, hdc in next st, sc in next st, sl st in each of next 4 sts, sc in next st, hdc in next st, dc in next st, tr in next st, dc in next st, hdc in next st, sc in each of next 2 sts *, work 50 sc evenly sp up opposite edge of stocking

(place a marker in last sc), rep from * to * across Row 50, sl st to join in beg sc, fasten off.

Back

Rows 1–50: Rep Rows 1–50 of front.

Rnd 51: Rep Rnd 51 of front.

Finishing

Holding front and back tog, leaving top open, starting at first marker, sew stocking tog, ending at 2nd marker.

Cut ribbon into 3 equal lengths. Fold each into a bow. Glue bows evenly sp down center front of stocking. Glue a novelty button to the center of each bow.

For hanging lp, attach lace with sl st at center top back of stocking, ch 12, sl st in next st, fasten off. ★

Show some "puppy love" this holiday season by stitching this special stocking for the family dog. Chances are, Santa's got plenty of doggie treats for your loyal and furry friend!

Kitty's Christmas Stocking

By Cheryl Helbig

Skill Level: Beginner

Size: 12 inches long

Materials

✓ Caron Christmas Glitter worsted weight yarn (1¾ oz per skein): 3 skeins white #7201, small amount dark rose and light pink

✓ Size I/9 crochet hook or size needed to obtain gauge

✓ 2 (12mm) black cabochons

✓ 2 pieces 30-gauge white cloth-wrapped wire each 18 inches long

✓ 18 inches 1½-inch-wide silver wire-edged holiday ribbon

✓ ⅜-inch silver jingle bell

✓ 2 (12-inch) white chenille stems

✓ Hot-glue gun

✓ Wire cutters

✓ Tapestry needle

Let your favorite feline know it's Christmastime by crocheting this irresistible mouse stocking. Fill it with tasty treats, and your cat will be sure to appreciate your efforts!

Gauge

10 sc = 3 inches; 8 sc rows = 2 inches

Check gauge to save time.

Pattern Notes

Weave in loose ends as work progresses.

Join rnds with a sl st unless otherwise stated.

Front

Row 1: With dark rose, ch 2, 2 sc in 2nd ch from hook, turn. (2 sc)

Row 2: Ch 1, 2 sc in each st across, turn. (4 sc)

Row 3: Ch 1, 2 sc in first sc, sc in each st across to last sc, 2 sc in last sc, turn. (6 sc)

Row 4: Rep Row 3, fasten off, turn. (8 sc)

Row 5: Attach white, ch 1, sc in each sc across, turn.

Row 6: Rep Row 3. (10 sc)

Row 7: Ch 1, sc in each sc across, turn.

Rows 8–27: Rep Rows 6 and 7. (30 sc)

Rows 28–30: Rep Row 7.

Row 31: Ch 1, sc dec over next 2 sc, sc in each sc across to last 2 sc, sc dec over next 2 sc, turn. (28 sc)

Row 32: Rep Row 7.

Rows 33–40: Rep Rows 31 and 32. (20 sc)

Rows 41–44: Rep Row 31. (12 sc)

Row 45: Rep Row 7, do not turn.

Rnd 46: Ch 1, (place a marker in first sc) sc evenly sp down side edge of rows, work 3 sc in tip of nose, sc evenly sp up opposite edge (place a marker in last sc), working across Row 45, sc in first 2 sts, hdc in each of next 2 sts, dc in each of next 4 sts, hdc in next 2 sts, sc in last 2 sts, join in beg sc, fasten off.

Back

Rows 1–45: With white, rep Rows 1–45 of front.

Rnd 46: Rep Rnd 46 of front.

Ear

(Make 2)

Row 1: With light pink, ch 4, sc in 2nd ch from hook, sc in each of next 2 chs, turn. (3 sc)

Row 2: Ch 1, 2 sc in first sc, sc in next sc, 2 sc in last sc, turn. (5 sc)

Rows 3 & 4: Ch 1, 2 sc in

first sc, sc in each sc across to last sc, 2 sc in last sc, turn. (9 sc)

Row 5: Ch 1, sc in each sc across, turn.

Rows 6 & 7: Ch 1, sc dec over next 2 sc, sc in each sc across to last 2 sc, sc dec over next 2 sc, turn. (5 sc)

Row 8: Ch 1, sc dec over

next 2 sc, sc in next sc, sc dec over next 2 sc, do not turn. (5 sc)

Row 9: Ch 1, sc evenly sp across side edge of ear, across opposite side of foundation ch and across opposite side edge, ending at side edge of Row 8, fasten off, turn.

Row 10: Attach white in

first sc of previous row, ch 1, sc in each st of previous row, turn.

Row 11: Sl st in each st of previous row, leaving a length of yarn, fasten off.

Weave rem length through bottom sts of ear, pull tightly and secure; sew ears to front, 4 inches apart, over Row 23.

Tail

(Make 2)

With white, ch 45, sc in 2nd ch from hook, sc in each rem ch across, fasten off.

Holding 2 chenille stems tog, twist stems around each other. Bend each tip inward ¼-inch. With RS facing, sew tail section tog, inserting chenille stems before closing.

Sew tail to WS of back of stocking 2½ inches down on 3 sides to secure. Curl top of tail.

Whiskers

Hold 2 pieces of 30-gauge cloth-covered wire tog, fold in half and cut at center. Holding all 4 pieces tog, twist in center only and slide 1 end under center st of Row 5 above nose on front of stocking. Glue twisted center of whiskers on WS of front. Trim whiskers to desired length.

Finishing

Attach cabochons to front for eyes, 2½ inches apart, on Row 16.

Holding WS of front and back of stocking tog, starting at first marker, sew front and back tog, ending at last marker, leaving top of stocking open.

For hanging lp, with RS of back facing, attach white with a sl st to next st of back to the right side of tail, ch 10, sl st in next st on opposite side of tail on back, fasten off.

Glue center back of ear to front of stocking.

Make a bow with wired ribbon; attach jingle bell to center of bow. Attach bow to stocking as shown. ★

Mini Tree Skirt

By Vida Sunderman

Skill Level: Beginner

Size: 12½ inches in diameter

Materials

✓ Coats & Clark Red Heart sport weight pompadour yarn (6 oz per skein): 2 oz white #1001, 1 oz hot red #1390

✓ Size F/5 crochet hook or size needed to obtain gauge

✓ Yarn needle

This lovely tree skirt makes the perfect accent for a tabletop tree. It works equally well as a decorative base for a holiday lamp!

Gauge

4 dc = 1 inch

Check gauge to save time.

Pattern Notes

Weave in loose ends as work progresses.

Ch 3 counts as first dc throughout.

Ch 2 counts as first hdc throughout.

Pattern Stitch

V-st: [Dc, ch 2, dc] in indicated st.

Skirt

Row 1 (WS): With white, ch 18, dc in 4th ch from hook, 2 dc in each rem ch across, turn. (30 dc)

Row 2 (RS): Ch 3, dc in next dc, V-st in next dc, [dc in each of next 4 dc, V-st in next dc] 5 times, dc in next 2 dc, turn. (6 V-sts)

Row 3: Ch 3, dc in next 2 dc, [V-st in ch-2 sp of V-st, dc in each dc across to next V-st] 5 times, V-st in next ch-2 sp, dc in each of next 3 dc, turn.

Rows 4–6: Rep Row 3. (72 dc; 6 V-sts)

At the end of Row 6, fasten off, do not turn.

Row 7 (RS): Attach hot red in first st of previous row, ch 2, hdc in each st across to next ch-2 sp of V-st, [{hdc, ch 2, hdc} in ch-2 sp, hdc in each dc across to next ch-2 sp of V-st] 5 times, [hdc, ch 2, hdc] in ch-2 sp, hdc in each rem dc across, fasten off, do not turn.

Row 8 (RS): Attach white in first st of previous row, ch 3, dc in each hdc across to ch-2 sp, [V-st in ch-2 sp, dc in each hdc across to next ch-2 sp] 5 times, V-st in next ch-2 sp, dc in each rem hdc across, fasten off, do not turn.

Rows 9 & 10: Rep Rows 7 and 8. (120 dc; 6 V-sts)

Row 11 (RS): Attach hot red in first st of previous row, ch 1, sc in same st, [sc in next st, ch 3, sk next 2 sts] 3 times, *sc in next st, ch 3, sk ch-2 sp **, [sc in next st, ch 2, sk next 2 sts] 7 times, rep from * across, ending last rep at **, [sc in next st, ch 2, sk next 2 sts] 3 times, sc in each of next 2 sts, turn. (47 ch-3 sps)

Row 12 (WS): Ch 1, sc in each of next 2 sc, [{hdc, ch 3, hdc} in ch-3 sp, sc in next sc] 47 times, sc in next sc, fasten off. ★

Santa's Bag Ornament

By Beverly Mewhorter

Skill Level: Beginner

Size: 3 inches tall

Materials

- ✓ Worsted weight yarn: small amounts red and green
- ✓ Size G/6 crochet hook or size needed to obtain gauge
- ✓ 1¼-inch-square gift package
- ✓ 2 (⅜-inch) jingle bells
- ✓ Fiberfill
- ✓ Hot-glue gun
- ✓ Tapestry needle

This delightful ornament holds the promise of Christmas treasures! Make it as shown, or fill it with real goodies for the kids!

Gauge

4 sc = 1 inch

Check gauge to save time.

Pattern Notes

Weave in loose ends as work progresses.

Join rnds with a sl st unless otherwise stated.

Ch 3 counts as first dc throughout.

Bag

Rnd 1 (RS): With red, ch

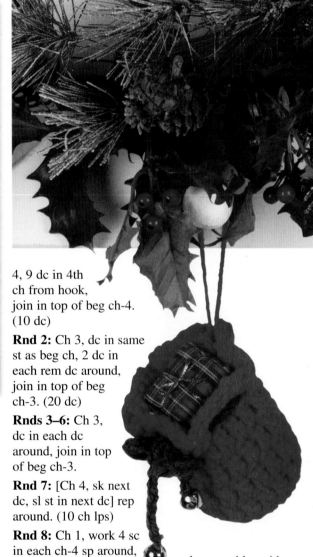

4, 9 dc in 4th ch from hook, join in top of beg ch-4. (10 dc)

Rnd 2: Ch 3, dc in same st as beg ch, 2 dc in each rem dc around, join in top of beg ch-3. (20 dc)

Rnds 3–6: Ch 3, dc in each dc around, join in top of beg ch-3.

Rnd 7: [Ch 4, sk next dc, sl st in next dc] rep around. (10 ch lps)

Rnd 8: Ch 1, work 4 sc in each ch-4 sp around, join in beg sc, fasten off. (40 sc)

Tie

With green, leaving a 2-inch length at beg, ch 60, leaving a 2-inch length, fasten off.

Finishing

Weave tie through ch sps of Rnd 7. Attach a jingle bell to rem length at beg and end of tie.

Stuff bag with fiberfill, insert package and tie ends of tie in a bow. Secure

package at sides with a small amount of glue.

For hanging lp, attach a 6-inch length of red to back side of back over Rnd 7. ★

Vibrant Christmas Stocking

By Colleen Sullivan

Skill Level: Beginner

Size: 21 inches long

Materials

- ✓ Coats & Clark Red Heart Super Saver worsted weight yarn (8 oz per skein): 3½ oz each cherry red #319 and paddy green #368, 1½ oz white #311
- ✓ Size G/6 crochet hook or size needed to obtain gauge
- ✓ Yarn needle

This charming stocking is so quick and easy to make, you'll soon have the mantel hung with one for every family member! What's more, it's large enough to hold plenty of Christmas goodies!

Gauge

11 sts = 2½ inches; 5 rows = 2 inches

Check gauge to save time.

Pattern Notes

Weave in loose ends as work progresses.

Join rnds with a sl st unless otherwise stated.

Carry yarn color not in use loosely on WS along edge of stocking rnds.

Ch 4 counts as first dc, ch 1 throughout.

Stocking

Upper portion

Rnd 1 (RS): With cherry red, ch 40, using care not to twist ch, join in beg ch to form a ring, ch 4, sk next ch, [dc in next ch, ch 1, sk next ch] rep around, join in 3rd ch of beg ch-4, drop cherry red, draw through a lp of paddy green. (20 dc; 20 ch-1 sps)

Rnd 2: With paddy green, ch 1, sc in same dc as joining, dc in skipped ch of Rnd 1 directly below, drawing up yarn level with working rnd, [sc in next dc, dc in skipped ch of Rnd 1 directly below, drawing up yarn level with working rnd] rep around, join in beg sc. (20 sc; 20 dc)

Rnd 3: Ch 4, sk next dc, [dc in next sc, ch 1, sk next dc] rep around, join in 3rd ch of beg ch-4, drop paddy green, draw through a lp of cherry red. (20 dc; 20 ch-1 sps)

Rnd 4: With cherry red, ch 1, sc in same dc as joining, dc in skipped dc directly below, [sc in next dc, dc in skipped dc directly below] rep around, join in beg sc.

Rnd 5: Ch 4, sk 1 next st, [dc in next st, ch 1, sk next st] rep around, join in 3rd ch of beg ch-4, drop cherry red, draw up a lp of paddy green.

Rnds 6–27: Continue in pattern Rnds 4 and 5, alternating 2 rnds paddy green and 2 rnds cherry red.

Rnd 28: With cherry red, rep Rnd 4, fasten off.

Heel shaping

Row 1 (RS): Attach white in first st of previous rnd, ch 1, sc in same st as beg ch, sc in each of next 19 sts, turn. (20 sc)

Rows 2–9: Ch 1, sk first sc, sc in each sc across to last 2 sc, sk next s, sc in last sc, turn. (4 sc)

Row 10: Ch 1, [sc dec over next 2 sc] twice, turn. (2 sc)

Row 11: Ch 1, sc in each sc across, turn. (2 sc)

Row 12: Ch 1, [2 sc in next sc] twice, turn. (4 sc)

Rows 13–20: Ch 1, 2 sc in first sc, sc in each sc across to last sc, 2 sc in last sc, turn. (20 sc)

Row 21: Ch 1, sc in each sc across, fasten off.

Foot

Rnd 1 (RS): Attach cherry red in next unworked st of Rnd 28, ch 1, sc in same st as beg ch, sc in each of next 19 sts, working across Row 21 of heel shaping, sc in each sc across, join in beg sc. (40 sc)

Rnd 2: Ch 4, sk next st, [dc in next st, ch 1, sk next st] rep around, join in 3rd ch of beg ch-4, drop cherry red, draw up a lp of paddy green.

Rnds 3–17: Work in pattern of Rnds 4 and 5 of upper portion, working 2 rnds paddy green and 2 rnds cherry red.

Rnd 18: With cherry red, rep Rnd 4 of upper portion, fasten off.

Toe shaping

Rnd 1 (RS): Attach white in any st of Rnd 18, ch 1, sc in each st around, do not join. (40 sc)

Note: Do not join rnds, use a scrap of CC yarn to mark rnds.

Rnd 2: [Sc in each of next 5 sc, sk next sc] rep around, sc in next 4 sc. (34 sc)

Rnd 3: [Sc in each of next

4 sc, sk next sc] rep around, sc in next 4 sc. (28 sc)

Rnd 4: [Sc in next 3 sc, sk next sc] rep around. (21 sc)

Rnd 5: [Sc in each of next 2 sc, sk next sc] rep around. (14 sc)

Rnd 6: [Sc in next sc, sk next sc] rep around, sl st to join in next sc, leaving a length of yarn, fasten off. (7 sc)

Sew opening of toe closed.

Cuff

Rnd 1 (RS): Attach white in opposite side of foundation ch at center back, ch 1, sc in same st as beg ch, sc in next 19 sts, 2 sc in next st, sc in each of next 19 sts, sc in same st as beg sc, join in beg sc. (42 sc)

Rnd 2: Working in back lps for this rnd only, ch 4, sk next st, [dc in next st, ch 1, sk next st] rep around, join in 3rd ch of beg ch-4.

Rnds 3–7: Sl st into ch-1 sp, ch 4, [dc in next ch-1 sp, ch 1] rep around, join in 3rd ch of beg ch-4.

Rnd 8: Ch 1, sc in same dc as beg ch, dc in dc row directly below, [sc in next dc, dc in next dc row directly below] rep around, join in beg sc, fasten off.

Rnd 9 (RS): Attach white in rem free lp of Rnd 1 of cuff at back edge directly in line with heel, ch 16 (hanging lp), sl st in same st, sl st in each rem free lp around, fasten off.

With length of white, sew heel side seams closed. ★

Poinsettia Afghan

By Robin Murphy

Skill Level: Intermediate

Size: 52 x 63 inches

Materials

✓ Coats & Clark Red Heart Super Saver worsted weight yarn (8 oz per skein): 4 oz pale yellow #322, 12 oz cherry red #319, 32 oz dark sage #633 and 32 oz aran #313

✓ Size H/8 crochet hook or size needed to obtain gauge

✓ Yarn needle

Vibrant red flowers bloom in winter, bringing warmth and cheer to the holiday season. Assemble these pretty poinsettia blocks for a lovely afghan with its own radiant glow!

Gauge

Rnds 1–13 of square = 10 inches; 6 V-sts = 4 inches

Check gauge to save time.

Pattern Notes

Weave in loose ends as work progresses.

Join rnds with a sl st unless otherwise stated.

Pattern Stitches

V-st: [Dc, ch 1, dc] in indicated sp.

Beg V-st: [Ch 4 (counts as first dc, ch 1), dc] in same st or sp.

Square

(Make 30)

Rnd 1 (RS): With pale yellow, ch 4, 16 dc in 4th ch from hook, sk beg ch, join in first dc, fasten off. (16 dc)

Rnd 2: Working in front lps for this rnd only, attach cherry red, ch 1 loosely, [2 dc, ch 2, 2 dc} in same st, sc in next st, [{2 dc, ch 2, 2 dc} in next st, sc in next st] rep around, join in first dc. (8 petals)

Rnd 3: Sl st into ch-2 sp, ch 1 loosely, [3 dc, ch 2, 3 dc] in same ch-2 sp, sc in next sc, [{3 dc, ch 2, 3 dc} in next ch-2 sp, sc in next sc] rep around, join in first dc.

Rnd 4: Sl st into ch-2 sp, ch 1, [{sc, ch 2, sc in 2nd ch from hook, sc} in ch-2 sp, ch 4, sl st in next sc, ch 4] rep around, join in beg sc, fasten off.

Rnd 5: Working in rem back lps of Rnd 1, attach dark sage in any st between cherry red petals, ch 1 loosely, [2 dc, ch 2, 2 dc] in same st, sc in next st, [{2 dc, ch 2, 2 dc} in next st, sc in next st] rep around, join in top of first dc. (8 leaves)

Rnd 6: Sl st into ch-2 sp, ch 1 loosely, [{3 dc, ch 2, 3 dc} in ch-2 sp, sc in next sc] rep around, join in top of first dc.

Rnd 7: Sl st into ch-2 sp, ch 1 loosely, [{4 dc, ch 2, 4 dc} in ch-2 sp, sc in next sc] rep around, join in top of first dc.

Rnd 8: Ch 1, sc in same st as joining, *ch 5, [sc, ch 2, sc in 2nd ch from hook, sc] in ch-2 sp, ch 5, sk next 3 dc, sc in next dc, ch 3, sk next sc **, sc in next dc, sk next 3 dc, rep from * around, ending last rep at **, join in beg sc, fasten off.

Rnd 9: Attach aran in any ch-3 sp and holding leaves forward, ch 1 loosely, [{4 dc, ch 2, 4 dc} in ch-3 sp, ch 2, 4 dc in next ch-3 sp, ch 2] rep around, join in top of first dc. (48 dc)

Rnd 10: Ch 4 (counts as first dc, ch 1 throughout), [dc in next dc, ch 1] 3 times, *ch 1, [V-st, ch 2, V-st] in corner ch-2 sp, [ch 1, dc in next dc] 4 times, [ch 1, dc in next ch] twice **, [ch 1, dc in next dc] 4 times, rep from * around, ending last rep at **, ch 1, join in 3rd ch of beg ch-4. (80 dc)

Rnd 11: Sl st into next ch-1 sp, beg V-st in same ch-1 sp, sk next ch-1 sp, V-st in next ch-1 sp, *[V-st, ch 2, V-st] in corner ch-2 sp **, [sk next ch-1 sp, V-st in next ch-1 sp] 9 times, sk next ch-1 sp, rep from * around, ending last rep at **, [sk next ch-1 sp, V-st in next ch-1 sp] 7 times, join in 3rd ch of beg ch-4. (88 dc)

Rnd 12: Sl st into ch-1 sp of V-st, beg V-st in same ch-1 sp, V-st in each ch-1 sp around, working [V-st, ch 2, V-st] in each corner ch-2 sp, join in 3rd ch of beg ch-4. (104 dc)

Rnd 13: Ch 1, sc in same st as beg ch, sc in each dc around entire outer edge, work 3 sc in each corner ch-2 sp, join in beg sc, fasten off. (116 sc)

Joining Squares

Note: Squares are joined in strips, 6 strips of 5 squares each and then strips are joined tog.

Holding 2 squares with WS tog, attach dark sage with sl st in center corner st of first square, ch 3, sl st in center corner st of 2nd square, [ch 3, sl st in next sc of first square, ch 3, sl

st in next sc of 2nd square] rep across edge, ending pattern in center corner sc of squares, fasten off.

Continue to join squares until 5 squares are joined. Rep until a total of 6 strips, 5 squares each, is completed. Holding first and 2nd strip WS tog, join in same manner as joining squares.

Border

Rnd 1 (RS): Attach dark sage in any center corner sc, *[ch 8, sl st] 3 times in center corner sc, [ch 8, sl st in next sc] rep across edge, ending with last sl st in center corner sc, rep from * around.

Rnd 2: Ch 4 (to bring yarn level with working rnd), reverse sc in each ch-8 lp around, join in beg sc, fasten off. ★

Snowman Centerpiece

By Lori Zeller

Skill Level: Beginner

Size: 8½ inches tall

Materials

- ✓ Worsted weight yarn: 3 oz white, 1 oz black, ½ oz red, small amount orange
- ✓ Sport weight yarn: 1 oz green
- ✓ Size F/5 crochet hook or size needed to obtain gauge
- ✓ 2½-inch in diameter vine wreath
- ✓ 18 inches ¼-inch-wide green picot edge ribbon
- ✓ Fiberfill
- ✓ 2 (½ x ⅜-inch) black oval buttons
- ✓ 2 (½-inch) black buttons
- ✓ 2 red ribbon roses
- ✓ Hot-glue gun
- ✓ Tapestry needle

This friendly snowman brings cheer to any table or sideboard. His simple trimmings make him suitable for display even beyond the season!

Gauge

With worsted weight yarn, 4 sc and 4 sc rnds = 1 inch

Check gauge to save time.

Pattern Notes

Weave in loose ends as work progresses.

Do not join rnds unless otherwise stated. Use a scrap of CC yarn to mark rnds.

Join rnds with a sl st unless otherwise stated.

Pattern Stitch

V-st: [Dc, ch 1, dc] in indicated st.

Snowman

Head & body

Rnd 1 (RS): With white, ch 2, 6 sc in 2nd ch from hook. (6 sc)

Rnd 2: Work 2 sc in each st around. (12 sc)

Rnd 3: [2 sc in next sc, sc in next sc] rep around. (18 sc)

Rnd 4: [Sc in each of next 2 sc, 2 sc in next sc] rep around. (24 sc)

Rnd 5: [Sc in each of next 3 sc, 2 sc in next sc] rep around. (30 sc)

Rnd 6: [Sc in each of next 4 sc, 2 sc in next sc] rep around. (36 sc)

Rnd 7: Sc in each sc around.

Rnds 8–13: Rep Rnd 7.

Rnd 14: [Sc in each of next 4 sc, sc dec over next 2 sc] rep around. (30 sc)

Rnd 15: [Sc in each of next 3 sc, sc dec over next 2 sc] rep around. (24 sc)

Rnd 16: [Sc in each of next 2 sc, sc dec over next 2 sc] rep around. (18 sc)

Rnd 17: Rep Rnd 7.

Rnds 18–20: Rep Rnds 3–5. (45 sc)

Rnds 21–33: Rep Rnd 7.

Rnd 34: [Sc in each of next 13 sc, sc dec over next 2 sc] rep across. (42 sc)

Rnd 35: Rep Rnd 7.

Rnd 36: Rep Rnd 6. (35 sc)

Rnd 37: Sc in each sc around, sl st in next sc, leaving a length of yarn, fasten off.

Base

Rnd 1: With white, ch 2, 7 sc in 2nd ch from hook. (7 sc)

Rnd 2: Work 2 sc in each sc around. (14 sc)

Rnds 3–5: Rep Rnds 3–5 of head and body. At the end of Rnd 5, sl st in next st, fasten off. (35 sc)

Arm

(Make 2)

Rnd 1: With white, ch 2, 6 sc in 2nd ch from hook. (6 sc)

Rnd 2: Work 2 sc in each sc around. (12 sc)

Rnds 3–14: Sc in each sc around.

Rnd 15: Sc in each sc around, sl st in next st, leaving a length of yarn, fasten off.

Hat

Rnd 1: With black, ch 2, 7 sc in 2nd ch from hook. (7 sc)

Rnds 2–5: Rep Rnds 2–5 of head and body. (35 sc)

Rnd 6: Working in back lps for this rnd only, sc in each st around.

Rnds 7–12: Sc in each sc around.

Rnd 13: Sc in each sc around, sl st in next sc.

Rnd 14: Working in front lps for this rnd only, ch 3, [dc in next st, 2 dc in next st] rep around, join in top of beg ch, leaving a length

of yarn, fasten off.

Hatband

Row 1: With green, ch 4, sc in 4th ch from hook, turn.

Rows 2–31: Ch 3, sc in next sc, turn.

Row 32: Ch 3, sc in sc, leaving a length of yarn, fasten off.

Sew hatband around hat just above brim.

Nose

Rnd 1: With orange, ch 2, 4 sc in 2nd ch from hook. (4 sc)

Rnd 2: [Sc in next sc, 2 sc in next sc] twice. (6 sc)

Rnd 3: Sc in each sc around, sl st in next sc, leaving a length of yarn, fasten off.

Assembly

Stuff snowman with fiberfill; leaving front lps of Rnd 37 of snowman free, sew base to bottom of snowman. Stuff arms lightly with fiberfill and sew to sides of body. Sew hat to top of head. Sew nose to center of face.

Base Ruffle

Rnd 1: Attach green in any rem free lp of Rnd 37, ch 1, sc in same st, ch 2, [sc in next st, ch 2] rep around, join in beg sc.

Rnd 2: Sl st into ch-2 sp, ch 4, dc in same ch-2 sp, ch 1, [V-st in next ch-2 sp, ch 1] rep around, join in 3rd ch of beg ch-4.

Rnd 3: Sl st in ch-1 sp, ch 1, sc in same ch sp, ch 2, [sc in next ch-1 sp, ch 2] rep around, join in beg sc.

Rnd 4: Sl st into ch-2 sp, ch 1, sc in same ch sp, ch 3, [sc in next ch-2 sp, ch 3]

rep around, join in beg sc.

Rnd 5: Sl st into ch-3 sp, ch 1, sc in same ch sp, ch 3, [sc in next ch-3 sp, ch 3] rep around, join in beg sc.

Rnd 6: Sl st into ch-3 sp, ch 1, [sc, ch 2, dc] in same ch-3 sp, [sc, ch 2, dc] in each rem ch-3 sp around, join in beg sc, fasten off.

Scarf

Row 1: With red, ch 6, sc in 2nd ch from hook, [ch 1, sk next ch, sc in next ch] twice, turn. (3 sc)

Rows 2–76: Ch 1, sc in first sc, [ch 1, sc in next sc] twice, turn.

At the end of Row 76, fasten off.

Fringe

Cut 10 strands each 3 inches long of green and red yarn. Hold 2 strands tog, fold in half, insert hook in st, draw fold through to form a lp on hook, draw cut ends through lp on hook, pull gently to secure. Rep fringe in each st across short ends. Trim ends evenly.

Wrap scarf around neck, tying over shoulder with 1 end in front and the other in back; tuck front end under arm.

Wreath

Wrap an 11-inch length of ribbon around wrath and

glue ends to secure. Tie rem length of ribbon in a bow and glue to front bottom of wreath. Glue ribbon rose to center of bow. Glue wreath to ends of snowman's arms.

Finishing

Glue ribbon rose to front hatband. For eyes, glue oval buttons to face. For body buttons, glue rem buttons to upper body. ★

STITCH GUIDE

Front Loop (a)
Back Loop (b)

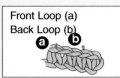

Chain (ch)
Yo, draw lp through

Slip Stitch Joining
Insert hook in beg ch, yo, draw lp through.

Front Post/Back Post Dc
Fpdc (a): Yo, insert hook from front to back and to front again around the vertical post (upright part) of next st, yo and draw yarn through, yo and complete dc.
Bpdc (b): Yo, reaching over top of piece and working on opposite side (back) of work, insert hook from back to front to back again

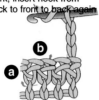

Single Crochet (sc)
Insert hook in st (a), yo, draw lp through (b), yo, draw through both lps on hook (c).

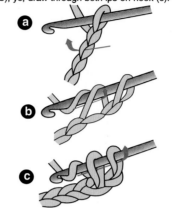

Half-Double Crochet (hdc)
Yo, insert hook in st (a), yo, draw lp through (b), yo, draw through all 3 lps on

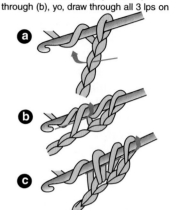

DECREASING

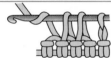

Single Crochet Decrease
Dec 1 sc over next 2 sts as follows: Draw up a lp in each of next 2 sts, yo, draw through all 3 lps on

Double Crochet Decrease
Dec 1 dc over next 2 sts as follows: [Yo, insert hook in next st, yo, draw up lp on hook, yo, draw through 2 lps] twice, yo, draw through all 3 lps on hook.

Double Crochet (dc)
Yo, insert hook in st (a), yo, draw lp through (b), [yo, draw through 2 lps] twice (c, d).

Treble Crochet (tr)
Yo hook twice, insert hook in st (a), yo, draw lp through (b), [yo, draw through 2 lps on hook] 3 times

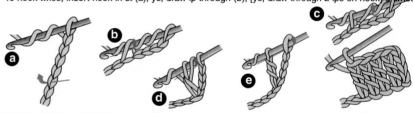

SPECIAL STITCHES

Chain Color Change (ch color change)

Double Crochet Color Change (dc color change)

Reverse Single Crochet (reverse sc)
Working from left to right, insert hook in next st to the right (a), yo, draw up lp on hook, com-

Stitch Abbreviations
The following stitch abbreviations are used throughout this publication.

beg	begin(ning)
bl(s)	block(s)
bpdc	back post dc
ch(s)	chain(s)
cl(s)	cluster(s)
CC	contrasting color
dc	double crochet
dec	decrease
dtr	double treble crochet
fpdc	front post dc
hdc	half-double crochet
inc	increase
lp(s)	loop(s)
MC	main color
p	picot
rem	remain(ing)
rep	repeat
rnd(s)	round(s)
RS	right side facing you
sc	single crochet
sk	skip
sl st	slip stitch
sp(s)	space(s)
st(s)	stitch(es)
tog	together
tr	treble crochet
trtr	triple treble crochet
WS	wrong side facing you
yo	yarn over

Crochet Hooks
METRIC
US

.60mm	14 steel
.75mm	12 steel
1.00mm	10 steel
1.25mm	8 steel
1.50mm	7 steel
1.75mm	5 steel
2.00mm	B/1
2.50mm	C/2
3.00mm	D/3
3.50mm	E/4
4.00mm	F/5
4.50mm	G/6
5.00mm	H/8

Yarn Conversion
OUNCES TO GRAMS

1	28.4
2	56.7
3	85.0
4	113.4

GRAMS TO OUNCES

25	⅞
40	1⅜
50	1¾
100	3½

Crochet Abbreviations

US	INTL
sc—single crochet	dc—double crochet
dc—double crochet	tr—treble crochet
hdc—half-double crochet	htr—half treble crochet
tr—treble crochet	dtr—double treble crochet
dtr—double treble crochet	trip—triple treble crochet
sk—skip	miss

YARNS

Bedspread weight	No. 10 cotton or Virtuoso
Sport weight	3-ply or thin DK
Worsted weight	Thick DK or Aran

General Instructions

Please review the following information before working the projects in this book. Important details about the abbreviations and symbols used are included.

Hooks

Crochet hooks are sized for different weights of yarn and thread. For thread crochet, you will usually use a steel crochet hook. Steel crochet hook sizes range from size 00 to 14. The higher the number of hook, the smaller your stitches will be. For example, a size 1 steel crochet hook will give you much larger stitches than a size 9 steel crochet hook. Keep in mind that the sizes given with the pattern instructions were obtained by working with the size thread or yarn and hook given in the materials list. If you work with a smaller hook, depending on your gauge, your project size will be smaller; if you work with a larger hook, your finished project's size will be larger.

Gauge

Gauge is determined by the tightness or looseness of your stitches, and affects the finished size of your project. If you are concerned about the finished size of the project matching the size given, take time to crochet a small section of the pattern and then check your gauge. For example, if the gauge called for is 10 dc = 1 inch, and your gauge is 12 dc to the inch, you should switch to a larger hook. On the other hand, if your gauge is only 8 dc to the inch, you should switch to a smaller hook.

If the gauge given in the pattern is for an entire motif, work one motif and then check your gauge.

Understanding Symbols

As you work through a pattern, you'll quickly notice several symbols in the instructions. These symbols are used to clarify the pattern for you: Brackets [], curlicue brackets { }, asterisks *.

Brackets [] are used to set off a group of instructions worked a number of times. For example, "[ch 3, sc in ch-3 sp] 7 times" means to work the instructions inside the [] seven times. Brackets [] also set off a group of stitches to be worked in one stitch, space or loop. For example, the brackets [] in this set of instructions, "Sk 3 sc, [3 dc, ch 1, 3 dc] in next st" indicate that after skipping 3 sc, you will work 3 dc, ch 1 and 3 more dc all in the next stitch.

Occasionally, a set of instructions inside a set of brackets needs to be repeated too. In this case, the text within the brackets to be repeated will be set off with curlicue brackets { }. For example, "[Ch 9, yo twice, insert hook in 7th ch from hook and pull up a lp, sk next dc, yo, insert hook in next dc and pull up a lp, {yo and draw through 2 lps on hook} 5 times, ch 3] 8 times." In this case, in each of the eight times you work the instructions included in brackets, you will work the section included in curlicue brackets five times.

Asterisks * are also used when a group of instructions is repeated. They may either be used alone or with brackets. For example, "*Sc in each of the next 5 sc, 2 sc in next sc, rep from * around, join with a sl st in beg sc" simply means you will work the instructions from the first * around the entire round.

"*Sk 3 sc, [3 dc, ch 1, 3 dc] in next st, rep from * around" is an example of asterisks working with brackets. In this set of instructions, you will repeat the instructions from the asterisk around, working the instructions inside the brackets together. ★

Special Thanks

A special note of appreciation goes to each of the crochet designers whose work appears in this book. Thanks!

Sandy Abbate
In Leaf Baby Layette; Flower Power Child's Afghan; Mini Purse Necklace; Sunflower Jewelry

Carol Alexander for Crochet Trends and Traditions
Regency Floral Afghan; Victorian Hearts Baby Coverlet

Mary Betz
Keepsake Box & Gift Bag

Vicki Blizzard
Elegant Christmas Cardigan

Carol Carlile
Mix-and-Match Outfits

Maggie Petsch Chasalow
His & Her Kewpie Outfits

Sue Childress
Baby Announcement Wreaths; Bouncing Baby Jackets; Drawstring Purses; Floral Candle Centerpiece; Flower Face Pins; Linen Heart Doilies; Poinsettia Plaid Wreath; Pretty Pillowcases; Summertime Kitchen Set

Donna Collinsworth
Inside-Out Eggs

JoHanna Dzikowski
Crocheted Wire Earrings

Katherine Eng
Kitchen Naturals; Natural Star Ornaments

Darla Fanton
Kitty's Favorite Mouse; Kitty's Pup Tent

Nazanin Fard
Guest Towel Edgings; Silk Roses Bouquet; Straw Hat Pin

Charlene Finiello
Country Checks Breakfast Set

Connie Folse
Canine Comfort Dog Sweater; Cat Play Tunnel; Cozy Pet Pad; Dapper Dog Sweater; Domed Pet Bed

Jamie Folse
Fancy Collar

Laura Gebhardt
Bouclé Shrug; Dapper Duckling; Holly Jolly Apron; Shoe Bag & Toe Sachets

Janet Giese
Ruffled Sachets

Dawn Goodan
Garnet Purse

Gloria Graham
Golden Angel Ornament; Happy Holidays Pin; Pineapple Bell Ornament; Pineapple Teardrop Ornament; String of Lights Garland

Stacey Graham
Bouquet of Lilies; Butterfly Magnets; "Catch Me!" Mouse; Dainty Dishcloths; Diamond Dog Collar; Doggie Barrettes; Flying Disc Toy; Tennis Ball Snake

Anne Halliday
Rainbow Stripes Baby Afghan

Cheryl Helbig
Canine Christmas Stocking; Kitty's Christmas Stocking

Melissa Leapman
Dainty Shells Baby Afghan

Roberta Maier
Bath Gift Basket; Window Soap Bags

Darla McGuire for Women of Design
Checks 'n' Cherries

Beverly Mewhorter
Baby Angel Ornament; Baby's Spring Outfit; Choo-Choo Train Afghan; Clowning Around Bear; Fourth of July Picnic Dress; Froggie Bath Mitt; Goldfish Bath Set; Hide-Away Bed; Louie Lizard; "Nip" the Mouse; Patriotic Coasters; Pretty in Pink Baby Doll & Pillow; Santa Air Freshener; Santa's Bag Ornament

Robin Murphy
Poinsettia Afghan

Margaret Nobles
Bath Powder Bottle Collar

Diane Poellot
Christmas Candy Afghan; Heart's Fancy Trivets

Ruth Shepherd
Handy Eyeglasses Holder Pin; Peach Blossom Doily

Irene Stock
Deluxe Lap Robe

Brenda Stratton for Crochet Trends & Traditions
Caitlin Victorian Doll; Summer Afternoon Afghan

Colleen Sullivan
Vibrant Christmas Stocking

Vida Sunderman
Mini Tree Skirt

Aline Suplinskas
Soft & Simple Face Cloth

Angela Tate
Scrap Thread Pot Holders

Michele Wilcox
Baby Bunny in Bunting; Little Red Riding Hood Costume; Spring Floral Pillow; Teddy Bear

Debi Yorston
Tooth-Saver Pillow

Lori Zeller
Crawly Critters; Snowman Centerpiece; Teach Me Shapes & Colors